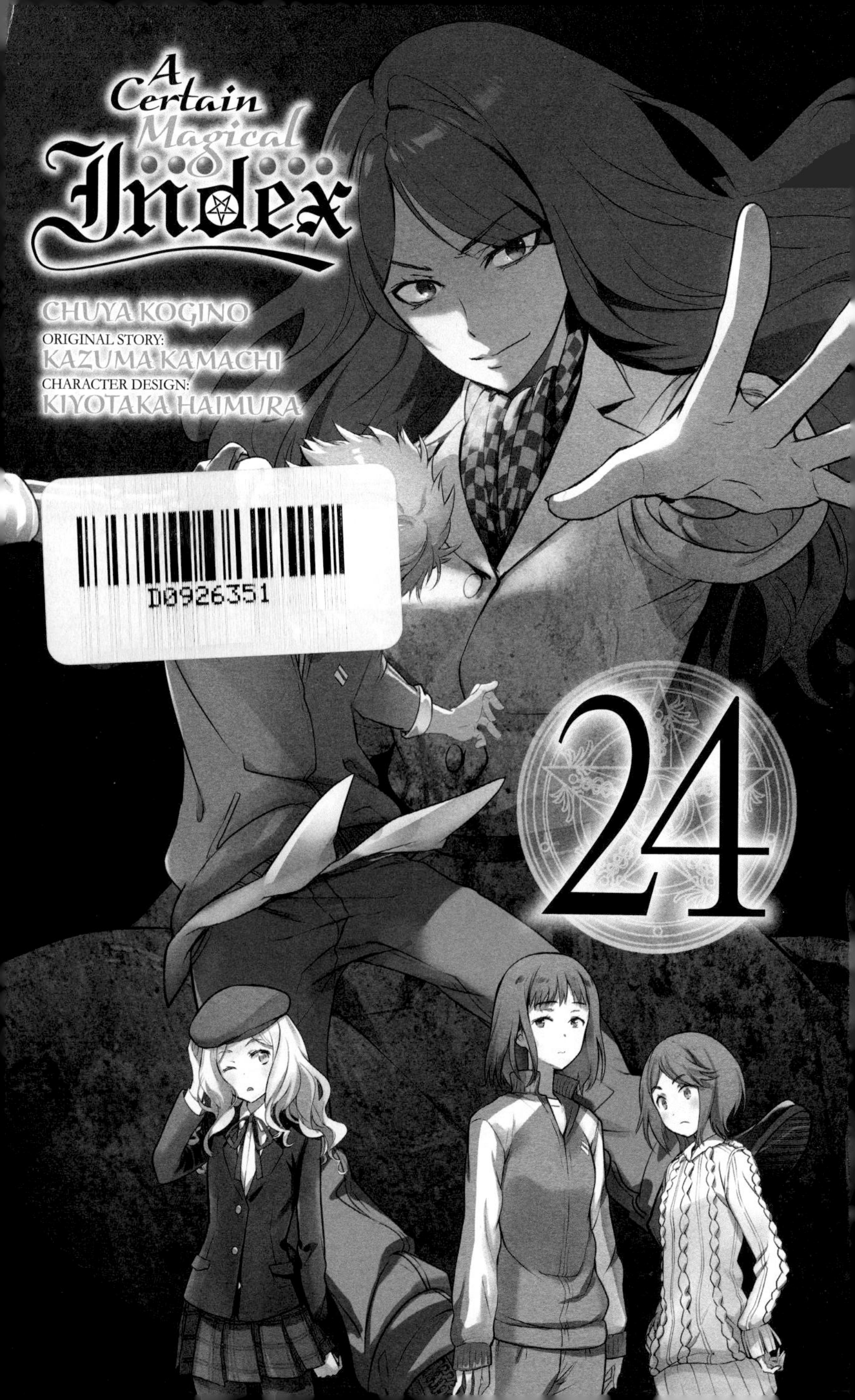
A Certain Magical Index
CHUYA KOGINO
ORIGINAL STORY:
KAZUMA KAMACHI
CHARACTER DESIGN:
KIYOTAKA HAIMURA
D0926351
24

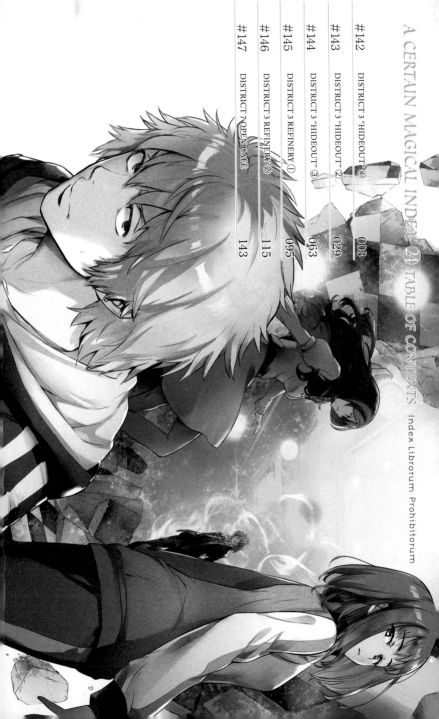

A CERTAIN MAGICAL INDEX 24 TABLE OF CONTENTS

Index Librorum Prohibitorum

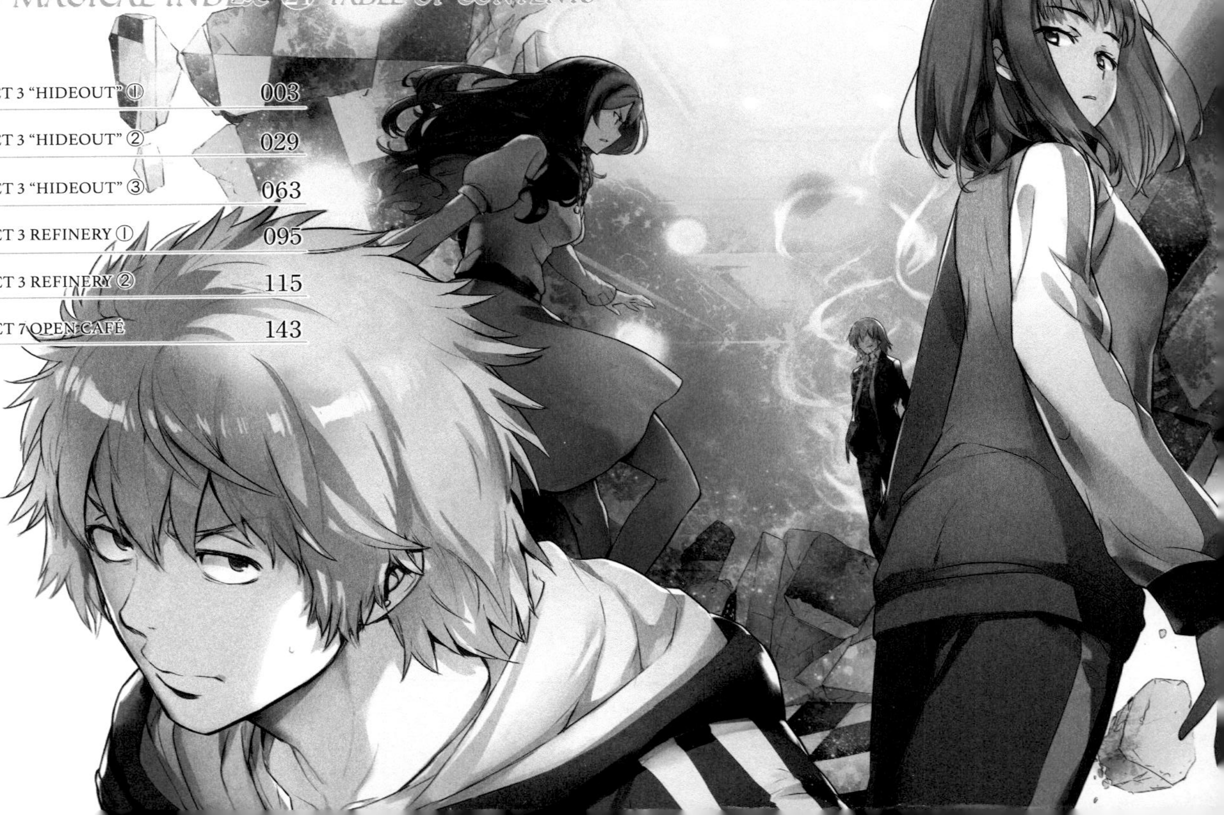

#142 DISTRICT 3 "HIDEOUT" ①

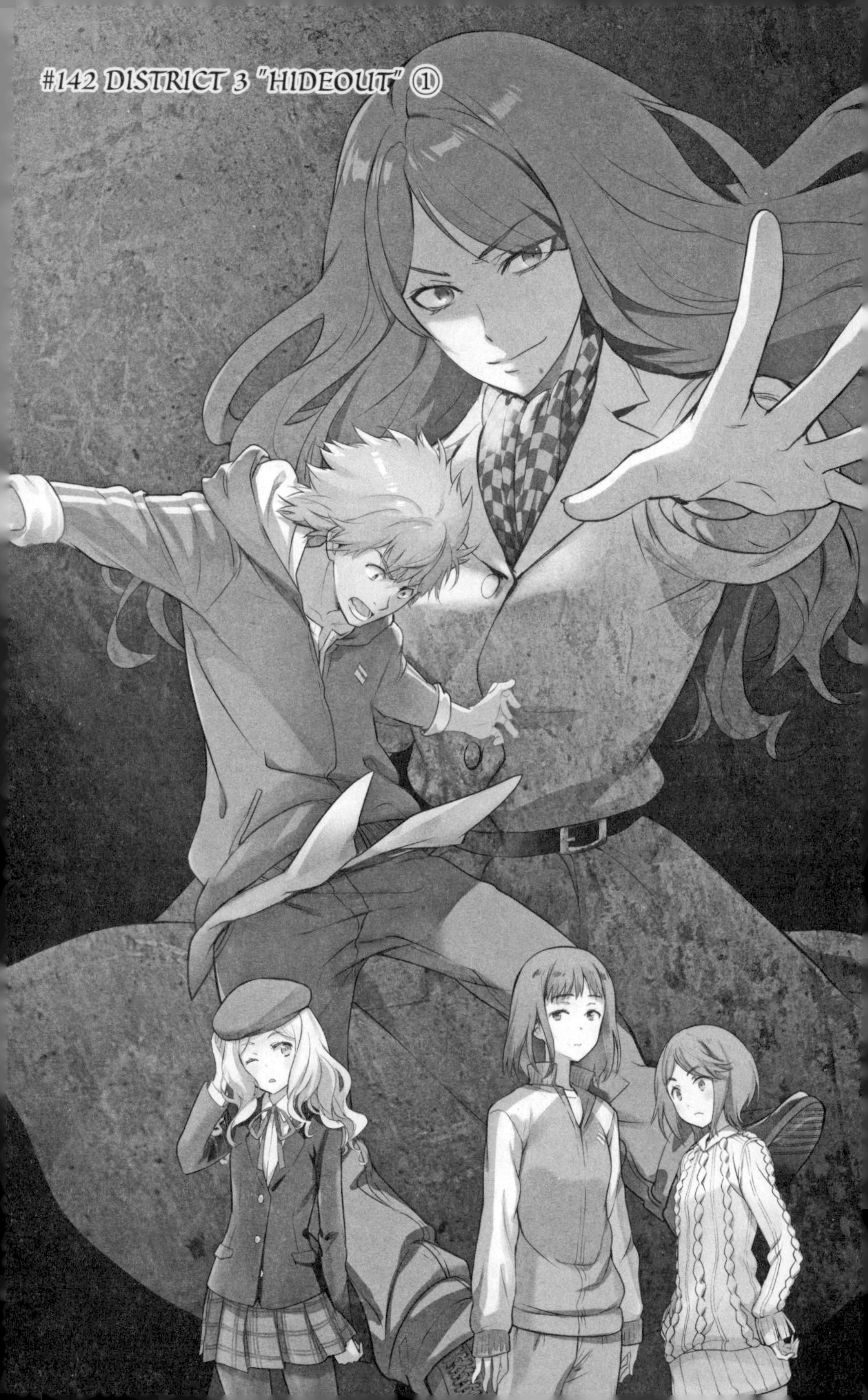

A
Certain
Magical
Index

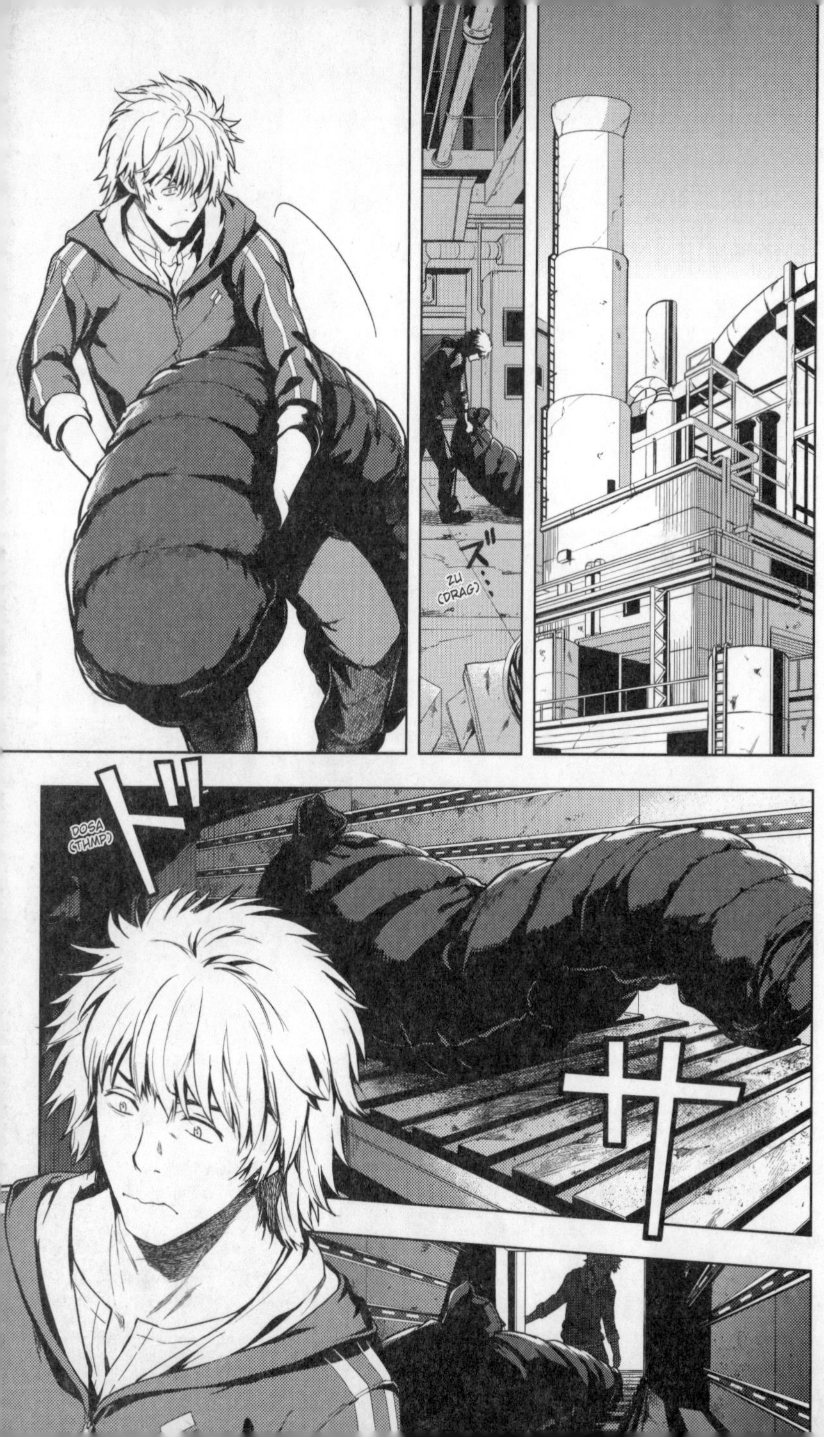
ズ…
ZU
(DRAG)
ドサ
DOSA
(THMP)

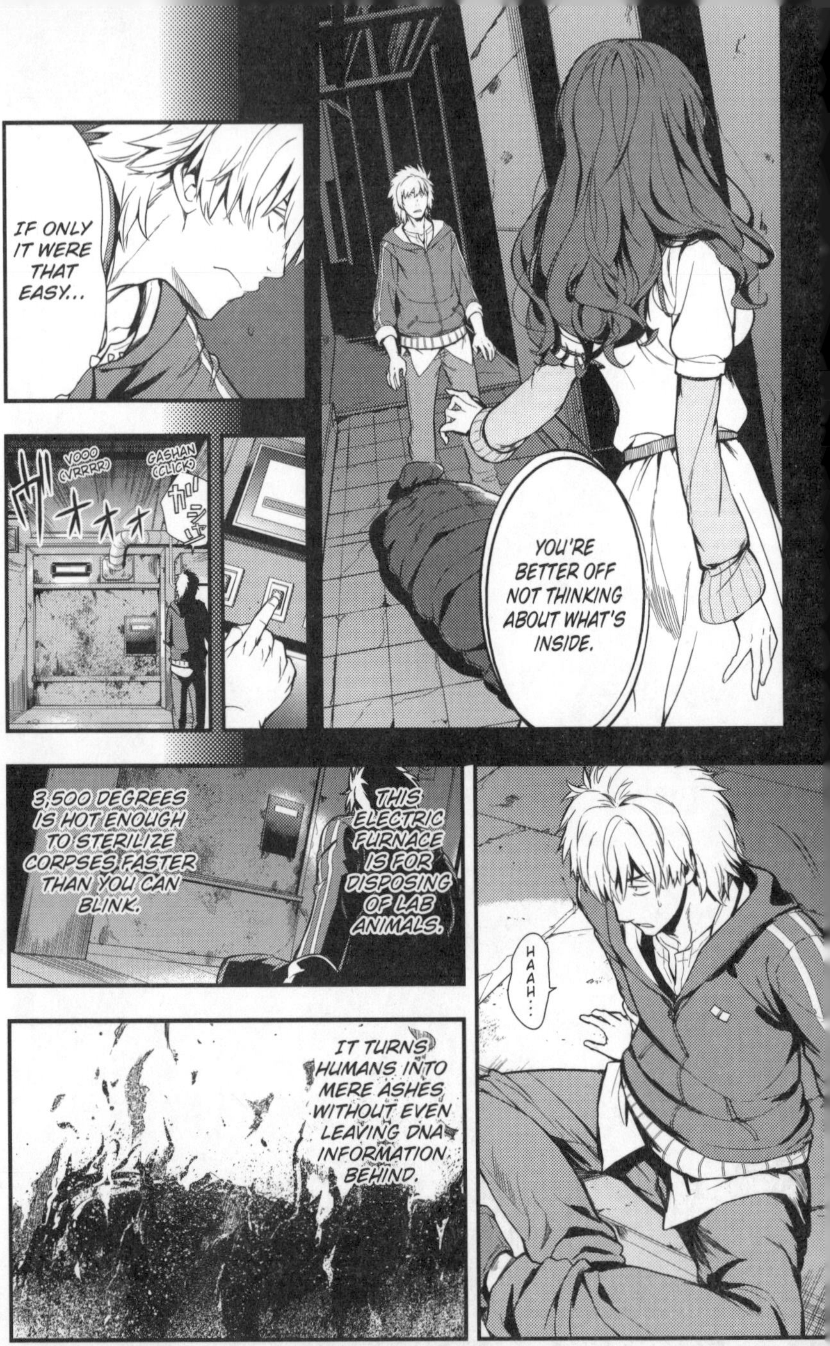
YOU'RE BETTER OFF NOT THINKING ABOUT WHAT'S INSIDE.
IF ONLY IT WERE THAT EASY...
GASHAN (CLICK)
VOOO (VRRRR)
THIS ELECTRIC FURNACE IS FOR DISPOSING OF LAB ANIMALS.
3,500 DEGREES IS HOT ENOUGH TO STERILIZE CORPSES FASTER THAN YOU CAN BLINK.
HAAH...
IT TURNS HUMANS INTO MERE ASHES WITHOUT EVEN LEAVING DNA INFORMATION BEHIND.

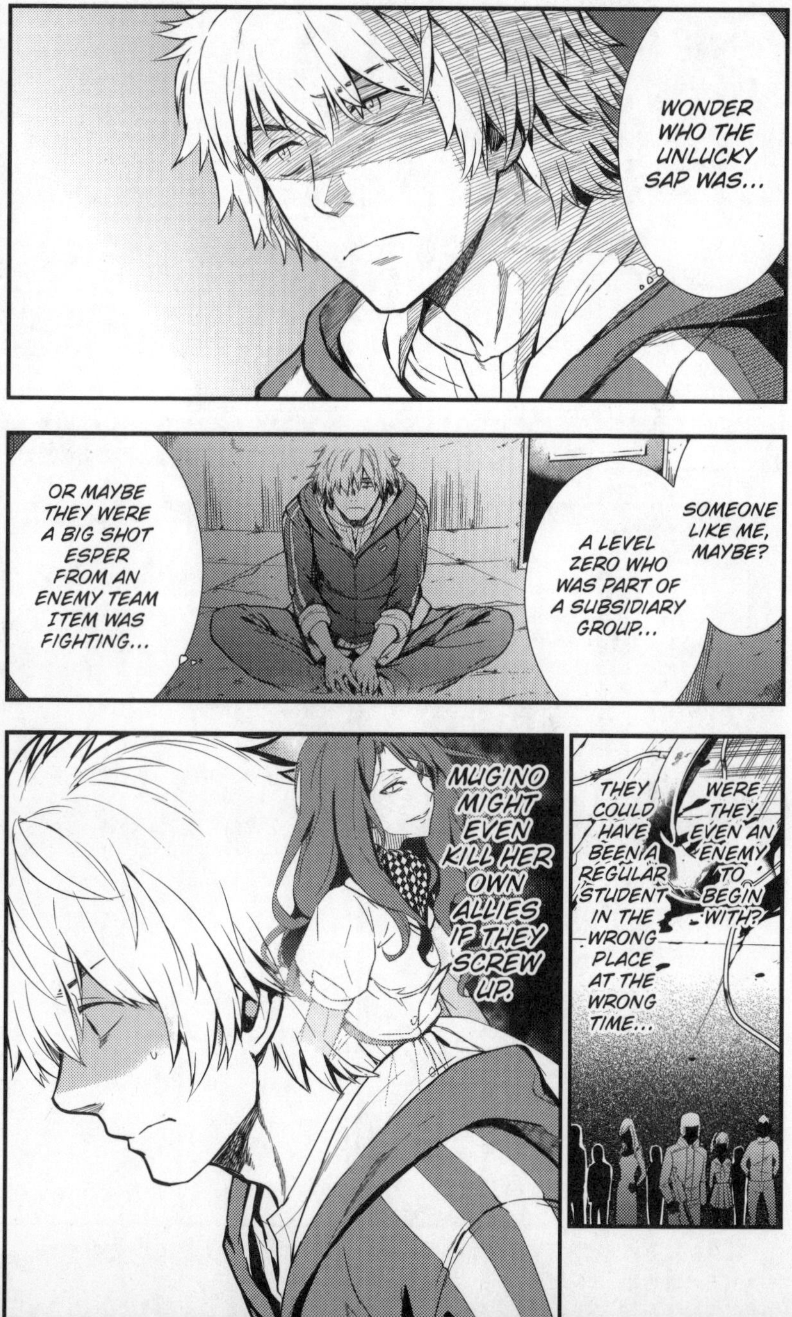
WONDER WHO THE UNLUCKY SAP WAS...
SOMEONE LIKE ME, MAYBE?
A LEVEL ZERO WHO WAS PART OF A SUBSIDIARY GROUP...
OR MAYBE THEY WERE A BIG SHOT ESPER FROM AN ENEMY TEAM ITEM WAS FIGHTING...
WERE THEY EVEN AN ENEMY TO BEGIN WITH?
THEY COULD HAVE BEEN A REGULAR STUDENT IN THE WRONG PLACE AT THE WRONG TIME...
MUGINO MIGHT EVEN KILL HER OWN ALLIES IF THEY SCREW UP.

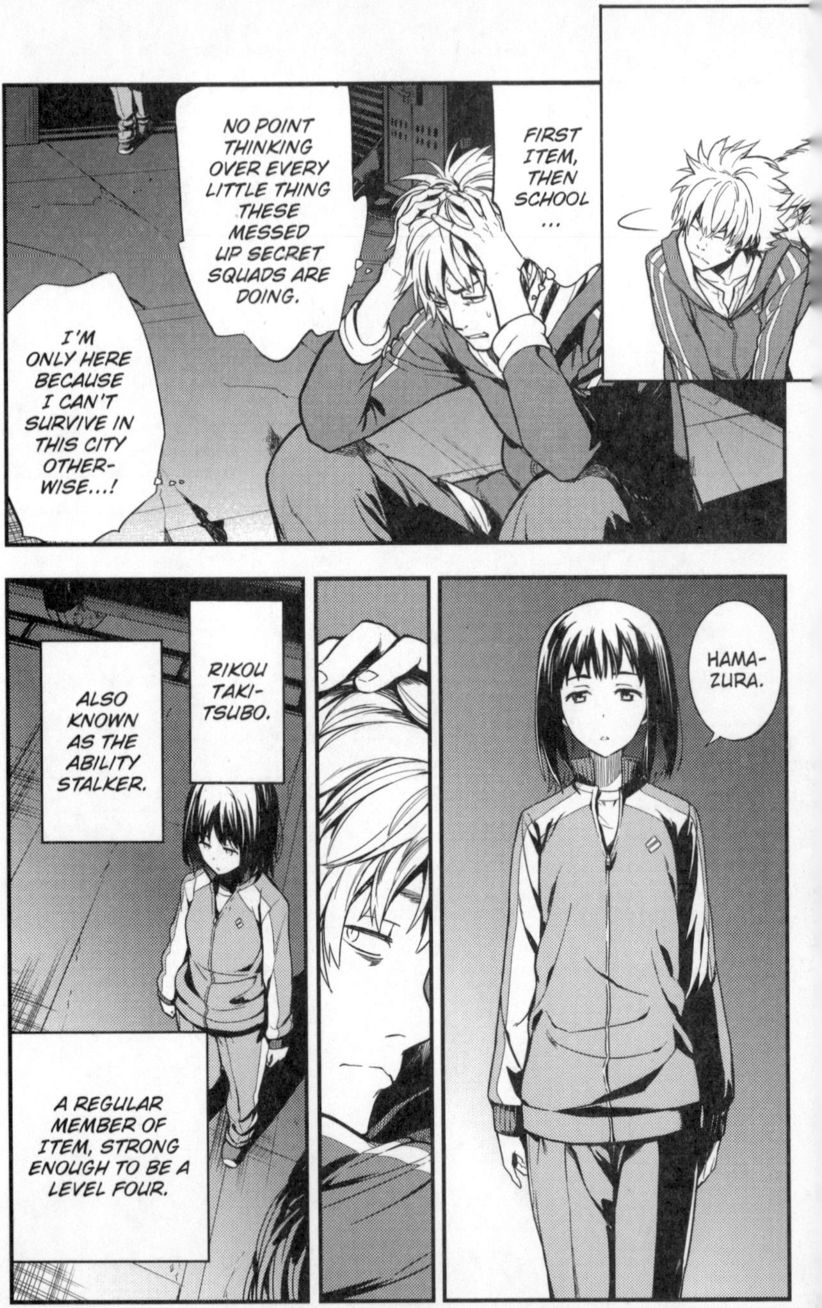
FIRST ITEM, THEN SCHOOL...
NO POINT THINKING OVER EVERY LITTLE THING THESE MESSED UP SECRET SQUADS ARE DOING.
I'M ONLY HERE BECAUSE I CAN'T SURVIVE IN THIS CITY OTHER-WISE...!
HAMA-ZURA.
RIKOU TAKI-TSUBO.
ALSO KNOWN AS THE ABILITY STALKER.
A REGULAR MEMBER OF ITEM, STRONG ENOUGH TO BE A LEVEL FOUR.

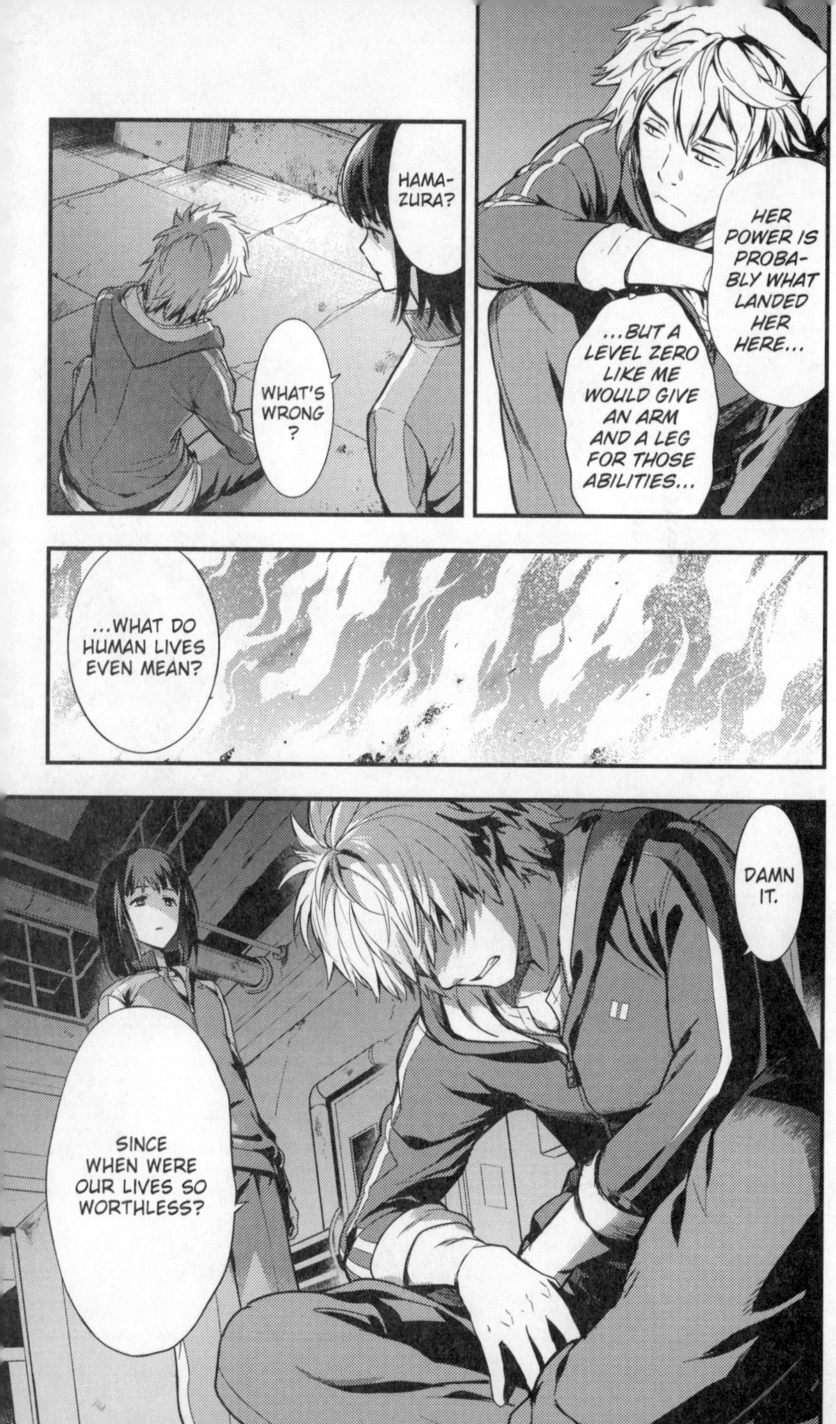
HER POWER IS PROBA-BLY WHAT LANDED HER HERE...
...BUT A LEVEL ZERO LIKE ME WOULD GIVE AN ARM AND A LEG FOR THOSE ABILITIES...
HAMA-ZURA?
WHAT'S WRONG?
...WHAT DO HUMAN LIVES EVEN MEAN?
DAMN IT.
SINCE WHEN WERE OUR LIVES SO WORTHLESS?

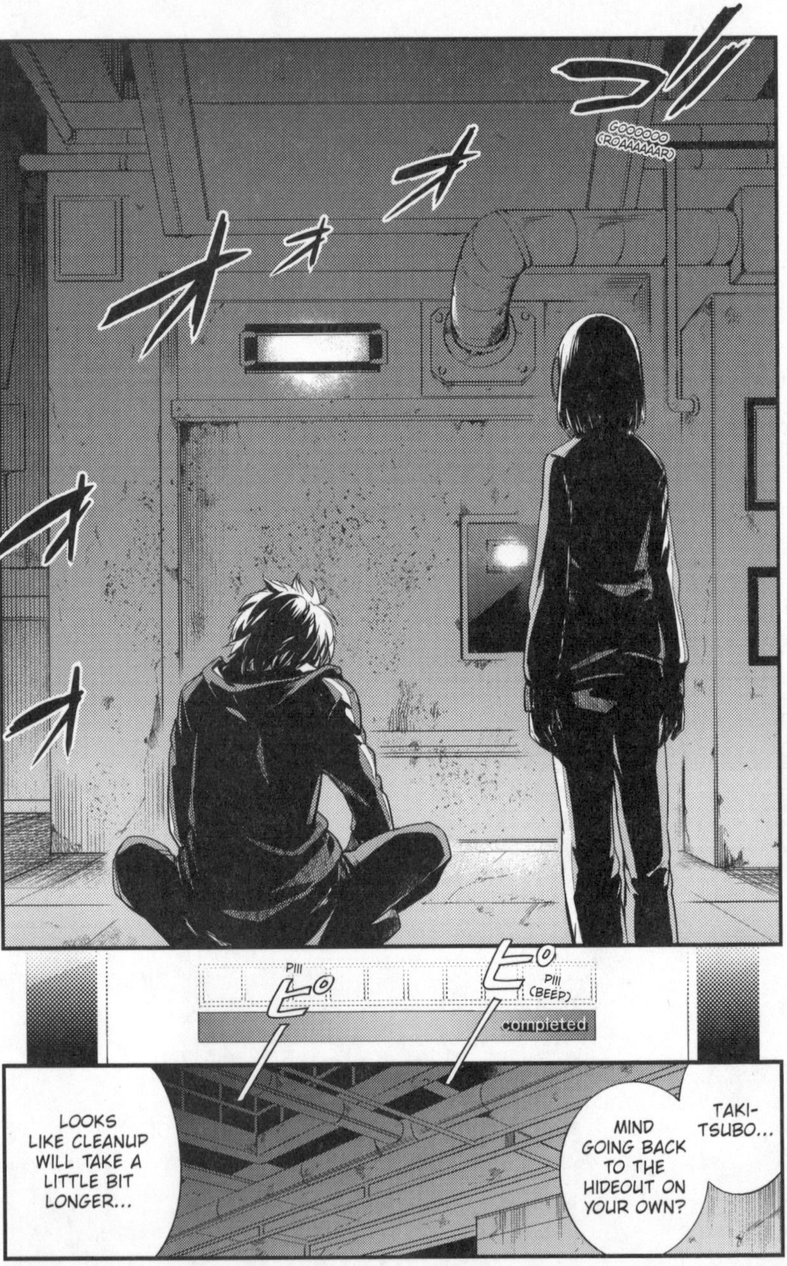
GOOOOOOO
(ROAAAAAAR)
PIII
(BEEP)
PIII
completed
TAKI-TSUBO...
MIND GOING BACK TO THE HIDEOUT ON YOUR OWN?
LOOKS LIKE CLEANUP WILL TAKE A LITTLE BIT LONGER...

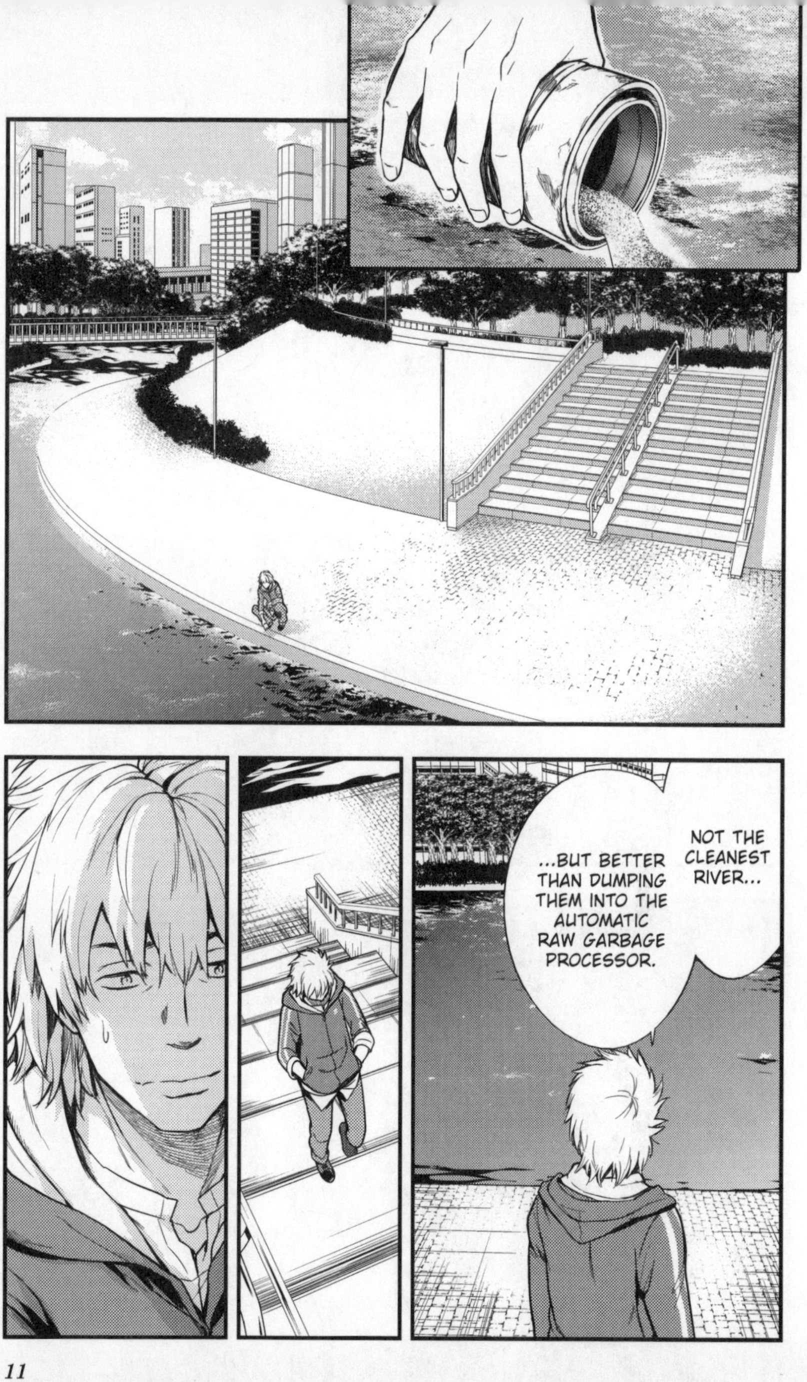
NOT THE CLEANEST RIVER...
...BUT BETTER THAN DUMPING THEM INTO THE AUTOMATIC RAW GARBAGE PROCESSOR.

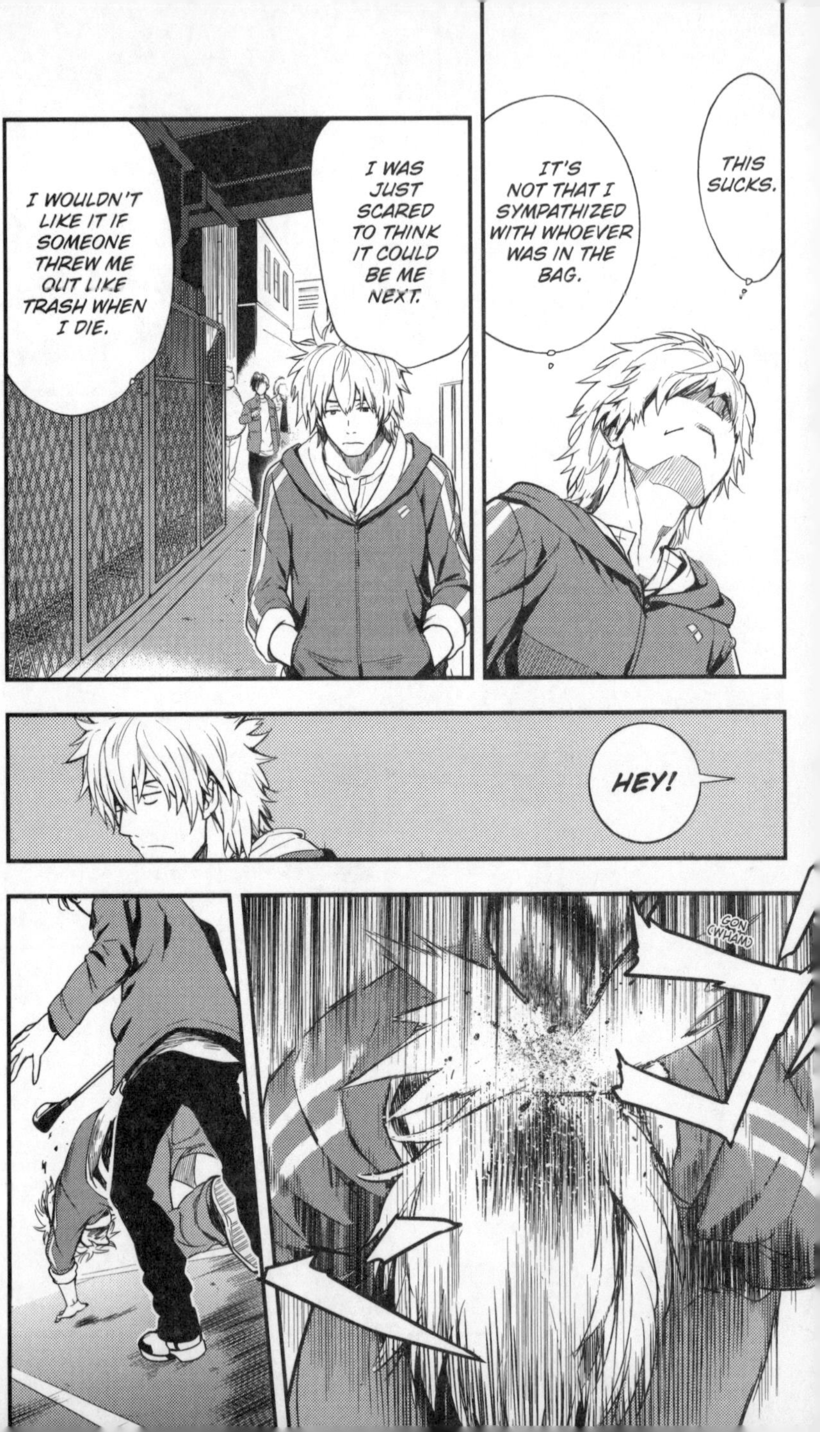
THIS SUCKS.
IT'S NOT THAT I SYMPATHIZED WITH WHOEVER WAS IN THE BAG.
I WAS JUST SCARED TO THINK IT COULD BE ME NEXT.
I WOULDN'T LIKE IT IF SOMEONE THREW ME OUT LIKE TRASH WHEN I DIE.
HEY!
GON (WHAM)

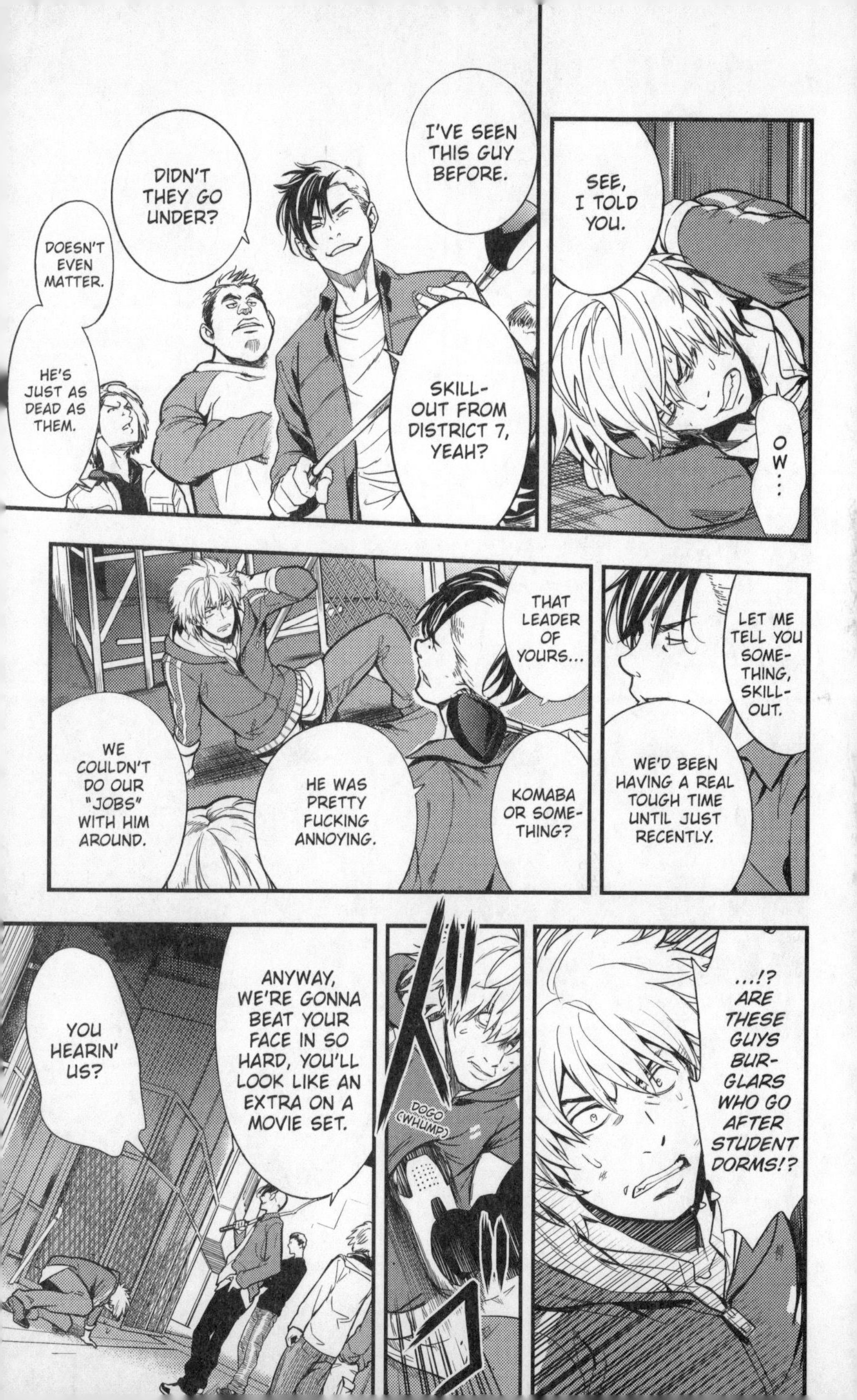
SEE, I TOLD YOU.
OW...
I'VE SEEN THIS GUY BEFORE.
SKILL-OUT FROM DISTRICT 7, YEAH?
DIDN'T THEY GO UNDER?
DOESN'T EVEN MATTER.
HE'S JUST AS DEAD AS THEM.
LET ME TELL YOU SOMETHING, SKILL-OUT.
WE'D BEEN HAVING A REAL TOUGH TIME UNTIL JUST RECENTLY.
THAT LEADER OF YOURS...
KOMABA OR SOME-THING?
HE WAS PRETTY FUCKING ANNOYING.
WE COULDN'T DO OUR "JOBS" WITH HIM AROUND.
...!? ARE THESE GUYS BUR-GLARS WHO GO AFTER STUDENT DORMS!?
DOGO (WHUMP)
ANYWAY, WE'RE GONNA BEAT YOUR FACE IN SO HARD, YOU'LL LOOK LIKE AN EXTRA ON A MOVIE SET.
YOU HEARIN' US?

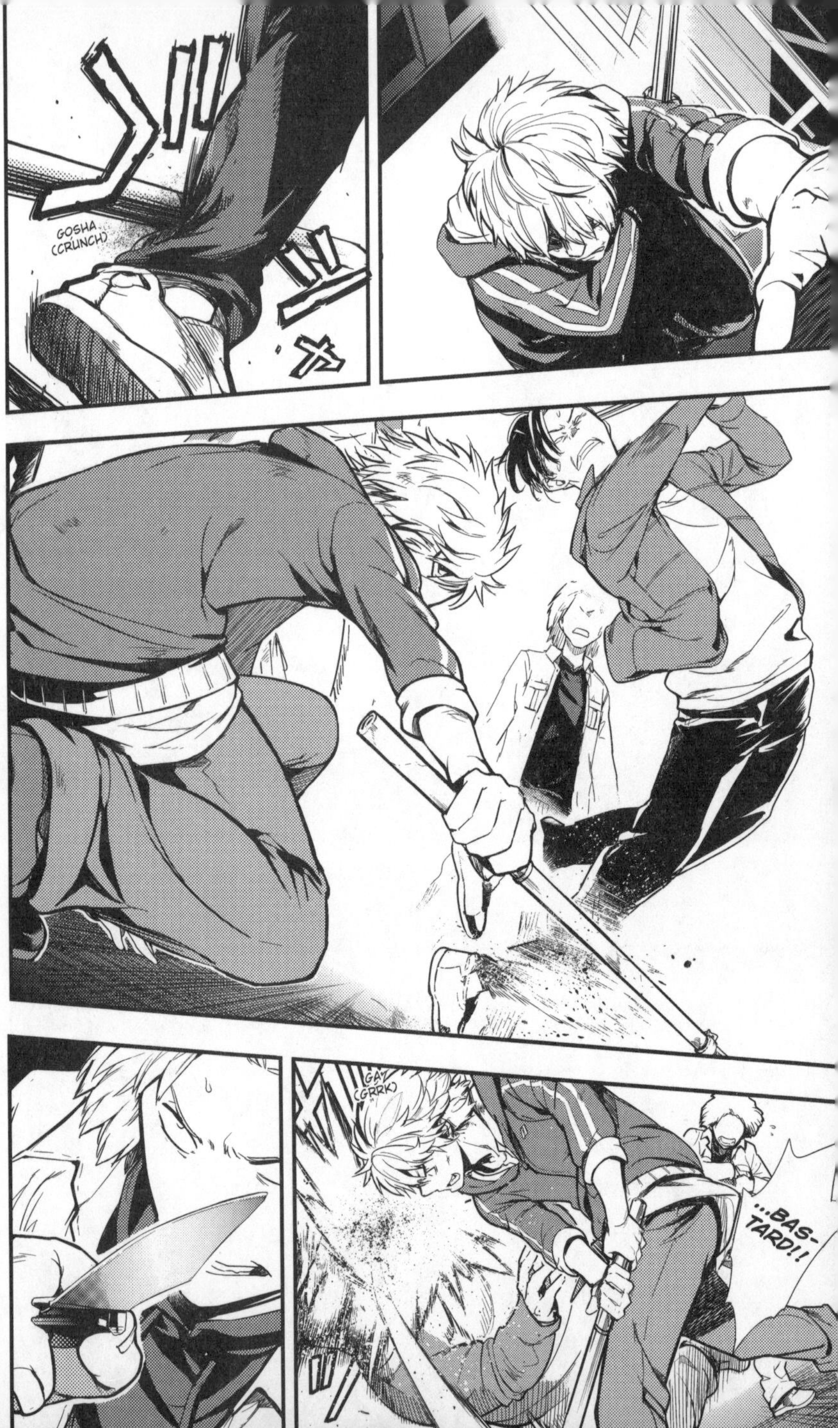
GOSHA
(CRUNCH)
GA
(GRRK)
...BAS-
TARD!!

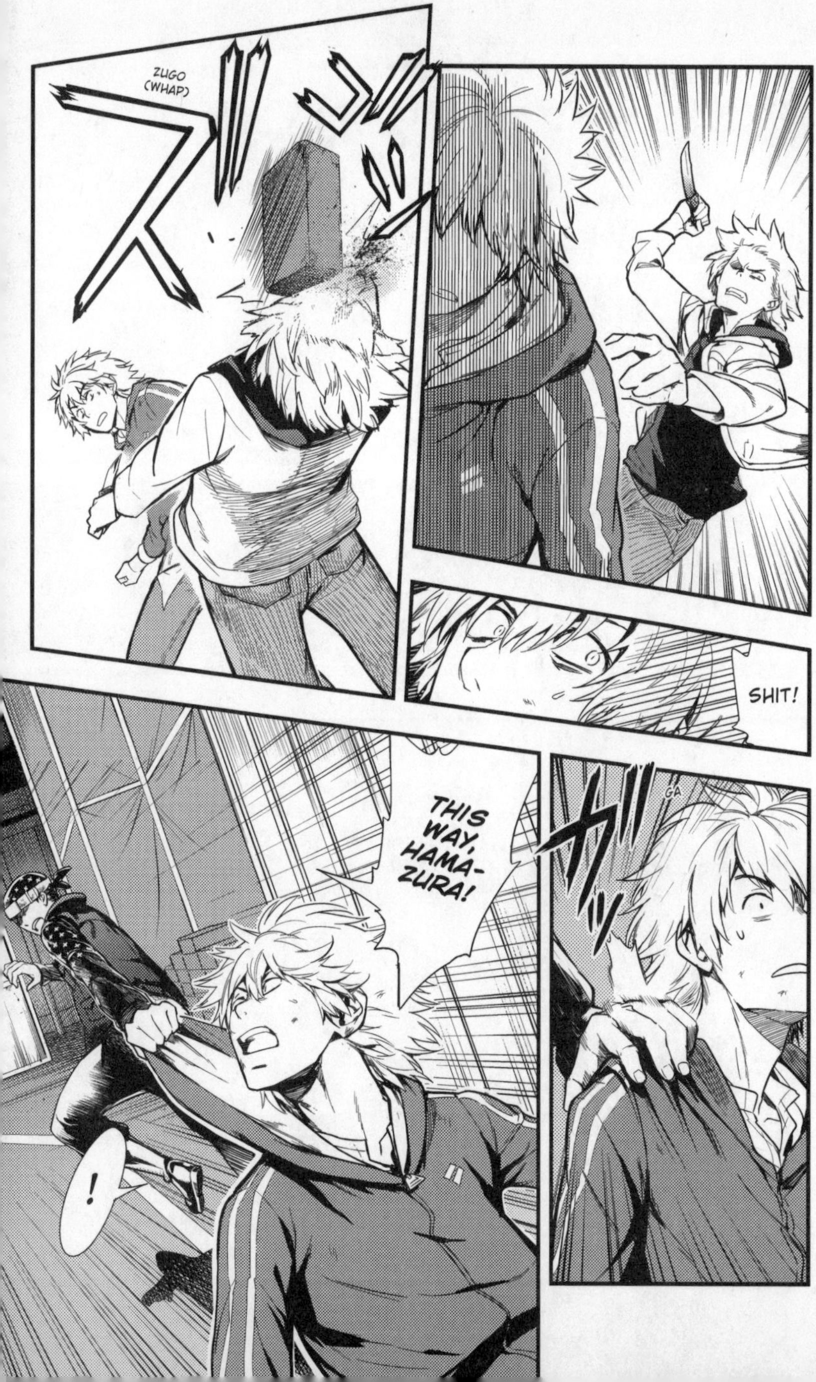
SHIT!
ZUGO (WHAP)
GA
THIS WAY, HAMA-ZURA!
!

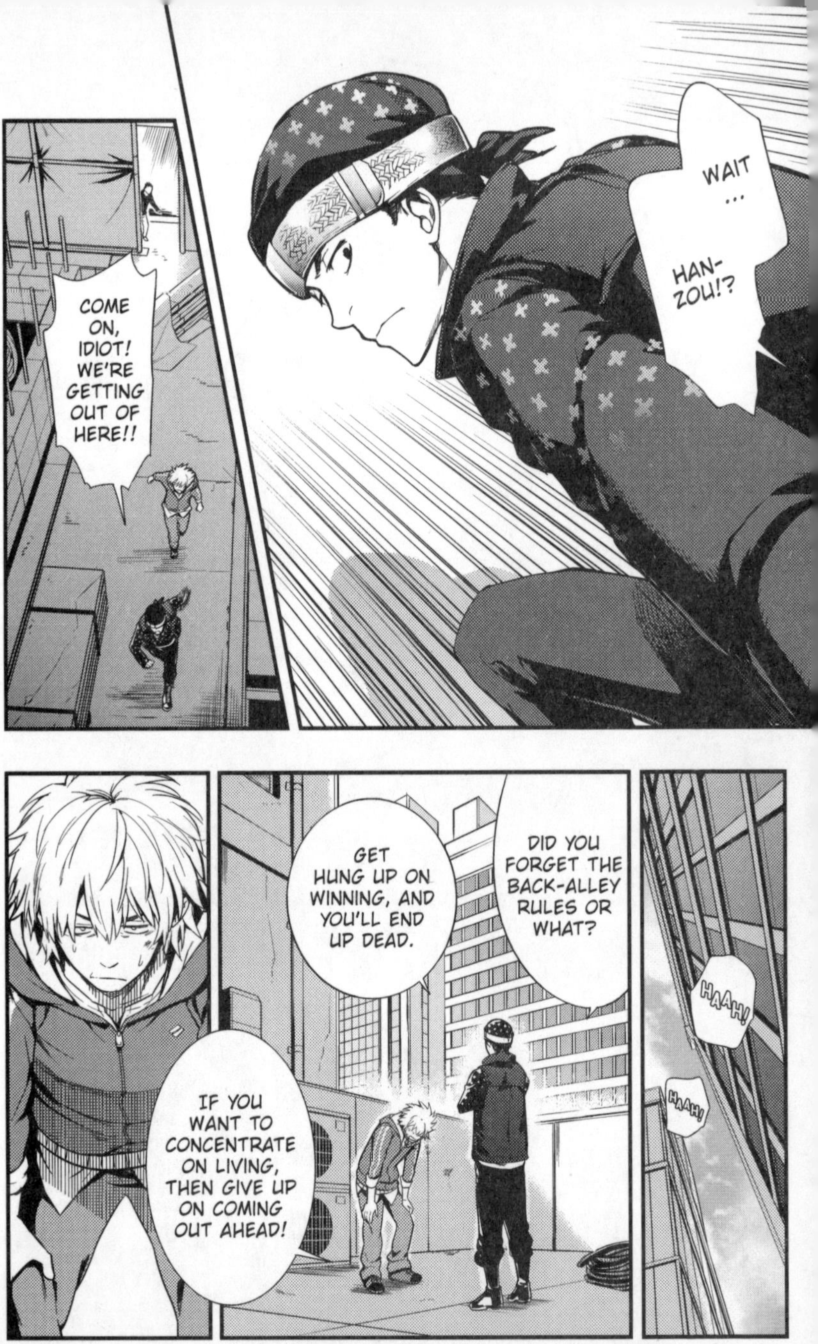
WAIT ...
HAN-ZOU!?
COME ON, IDIOT! WE'RE GETTING OUT OF HERE!!
HAAH!
HAAH!
DID YOU FORGET THE BACK-ALLEY RULES OR WHAT?
GET HUNG UP ON WINNING, AND YOU'LL END UP DEAD.
IF YOU WANT TO CONCENTRATE ON LIVING, THEN GIVE UP ON COMING OUT AHEAD!

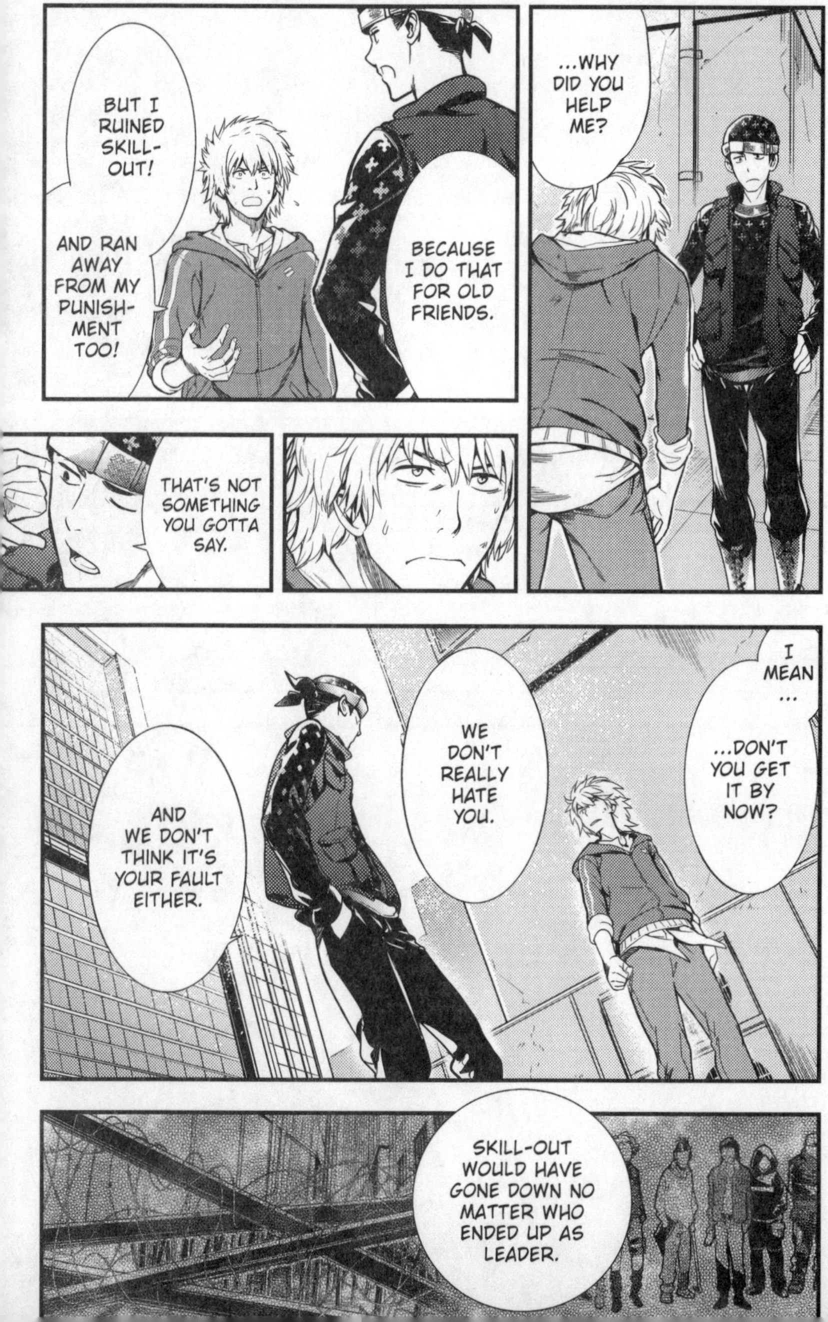
...WHY DID YOU HELP ME?
BECAUSE I DO THAT FOR OLD FRIENDS.
BUT I RUINED SKILL-OUT!
AND RAN AWAY FROM MY PUNISHMENT TOO!
THAT'S NOT SOMETHING YOU GOTTA SAY.
I MEAN...
...DON'T YOU GET IT BY NOW?
WE DON'T REALLY HATE YOU.
AND WE DON'T THINK IT'S YOUR FAULT EITHER.
SKILL-OUT WOULD HAVE GONE DOWN NO MATTER WHO ENDED UP AS LEADER.

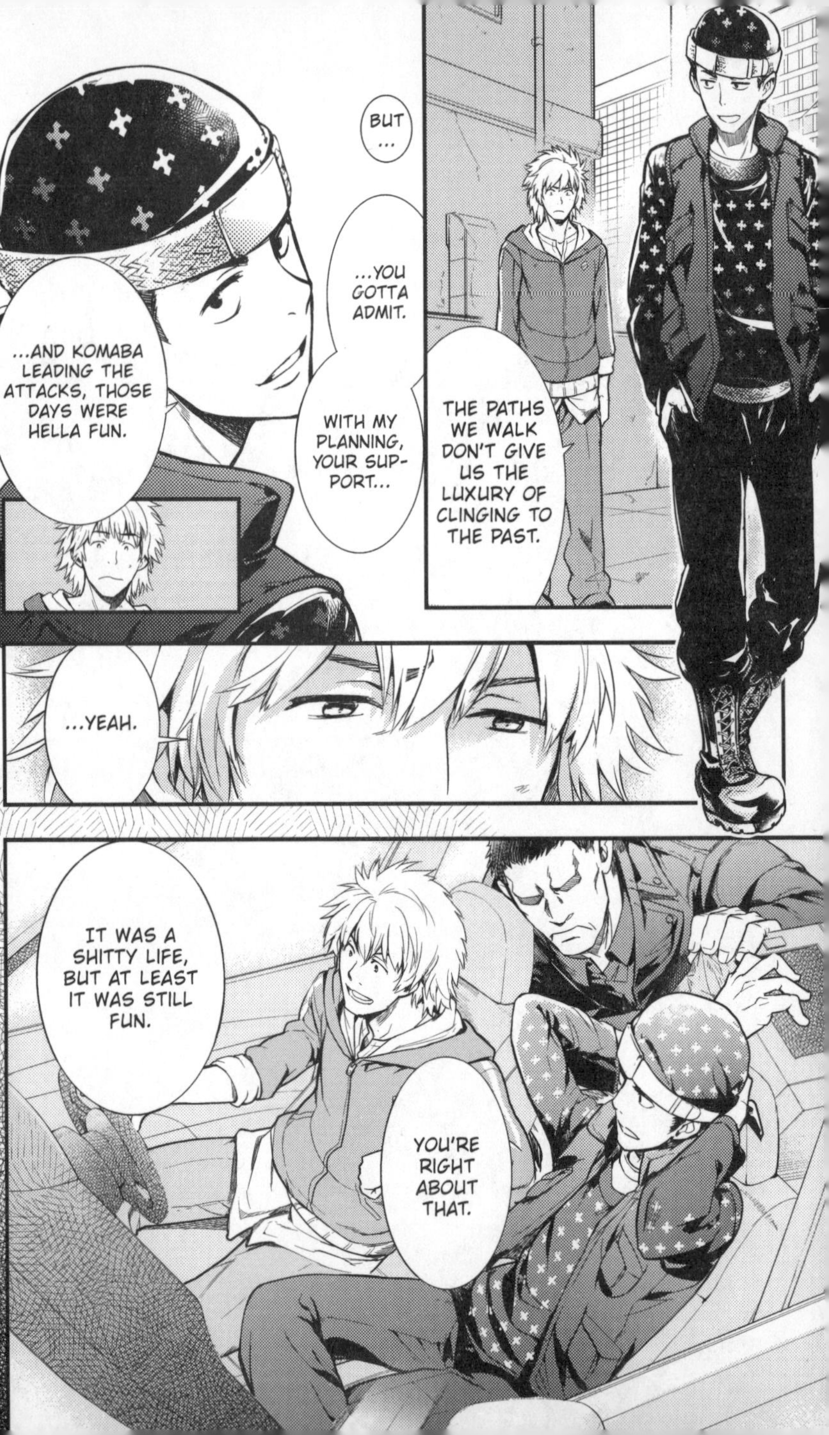
THE PATHS WE WALK DON'T GIVE US THE LUXURY OF CLINGING TO THE PAST.
BUT ...
...YOU GOTTA ADMIT.
WITH MY PLANNING, YOUR SUP-PORT...
...AND KOMABA LEADING THE ATTACKS, THOSE DAYS WERE HELLA FUN.
...YEAH.
IT WAS A SHITTY LIFE, BUT AT LEAST IT WAS STILL FUN.
YOU'RE RIGHT ABOUT THAT.

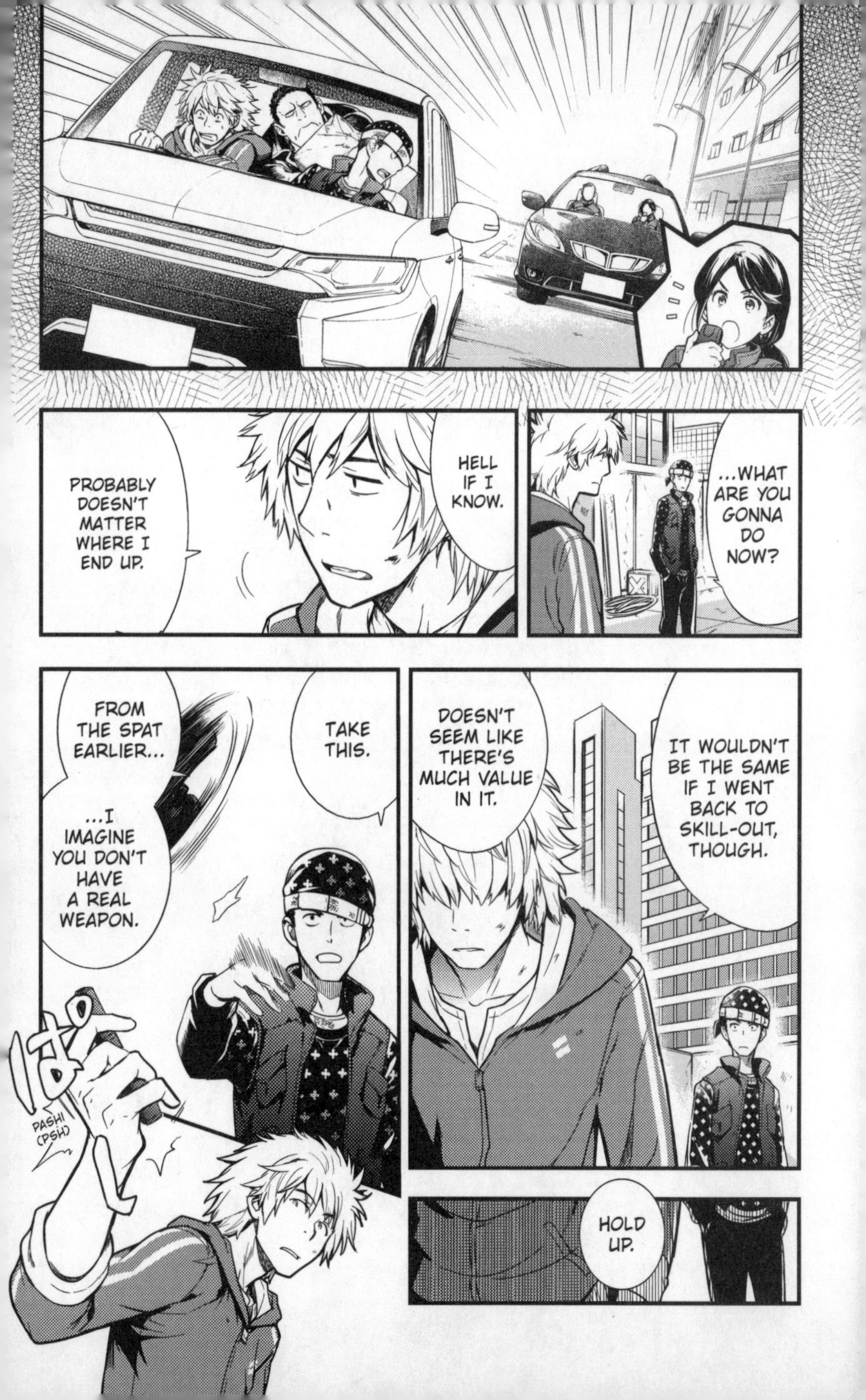
...WHAT ARE YOU GONNA DO NOW?
HELL IF I KNOW.
PROBABLY DOESN'T MATTER WHERE I END UP.
IT WOULDN'T BE THE SAME IF I WENT BACK TO SKILL-OUT, THOUGH.
DOESN'T SEEM LIKE THERE'S MUCH VALUE IN IT.
HOLD UP.
TAKE THIS.
FROM THE SPAT EARLIER...
...I IMAGINE YOU DON'T HAVE A REAL WEAPON.
ぱ
PASHI (PSH)

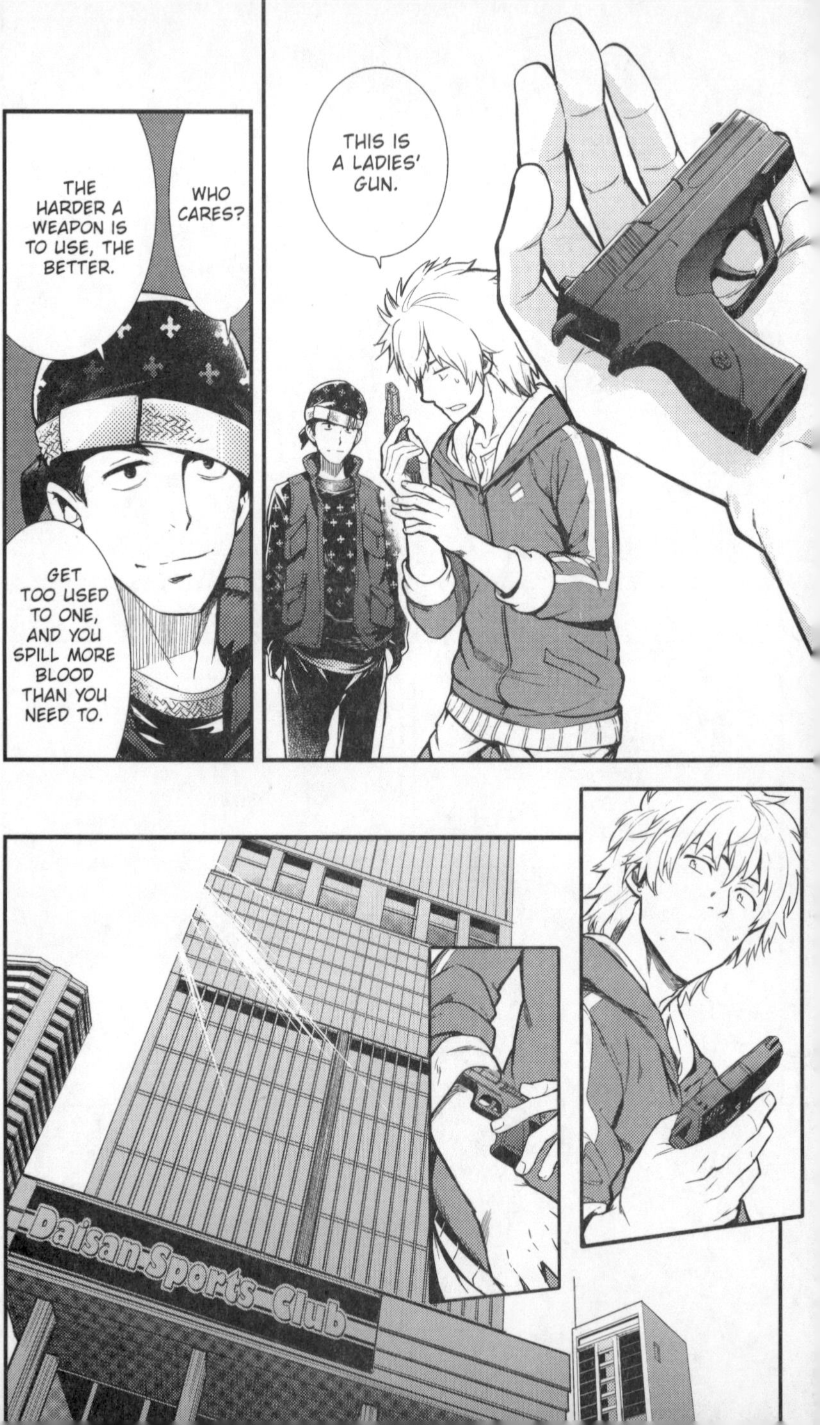
THIS IS A LADIES' GUN.
WHO CARES?
THE HARDER A WEAPON IS TO USE, THE BETTER.
GET TOO USED TO ONE, AND YOU SPILL MORE BLOOD THAN YOU NEED TO.
Daisan Sports Club

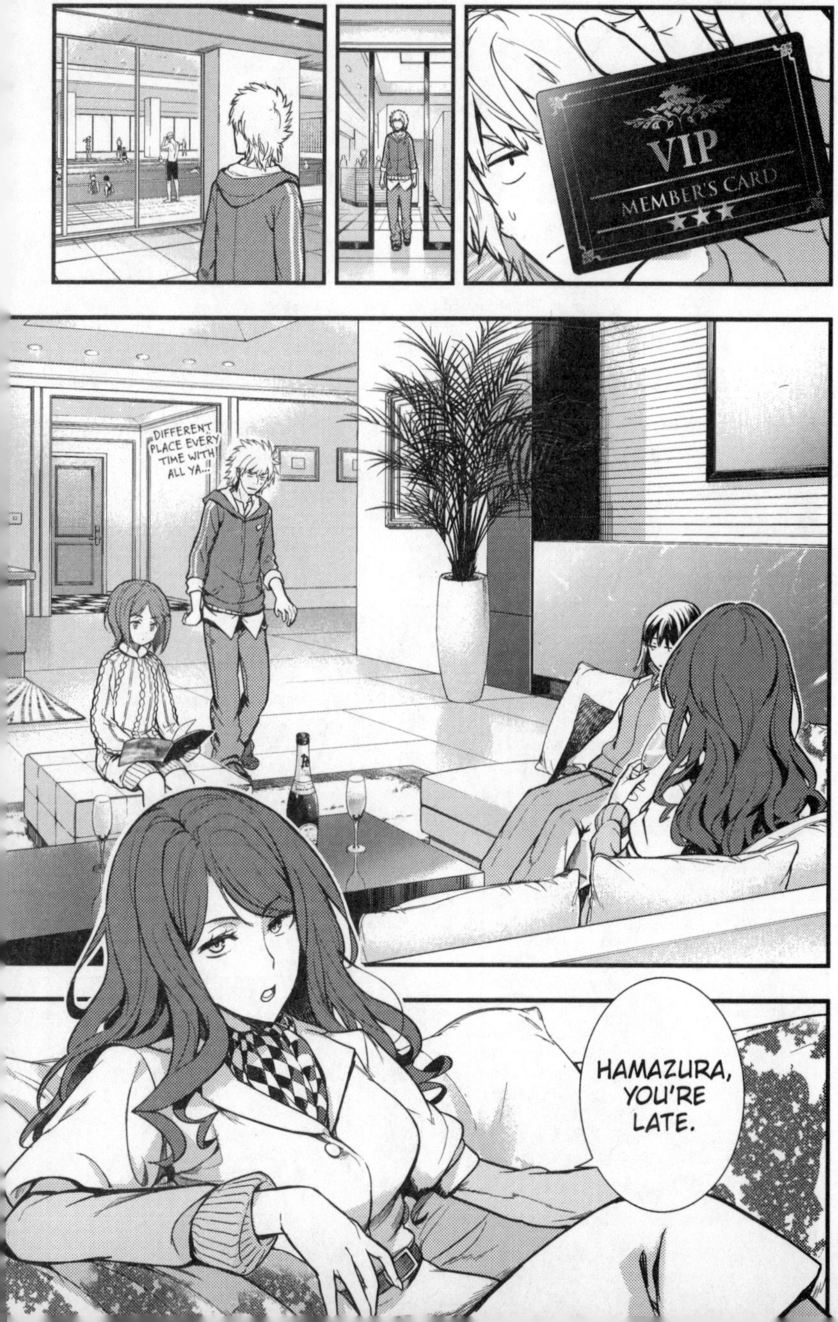
VIP
MEMBER'S CARD
DIFFERENT PLACE EVERY TIME WITH ALL YA...!
HAMAZURA, YOU'RE LATE.

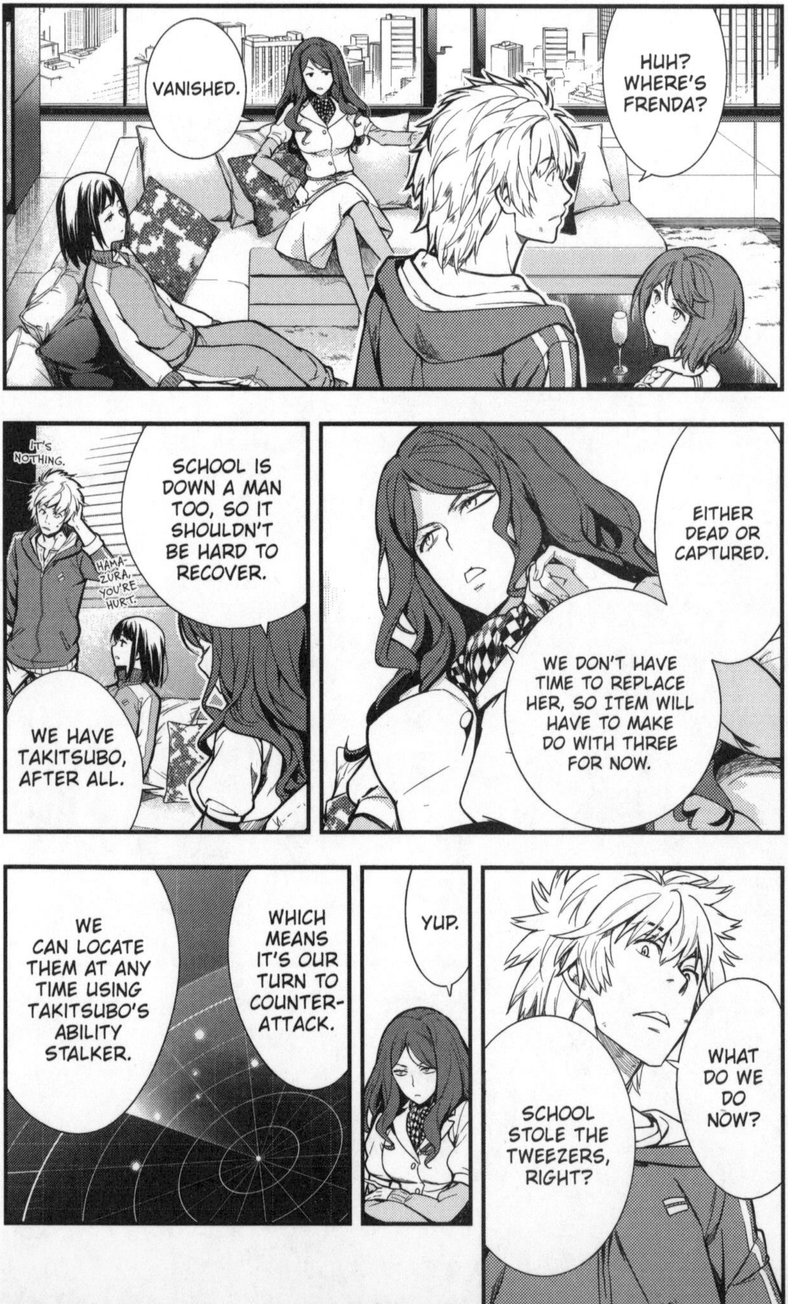
HUH? WHERE'S FRENDA?
VANISHED.
EITHER DEAD OR CAPTURED.
WE DON'T HAVE TIME TO REPLACE HER, SO ITEM WILL HAVE TO MAKE DO WITH THREE FOR NOW.
SCHOOL IS DOWN A MAN TOO, SO IT SHOULDN'T BE HARD TO RECOVER.
HAMA-ZURA, YOU'RE HURT.
IT'S NOTHING.
WE HAVE TAKITSUBO, AFTER ALL.
WHAT DO WE DO NOW?
SCHOOL STOLE THE TWEEZERS, RIGHT?
YUP.
WHICH MEANS IT'S OUR TURN TO COUNTER-ATTACK.
WE CAN LOCATE THEM AT ANY TIME USING TAKITSUBO'S ABILITY STALKER.

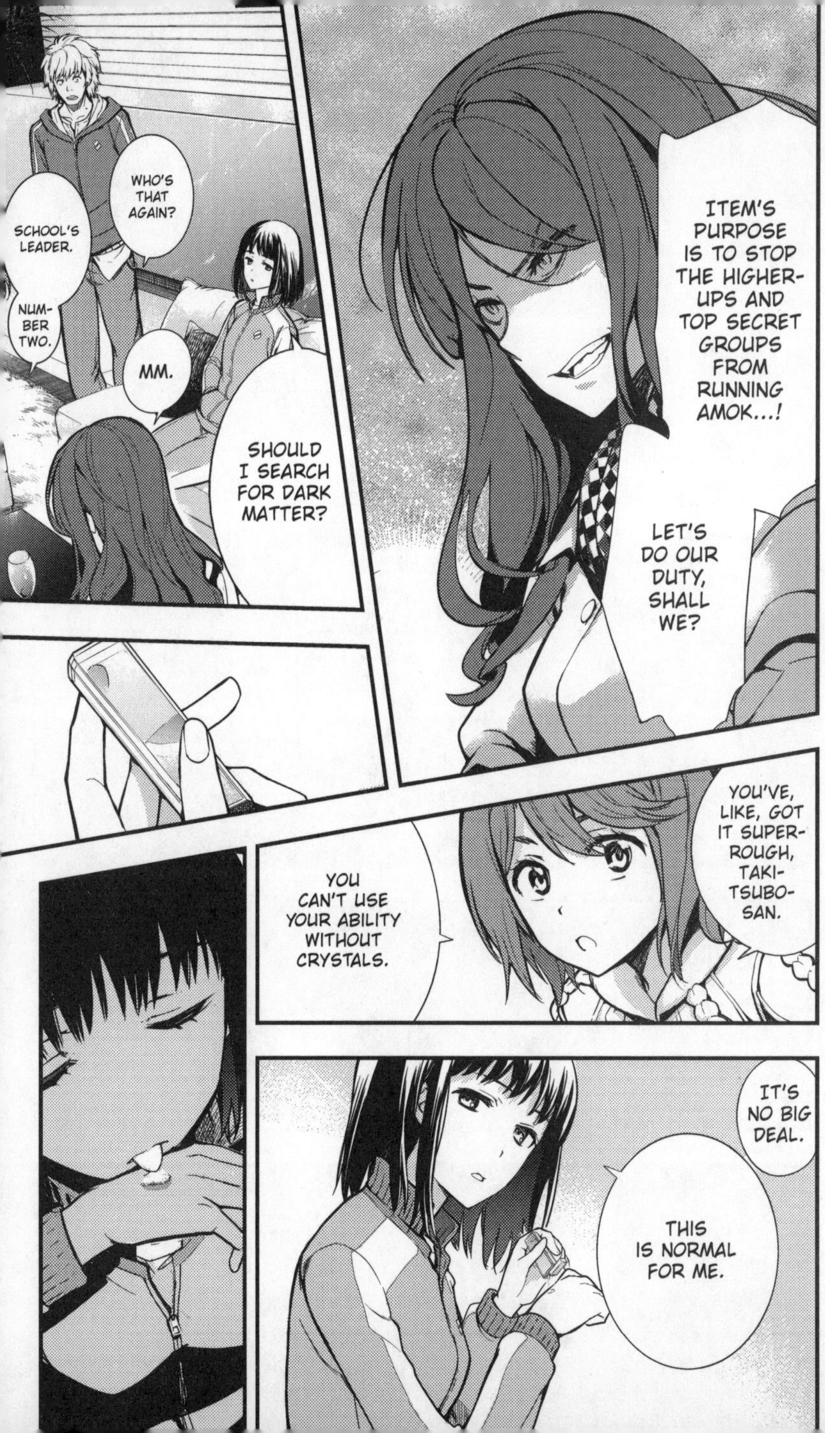
ITEM'S PURPOSE IS TO STOP THE HIGHER-UPS AND TOP SECRET GROUPS FROM RUNNING AMOK...!
LET'S DO OUR DUTY, SHALL WE?
WHO'S THAT AGAIN?
SCHOOL'S LEADER.
NUMBER TWO.
MM.
SHOULD I SEARCH FOR DARK MATTER?
YOU'VE, LIKE, GOT IT SUPER-ROUGH, TAKI-TSUBO-SAN.
YOU CAN'T USE YOUR ABILITY WITHOUT CRYSTALS.
IT'S NO BIG DEAL.
THIS IS NORMAL FOR ME.

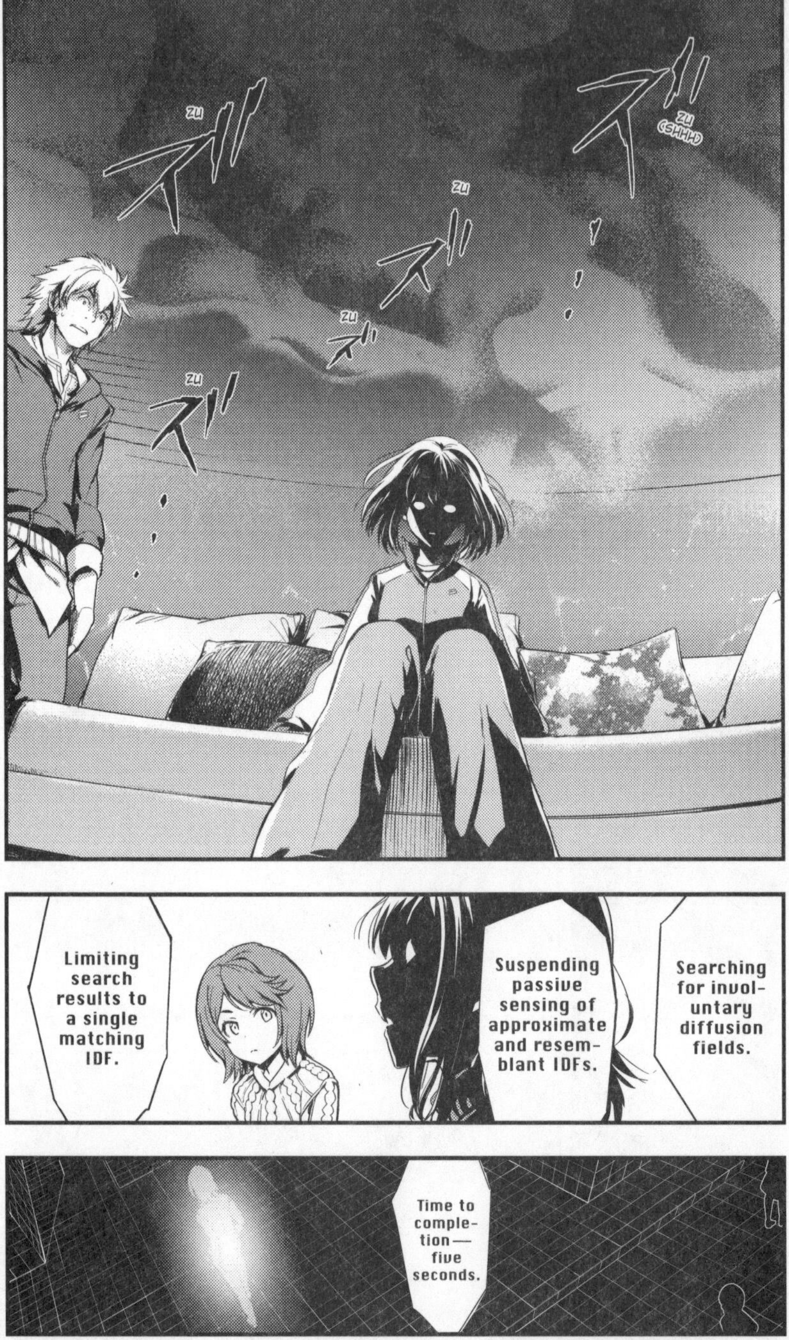
ZU (SHHH)
ZU
ZU
ZU
ZU
Searching for involuntary diffusion fields.
Suspending passive sensing of approximate and resemblant IDFs.
Limiting search results to a single matching IDF.
Time to completion—five seconds.

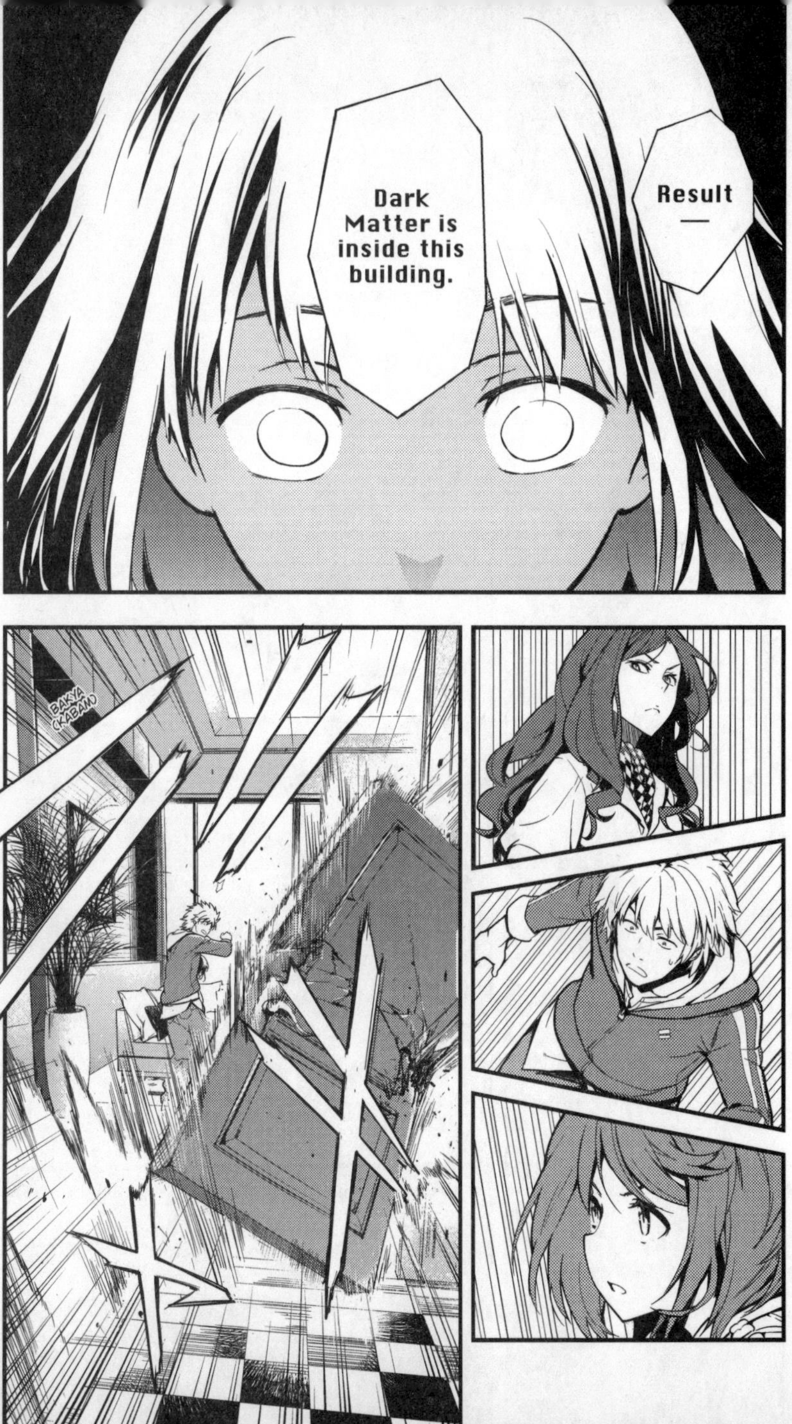
Result —
Dark Matter is inside this building.
BAKYA (KABAM)

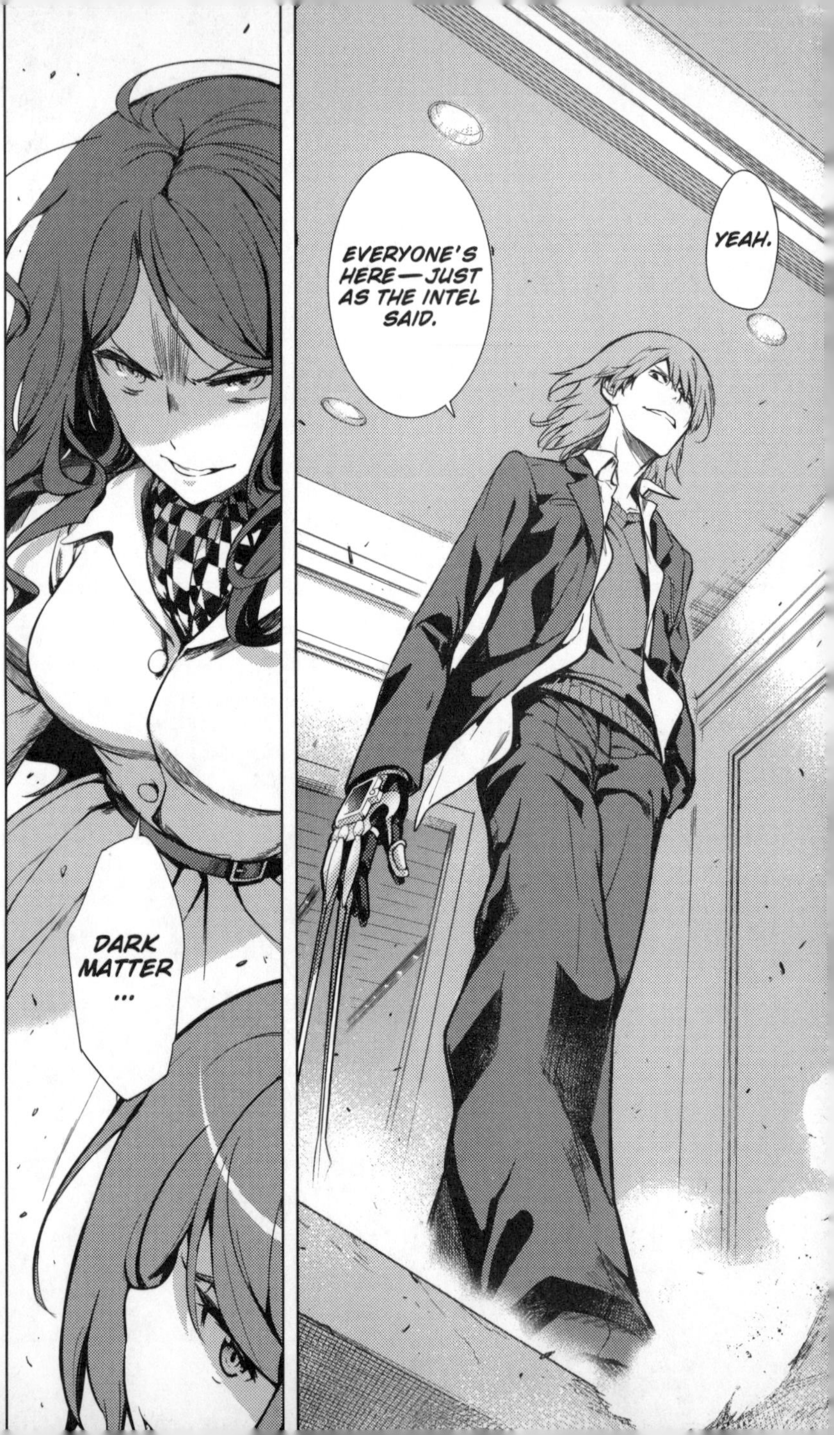
YEAH.
EVERYONE'S HERE—JUST AS THE INTEL SAID.
DARK MATTER ...

A Certain Magical Index

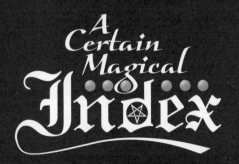

A Certain Magical Index

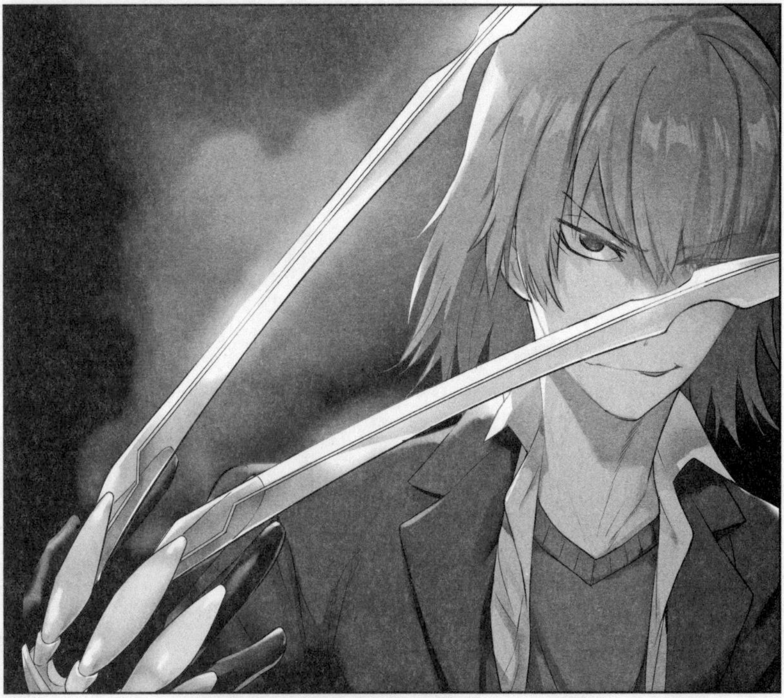

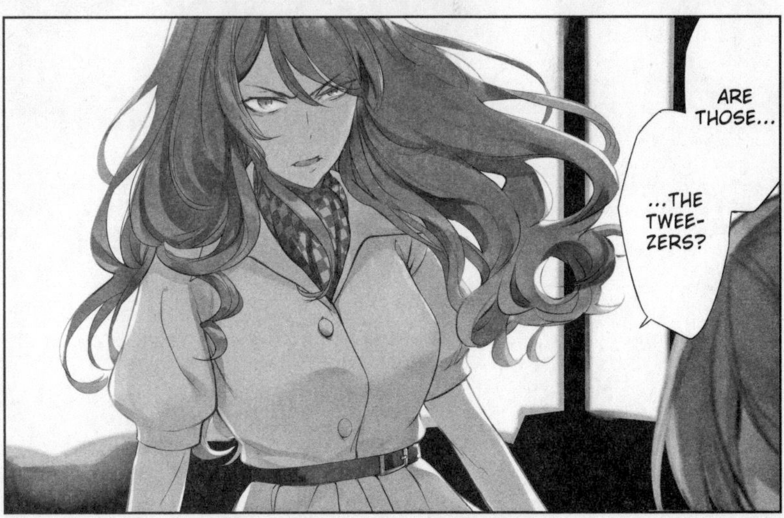
ARE THOSE...
...THE TWEE-ZERS?

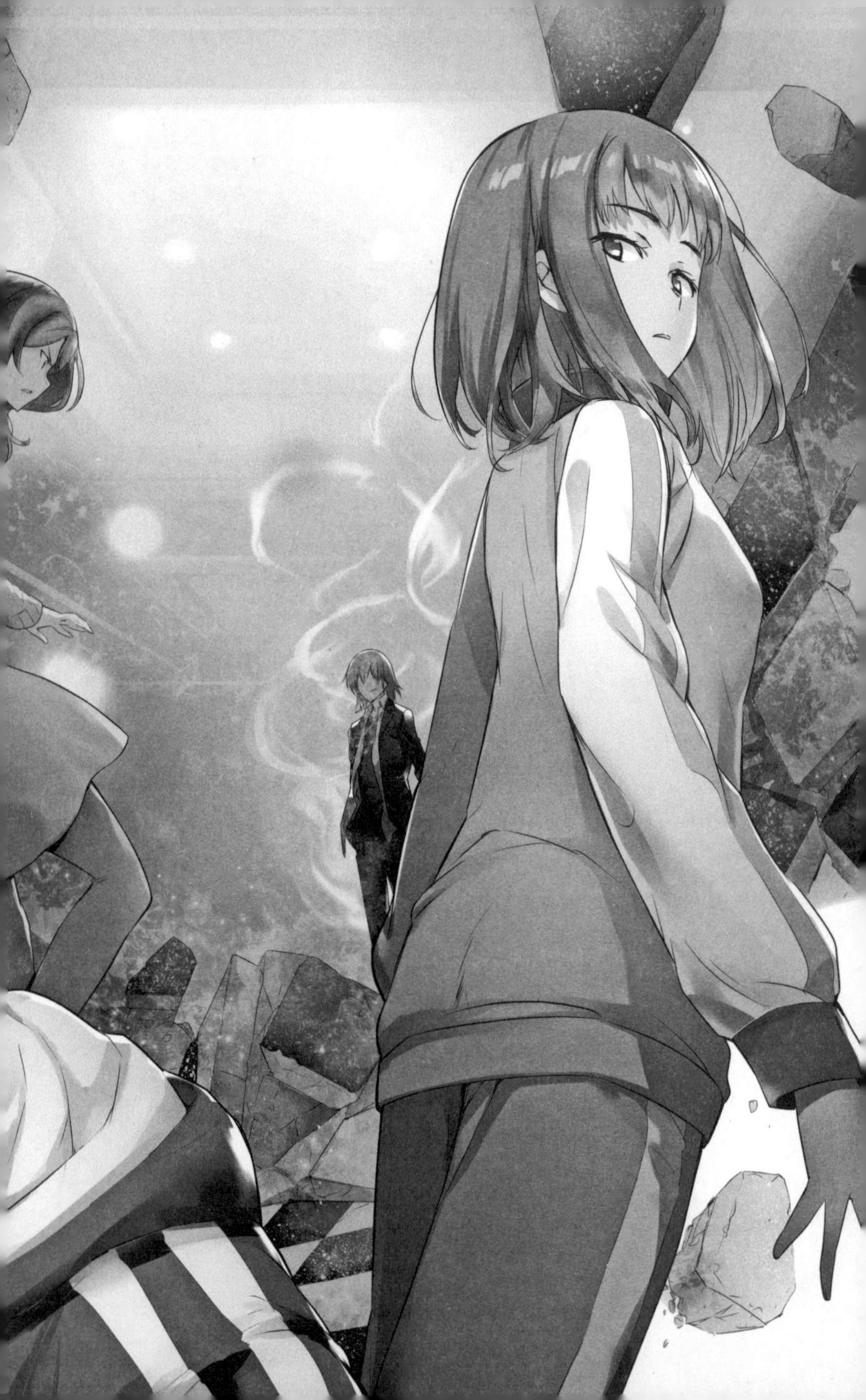

#143 DISTRICT 3 "HIDEOUT" ②

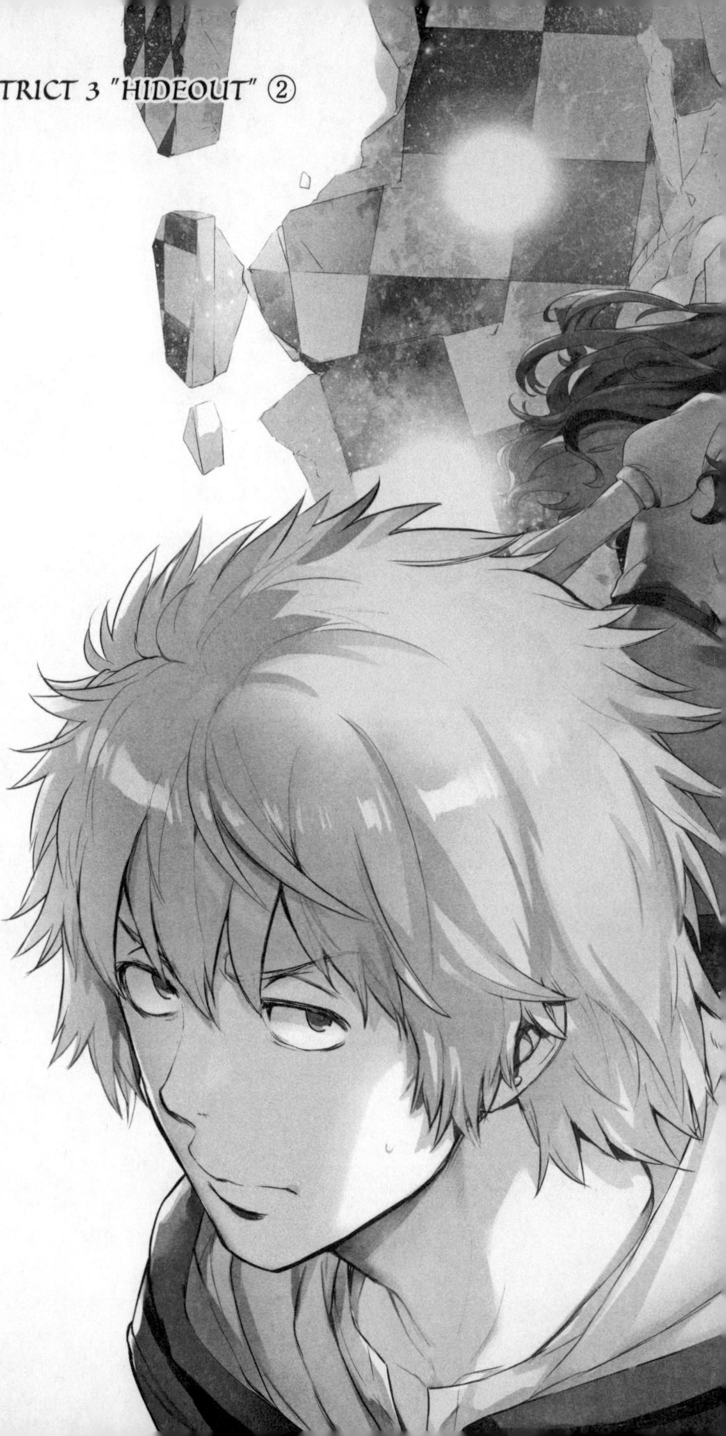

A Certain Magical Index

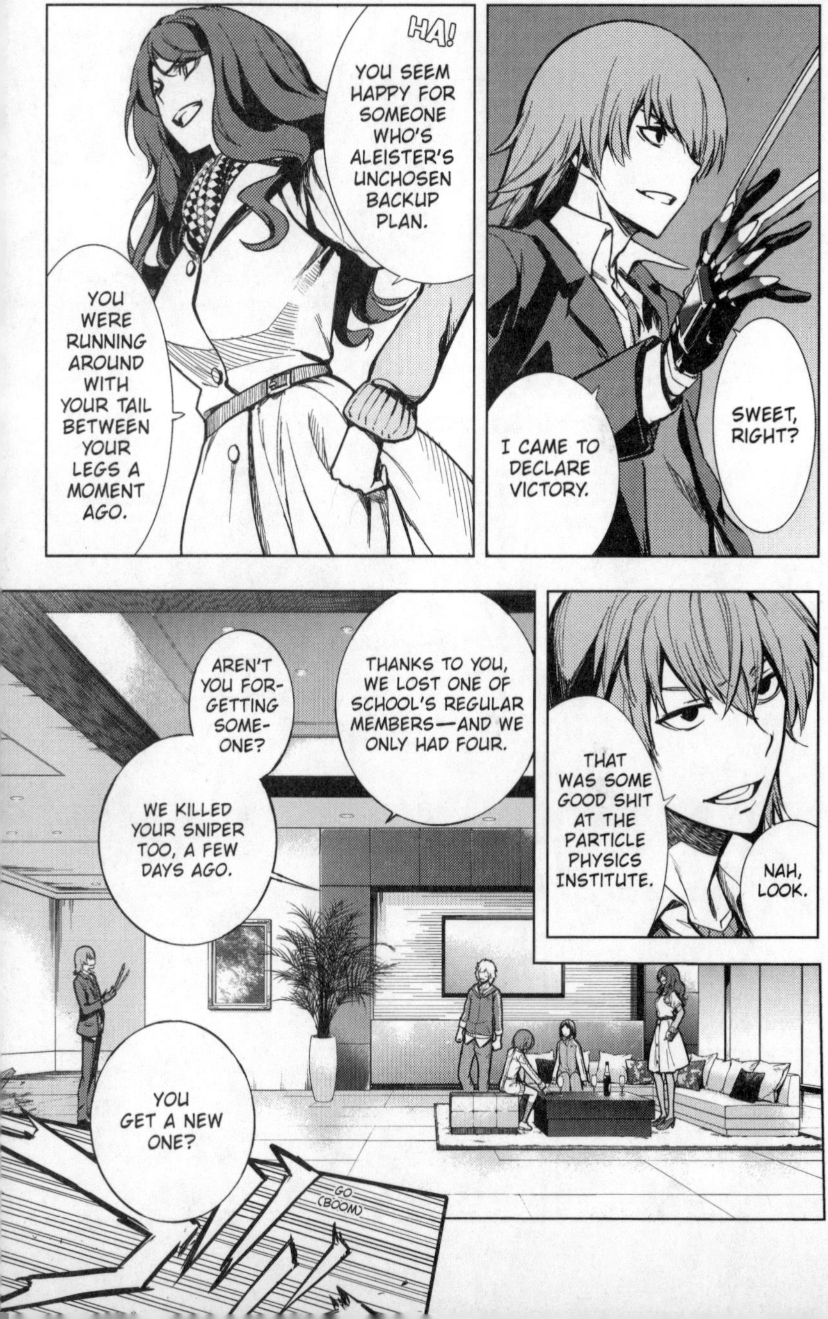
SWEET, RIGHT?
I CAME TO DECLARE VICTORY.
HA!
YOU SEEM HAPPY FOR SOMEONE WHO'S ALEISTER'S UNCHOSEN BACKUP PLAN.
YOU WERE RUNNING AROUND WITH YOUR TAIL BETWEEN YOUR LEGS A MOMENT AGO.
NAH, LOOK.
THAT WAS SOME GOOD SHIT AT THE PARTICLE PHYSICS INSTITUTE.
THANKS TO YOU, WE LOST ONE OF SCHOOL'S REGULAR MEMBERS—AND WE ONLY HAD FOUR.
AREN'T YOU FOR-GETTING SOME-ONE?
WE KILLED YOUR SNIPER TOO, A FEW DAYS AGO.
YOU GET A NEW ONE?
GO (BOOM)

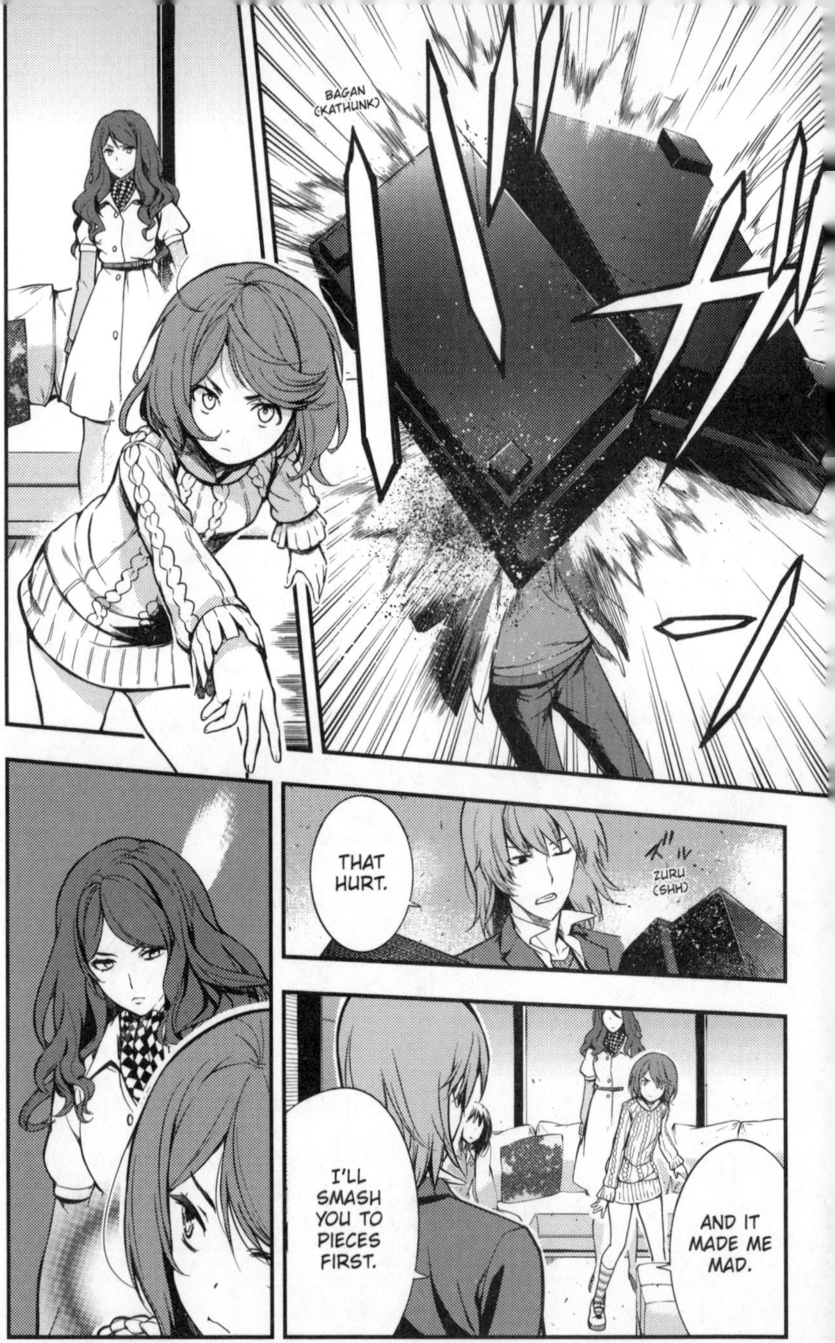
BAGAN (KATHUNK)
THAT HURT.
ズル
ZURU (SHH)
AND IT MADE ME MAD.
I'LL SMASH YOU TO PIECES FIRST.

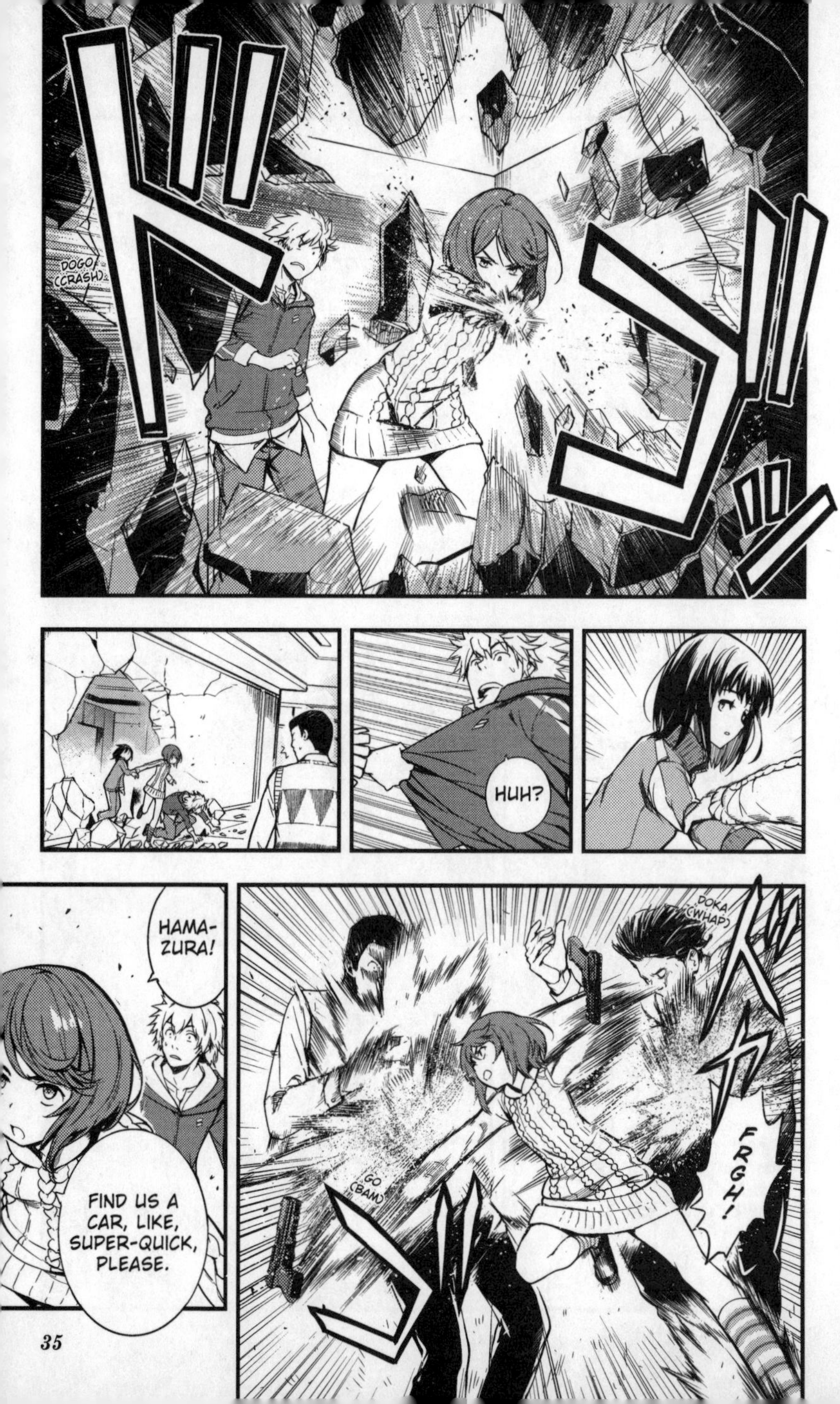
DOGO (CRASH)
HUH?
DOKA (WHAP)
FRGH!
GO (BAM)
HAMA-ZURA!
FIND US A CAR, LIKE, SUPER-QUICK, PLEASE.

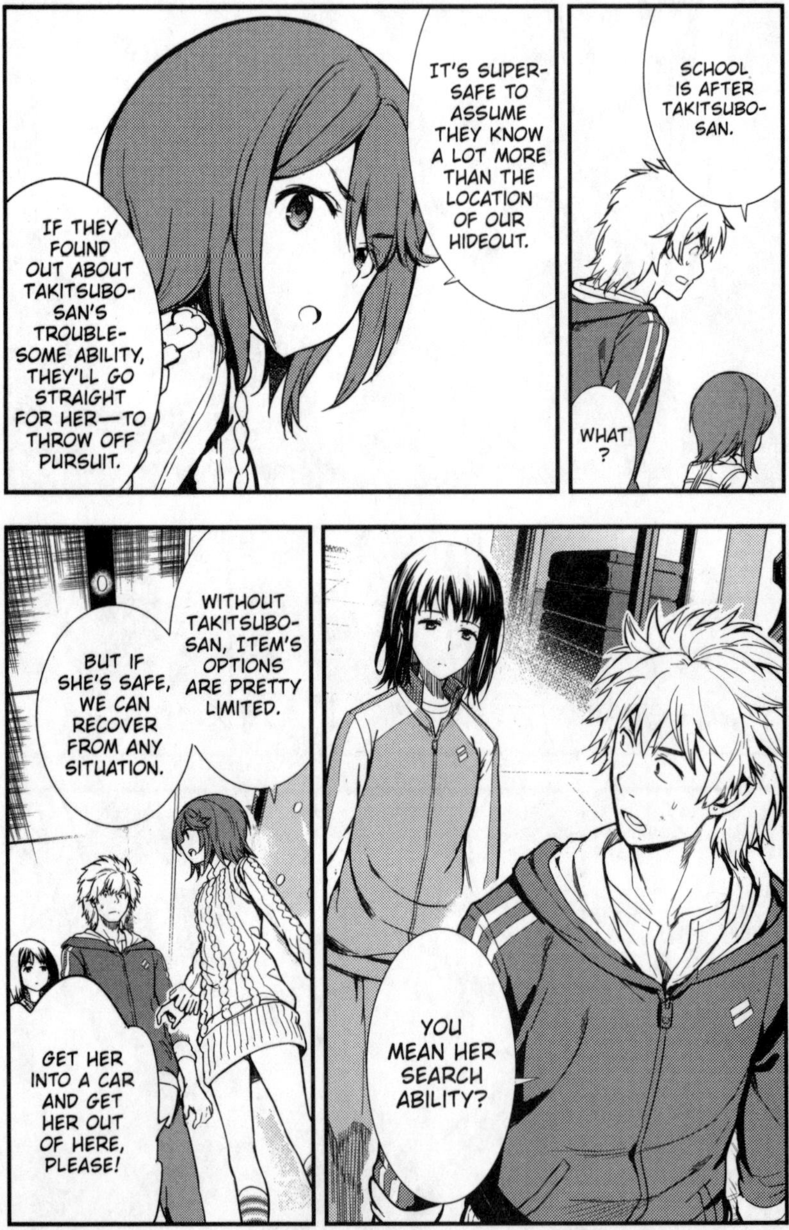
SCHOOL IS AFTER TAKITSUBO-SAN.
WHAT?
IT'S SUPER-SAFE TO ASSUME THEY KNOW A LOT MORE THAN THE LOCATION OF OUR HIDEOUT.
IF THEY FOUND OUT ABOUT TAKITSUBO-SAN'S TROUBLESOME ABILITY, THEY'LL GO STRAIGHT FOR HER—TO THROW OFF PURSUIT.
YOU MEAN HER SEARCH ABILITY?
WITHOUT TAKITSUBO-SAN, ITEM'S OPTIONS ARE PRETTY LIMITED.
BUT IF SHE'S SAFE, WE CAN RECOVER FROM ANY SITUATION.
GET HER INTO A CAR AND GET HER OUT OF HERE, PLEASE!

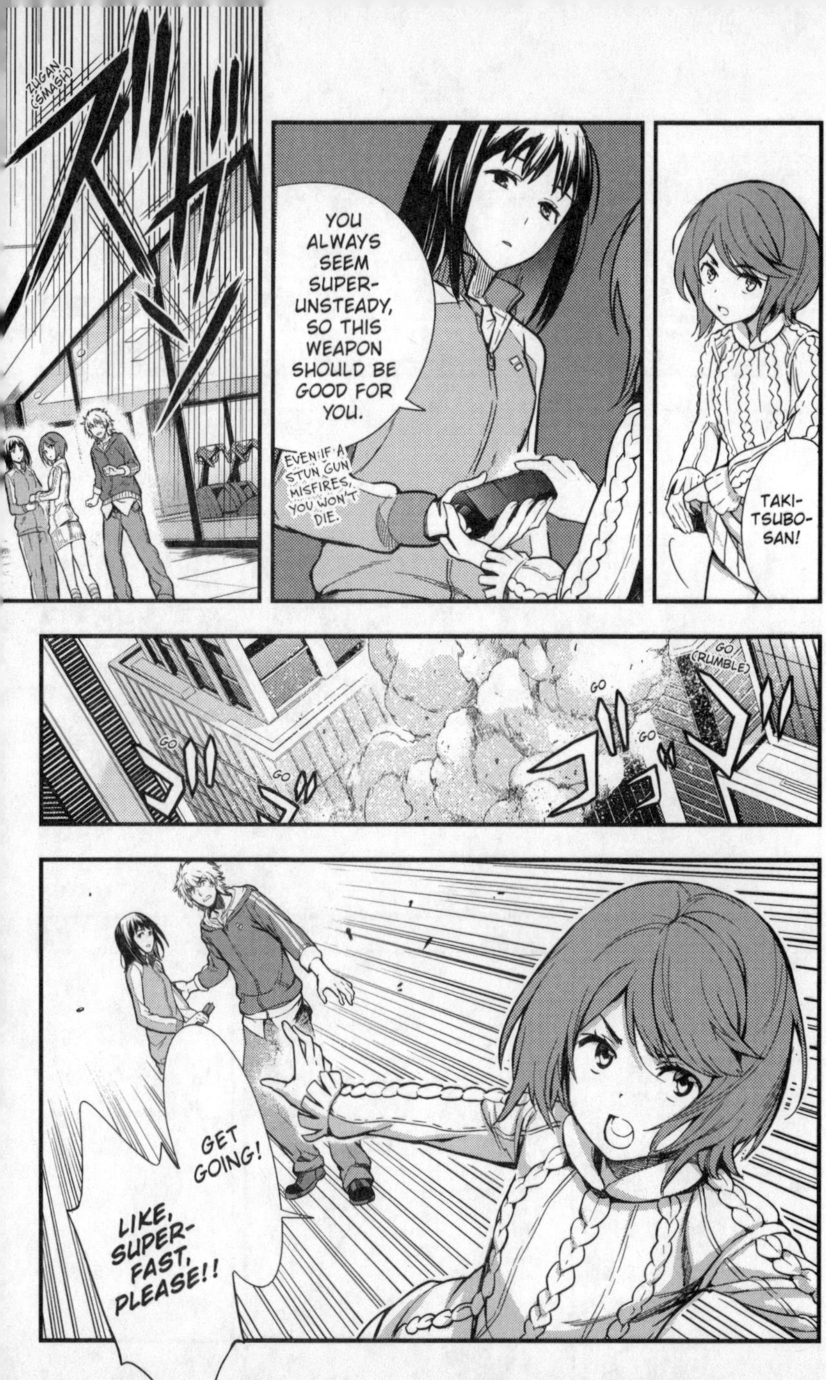
TAKI-TSUBO-SAN!
YOU ALWAYS SEEM SUPER-UNSTEADY, SO THIS WEAPON SHOULD BE GOOD FOR YOU.
EVEN IF A STUN GUN MISFIRES, YOU WON'T DIE.
ZUGAN (SMASH)
GO (RUMBLE)
GO
GO
GO
GO
GET GOING!
LIKE, SUPER-FAST, PLEASE!!

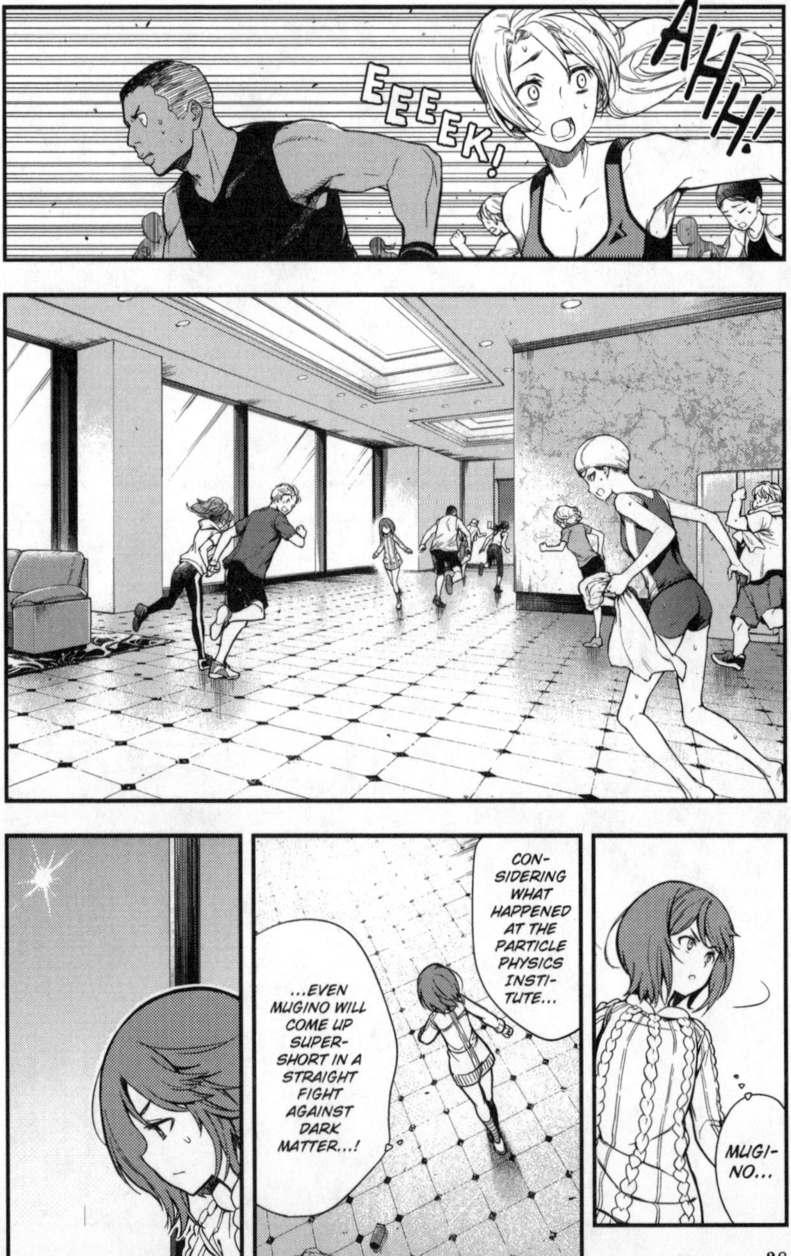
AHH!
EEEEK!
MUGI-NO...
CON-SIDERING WHAT HAPPENED AT THE PARTICLE PHYSICS INSTI-TUTE...
...EVEN MUGINO WILL COME UP SUPER-SHORT IN A STRAIGHT FIGHT AGAINST DARK MATTER...!

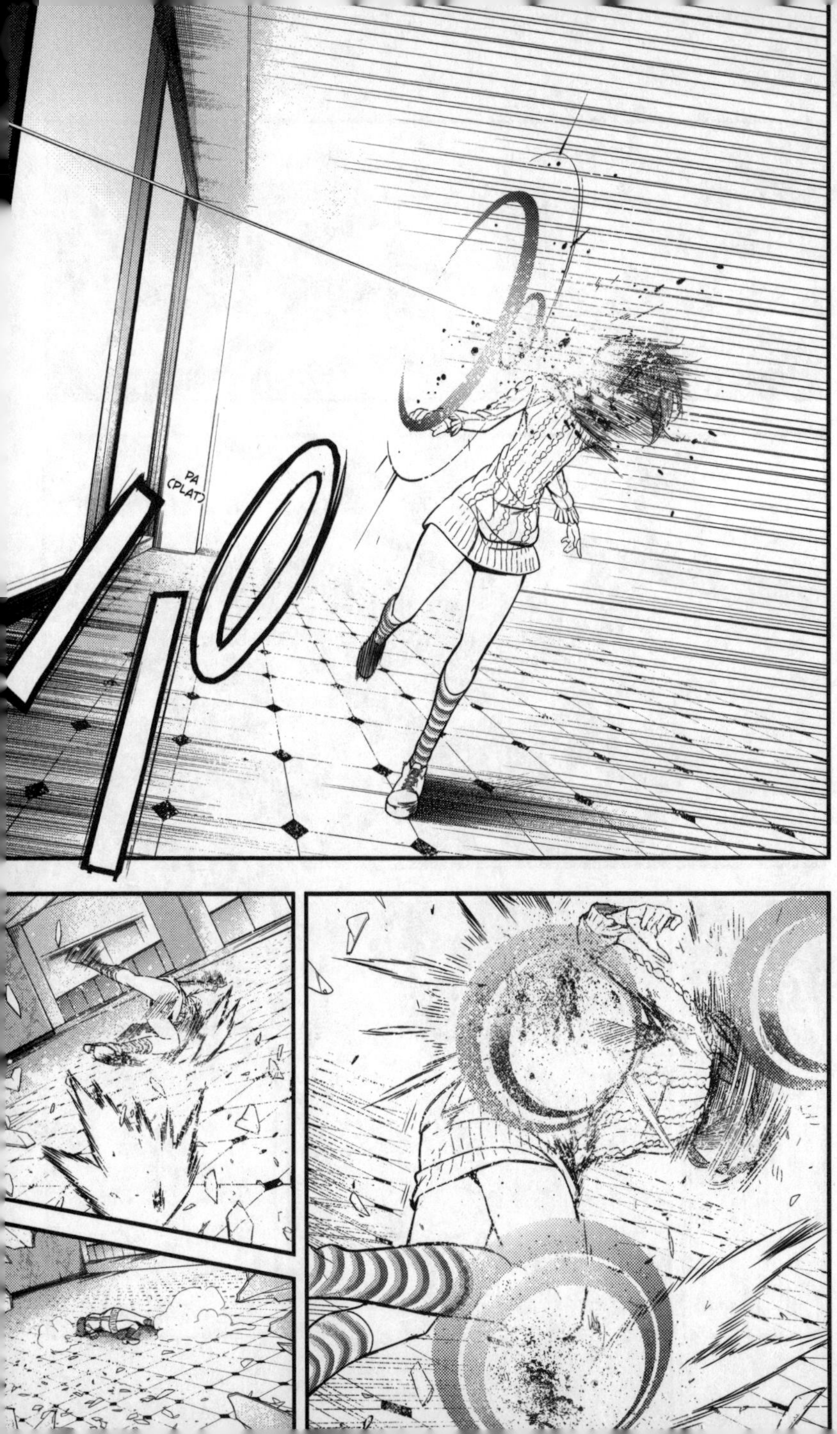
PA
(PLAT)

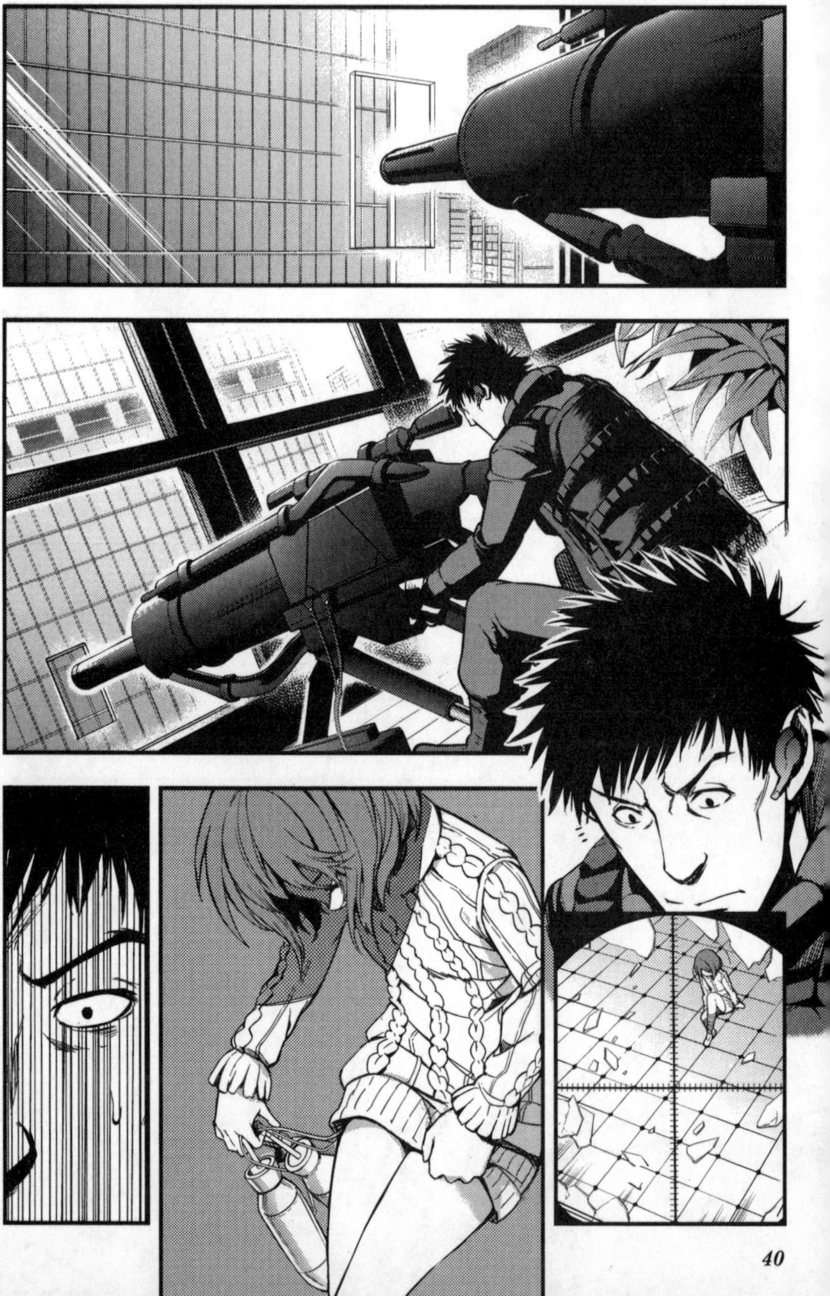

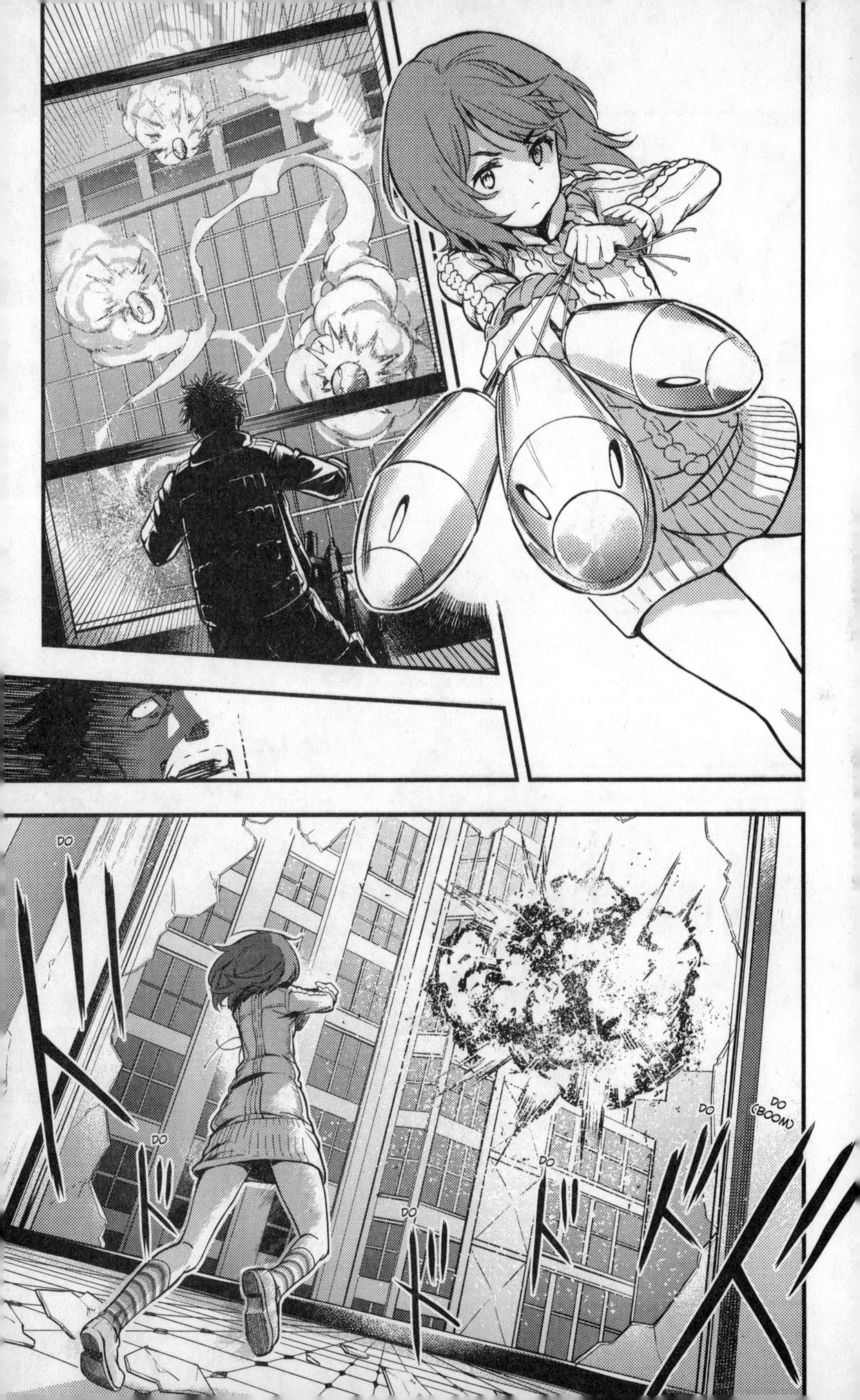
DO
(BOOM)
DO
DO
DO
DO
DO

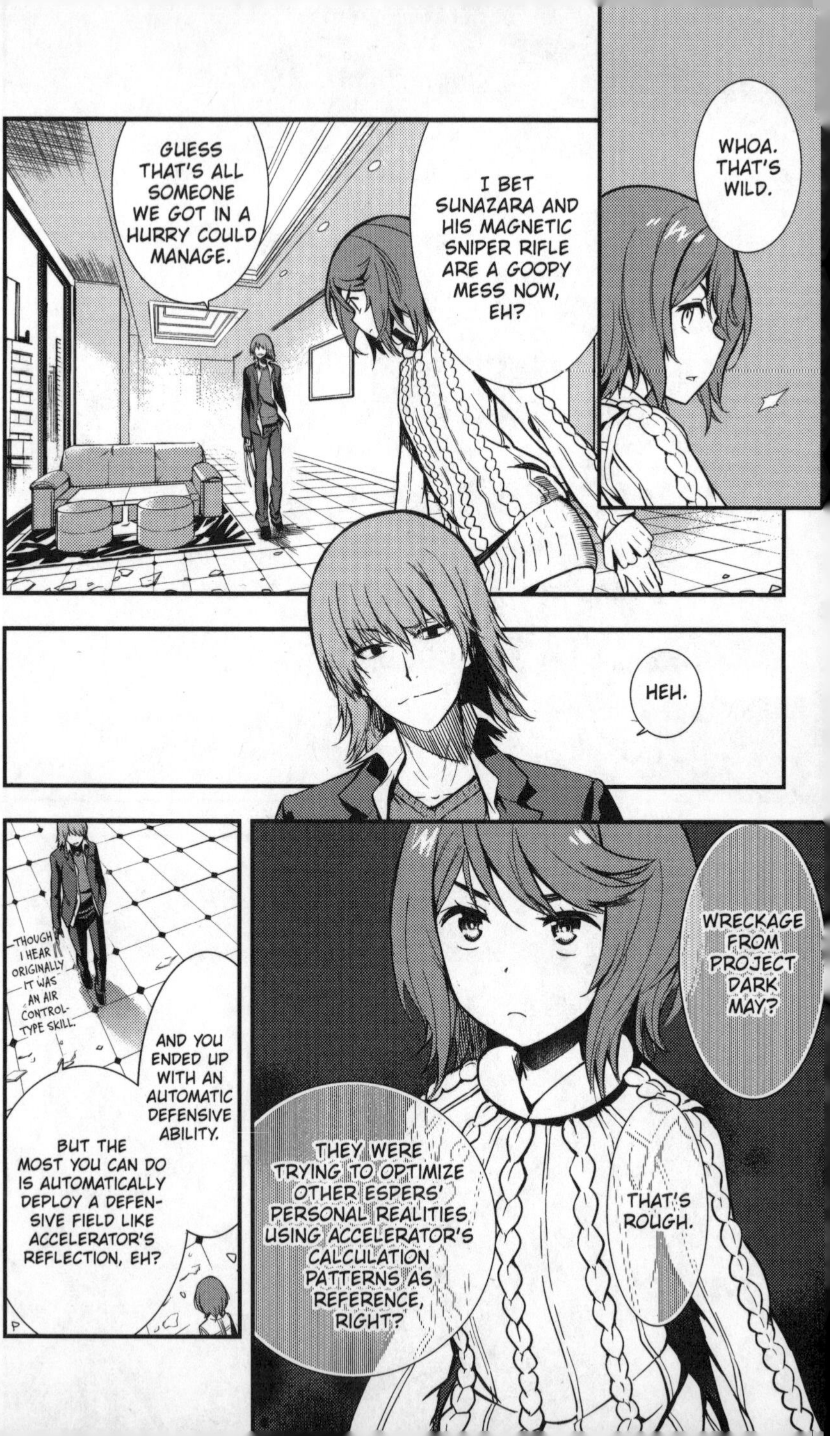
WHOA. THAT'S WILD.
I BET SUNAZARA AND HIS MAGNETIC SNIPER RIFLE ARE A GOOPY MESS NOW, EH?
GUESS THAT'S ALL SOMEONE WE GOT IN A HURRY COULD MANAGE.
HEH.
WRECKAGE FROM PROJECT DARK MAY?
THAT'S ROUGH.
THEY WERE TRYING TO OPTIMIZE OTHER ESPERS' PERSONAL REALITIES USING ACCELERATOR'S CALCULATION PATTERNS AS REFERENCE, RIGHT?
AND YOU ENDED UP WITH AN AUTOMATIC DEFENSIVE ABILITY.
THOUGH I HEAR ORIGINALLY IT WAS AN AIR CONTROL-TYPE SKILL.
BUT THE MOST YOU CAN DO IS AUTOMATICALLY DEPLOY A DEFEN-SIVE FIELD LIKE ACCELERATOR'S REFLECTION, EH?

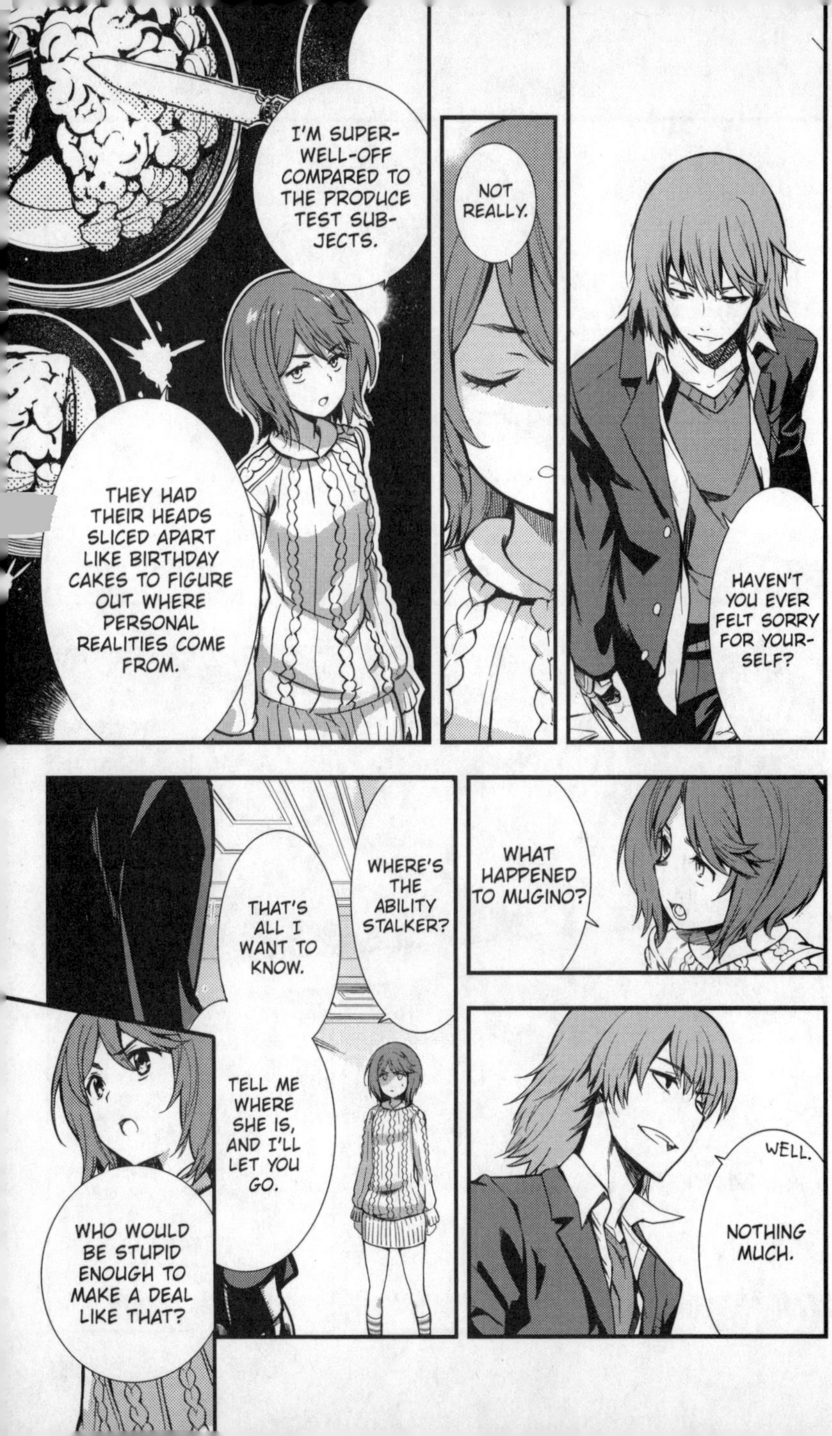
HAVEN'T YOU EVER FELT SORRY FOR YOURSELF?
NOT REALLY.
I'M SUPER-WELL-OFF COMPARED TO THE PRODUCE TEST SUBJECTS.
THEY HAD THEIR HEADS SLICED APART LIKE BIRTHDAY CAKES TO FIGURE OUT WHERE PERSONAL REALITIES COME FROM.
WHAT HAPPENED TO MUGINO?
WELL.
NOTHING MUCH.
WHERE'S THE ABILITY STALKER?
THAT'S ALL I WANT TO KNOW.
TELL ME WHERE SHE IS, AND I'LL LET YOU GO.
WHO WOULD BE STUPID ENOUGH TO MAKE A DEAL LIKE THAT?

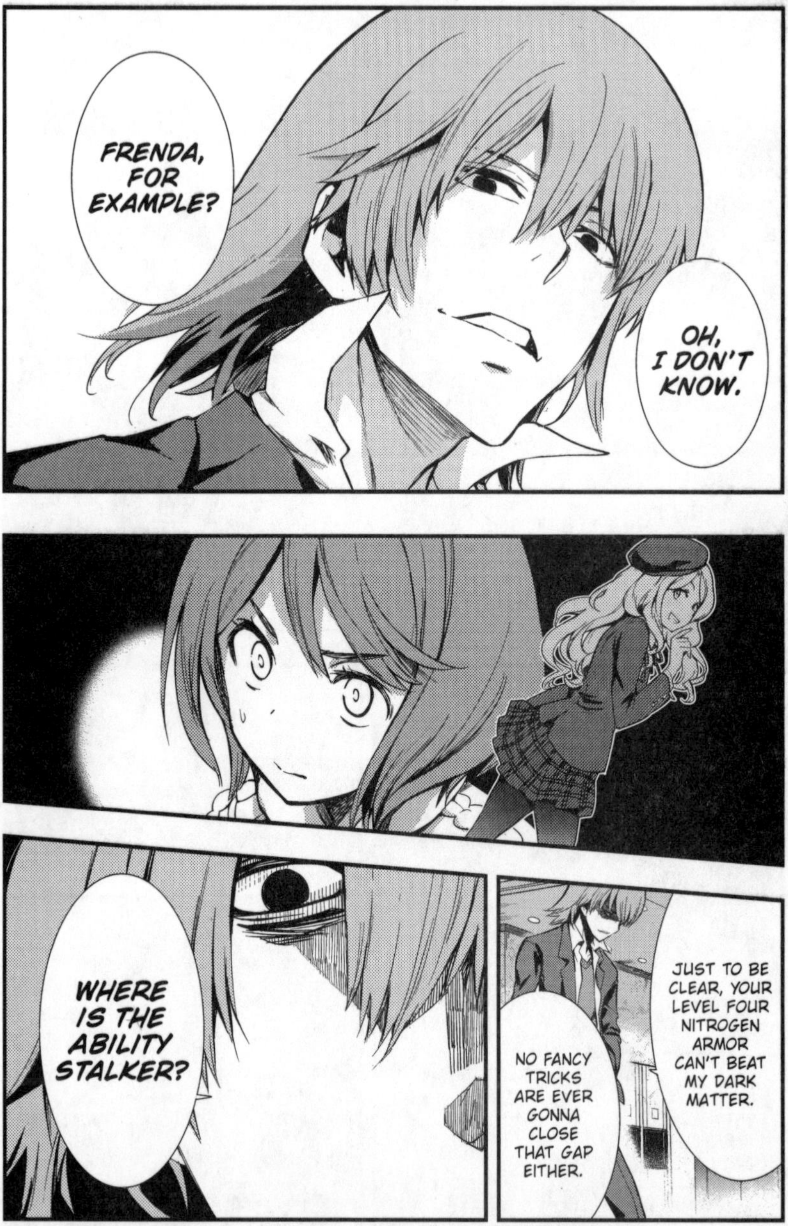
FRENDA, FOR EXAMPLE?
OH, I DON'T KNOW.
JUST TO BE CLEAR, YOUR LEVEL FOUR NITROGEN ARMOR CAN'T BEAT MY DARK MATTER.
NO FANCY TRICKS ARE EVER GONNA CLOSE THAT GAP EITHER.
WHERE IS THE ABILITY STALKER?

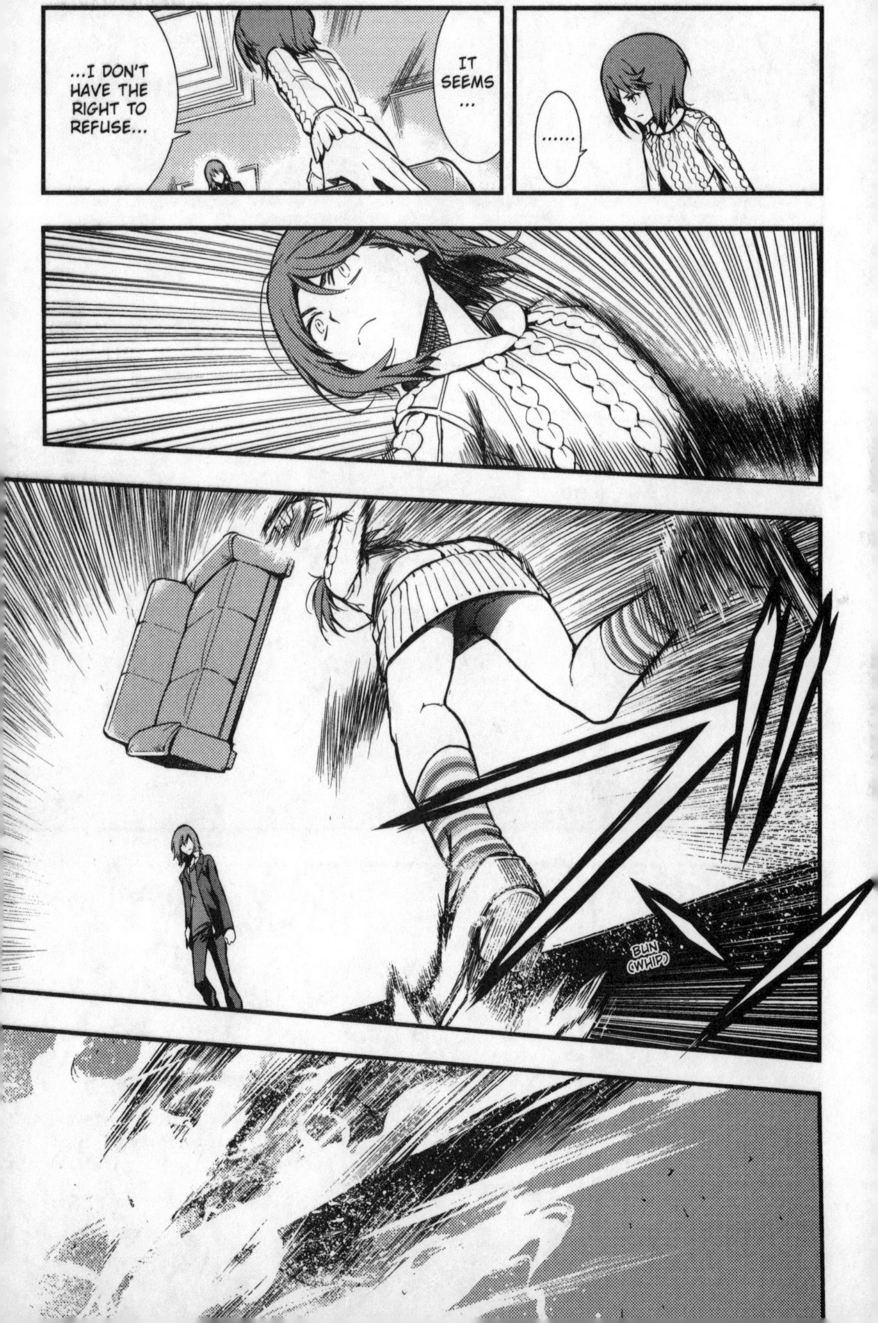
......
IT SEEMS ...
...I DON'T HAVE THE RIGHT TO REFUSE...
BUN (WHIP)

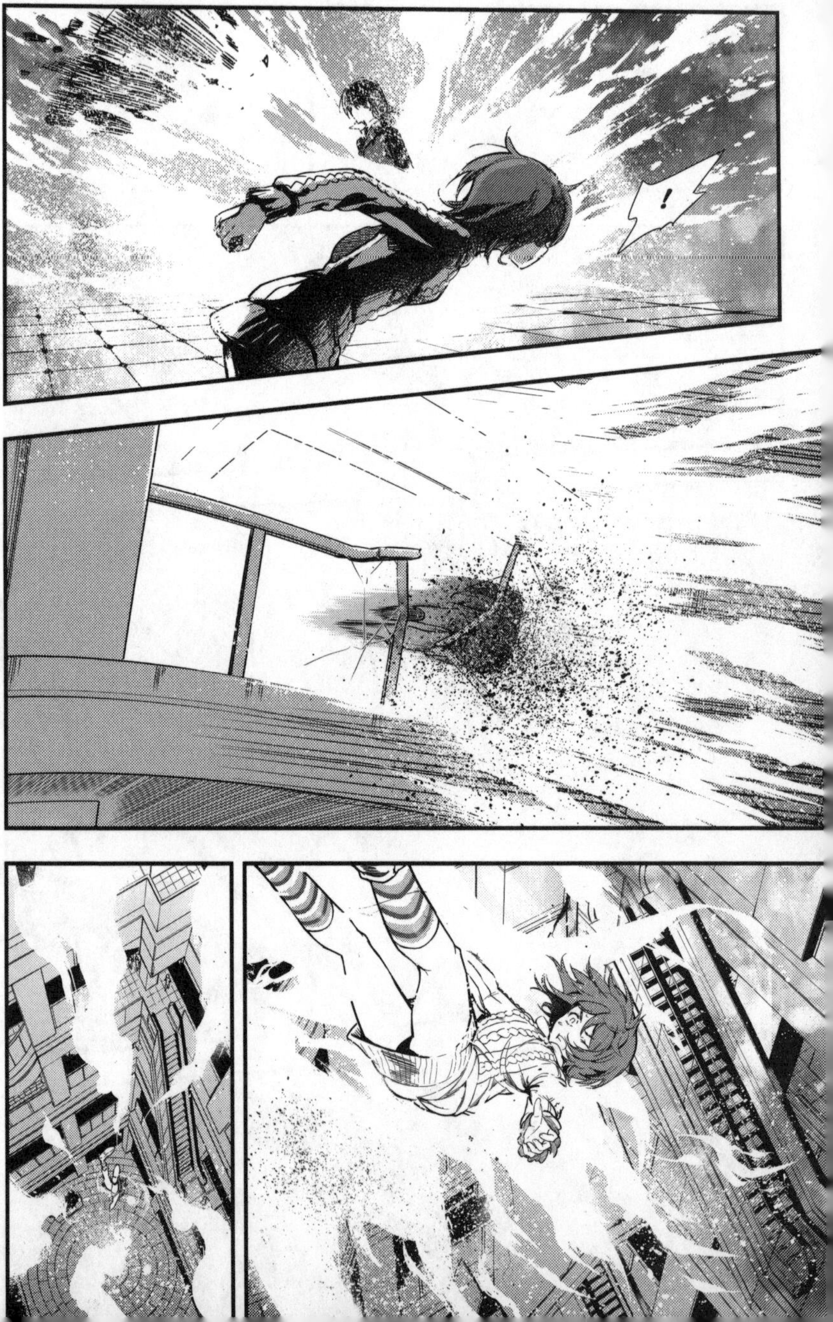
!

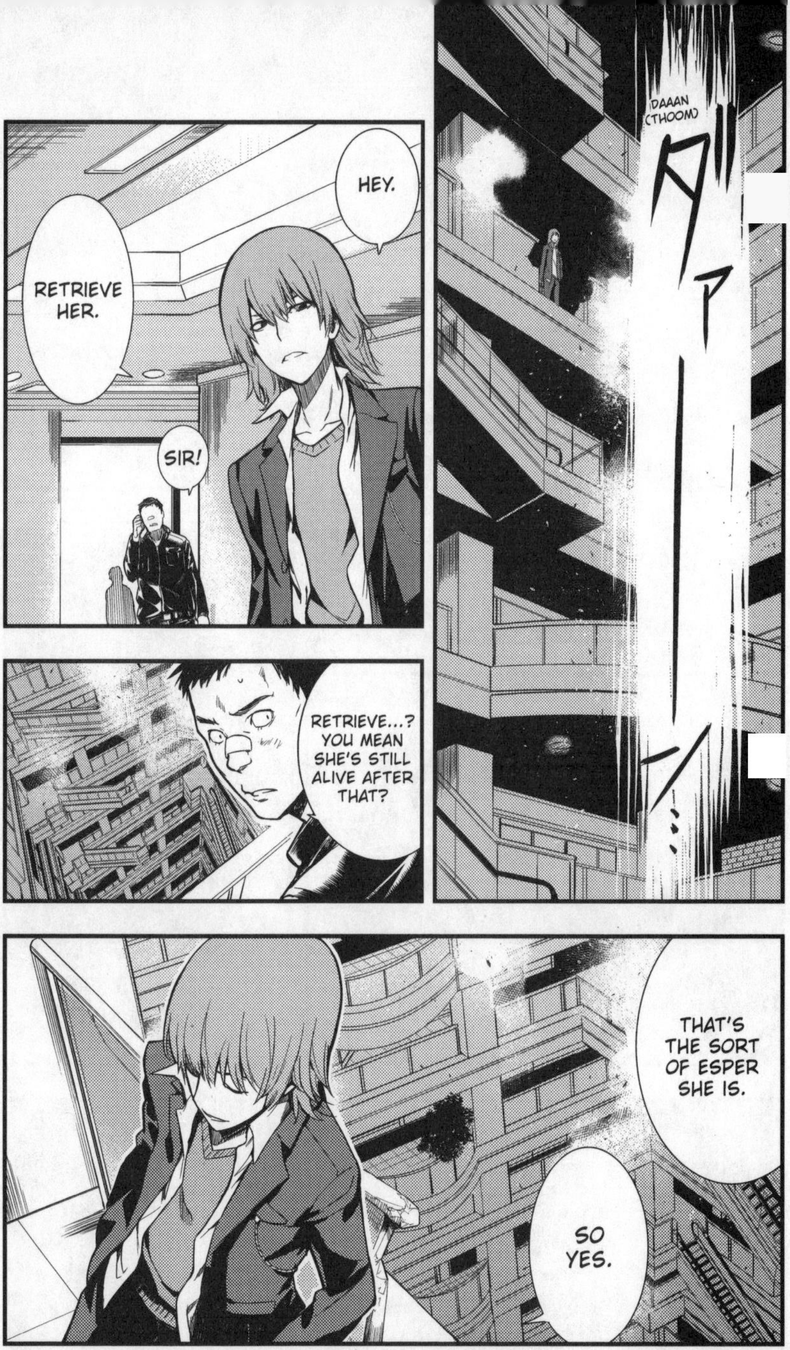
DAAAN (THOOM)
ダァーン…
HEY.
RETRIEVE HER.
SIR!
RETRIEVE...? YOU MEAN SHE'S STILL ALIVE AFTER THAT?
THAT'S THE SORT OF ESPER SHE IS.
SO YES.

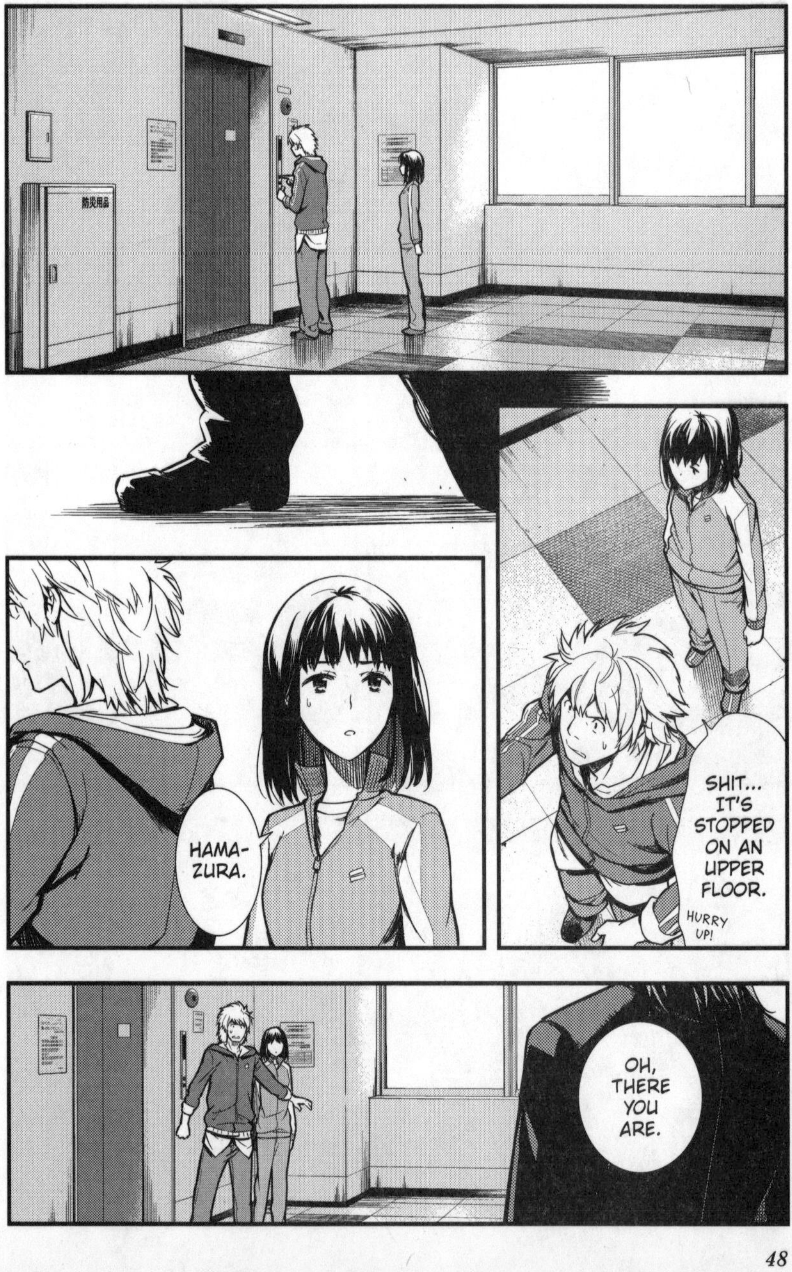
防災用品
SHIT... IT'S STOPPED ON AN UPPER FLOOR.
HURRY UP!
HAMA-ZURA.
OH, THERE YOU ARE.

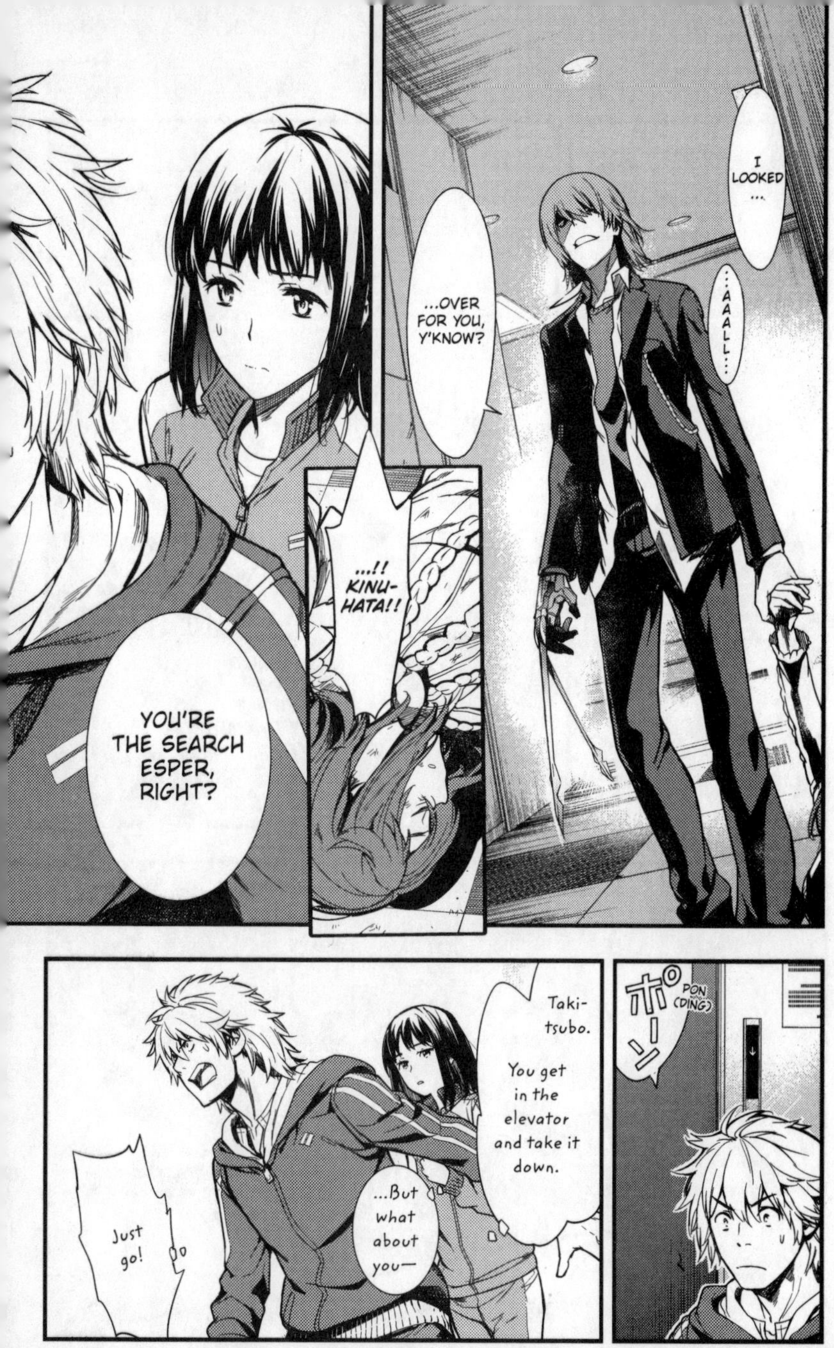
I LOOKED...
...AAALL...
...OVER FOR YOU, Y'KNOW?
...!! KINU-HATA!!
YOU'RE THE SEARCH ESPER, RIGHT?
ポーン
PON (DING)
Taki-tsubo.
You get in the elevator and take it down.
...But what about you—
Just go!

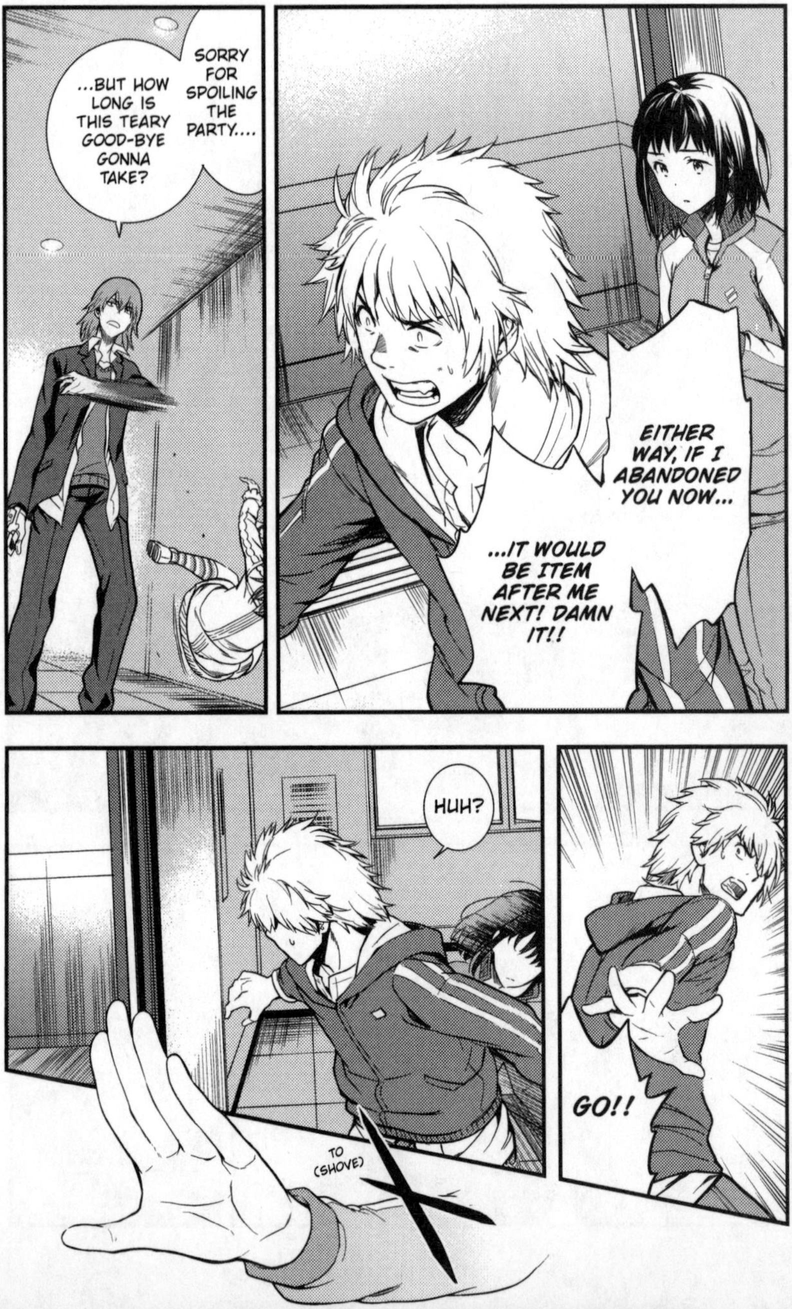
EITHER WAY, IF I ABANDONED YOU NOW...
...IT WOULD BE ITEM AFTER ME NEXT! DAMN IT!!
SORRY FOR SPOILING THE PARTY....
...BUT HOW LONG IS THIS TEARY GOOD-BYE GONNA TAKE?
GO!!
HUH?
TO (SHOVE)

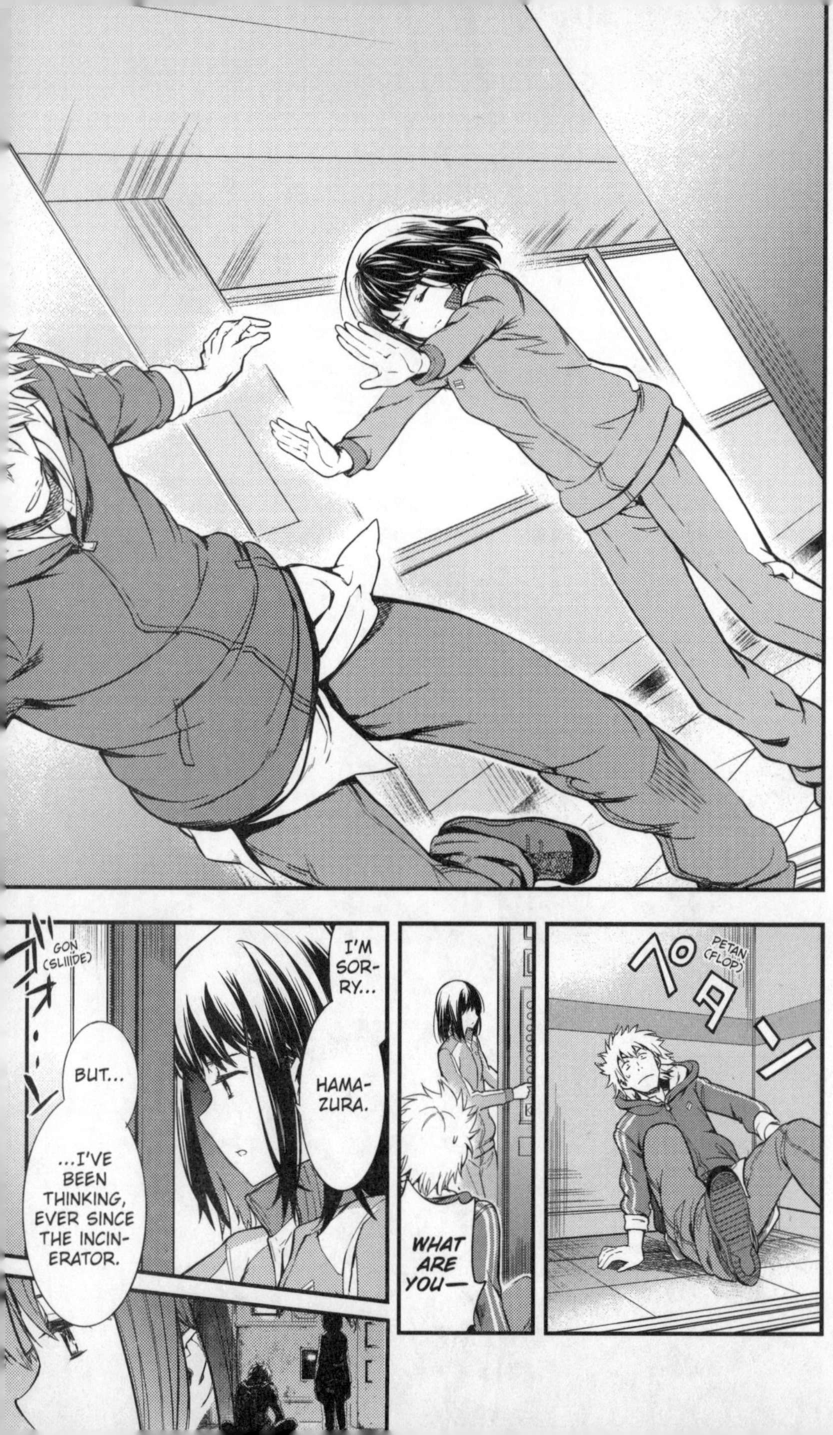
PETAN (FLOP)
WHAT ARE YOU—
I'M SORRY...
HAMA-ZURA.
GON (SLIIIDE)
BUT...
...I'VE BEEN THINKING, EVER SINCE THE INCIN-ERATOR.

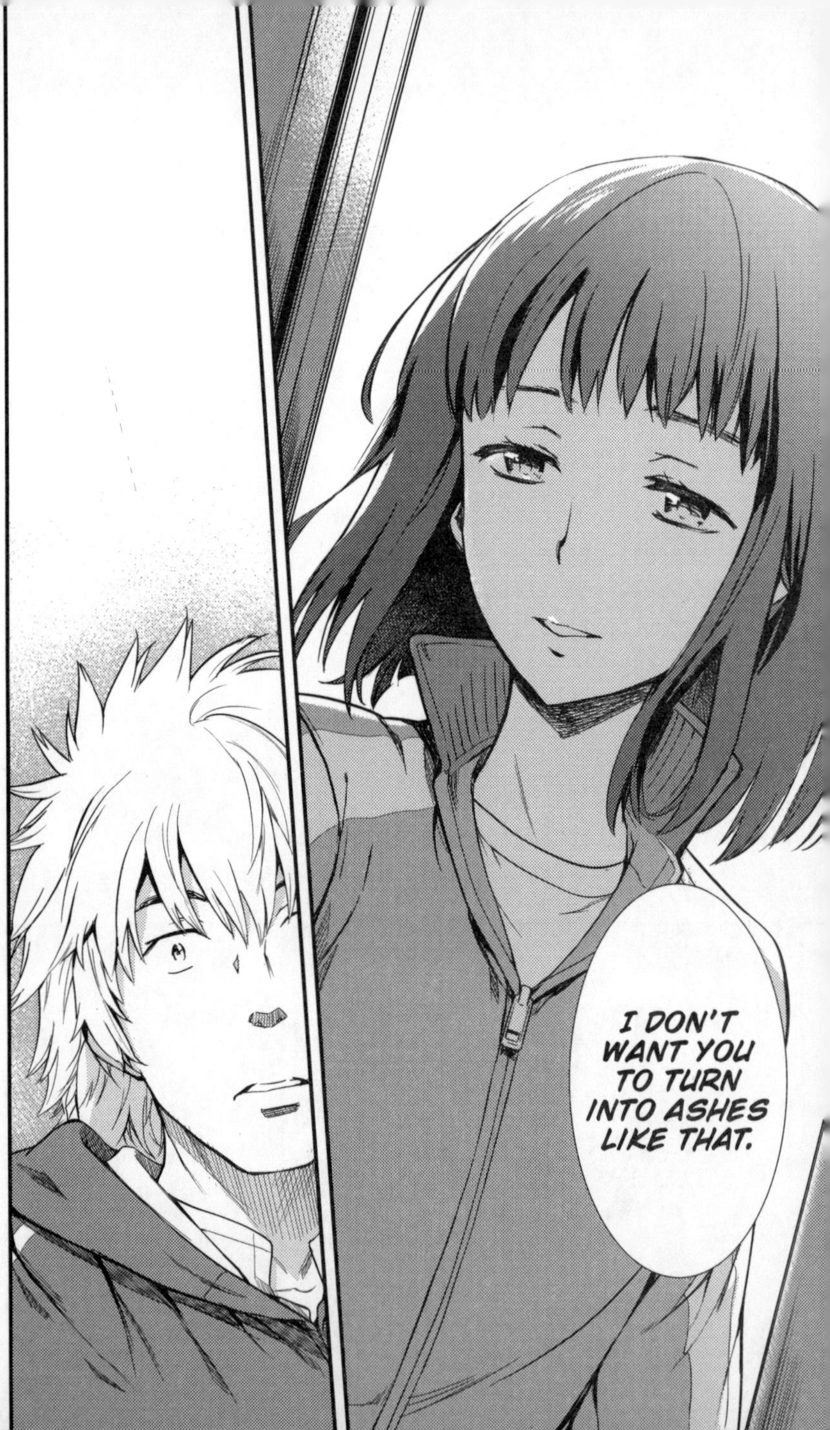
I DON'T WANT YOU TO TURN INTO ASHES LIKE THAT.

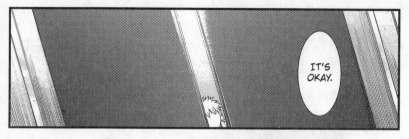

IT'S OKAY.

I'M A LEVEL FOUR.

AND I'LL PROTECT YOU—THE LEVEL ZERO.

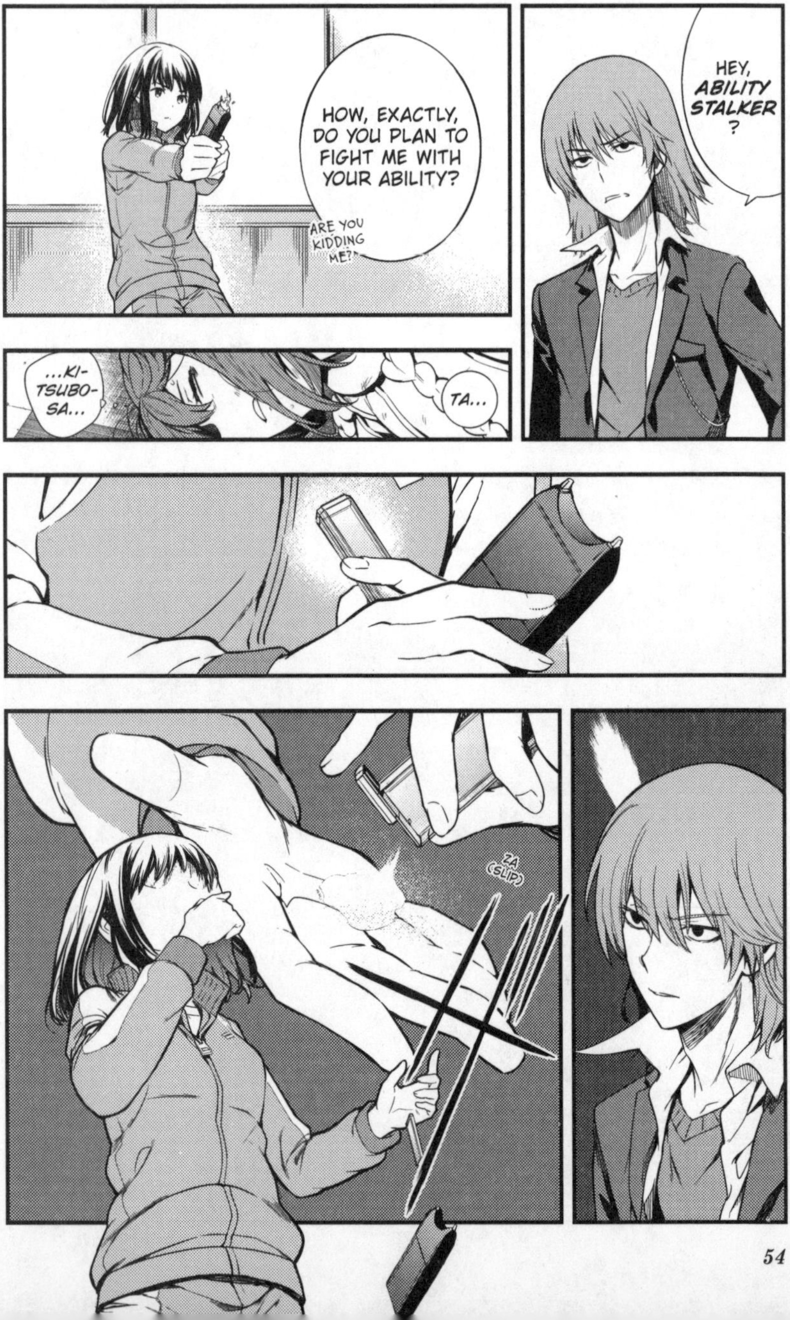
HEY, ABILITY STALKER?
HOW, EXACTLY, DO YOU PLAN TO FIGHT ME WITH YOUR ABILITY?
ARE YOU KIDDING ME?
...KI-TSUBO-SA...
TA...
ZA (SLIP)

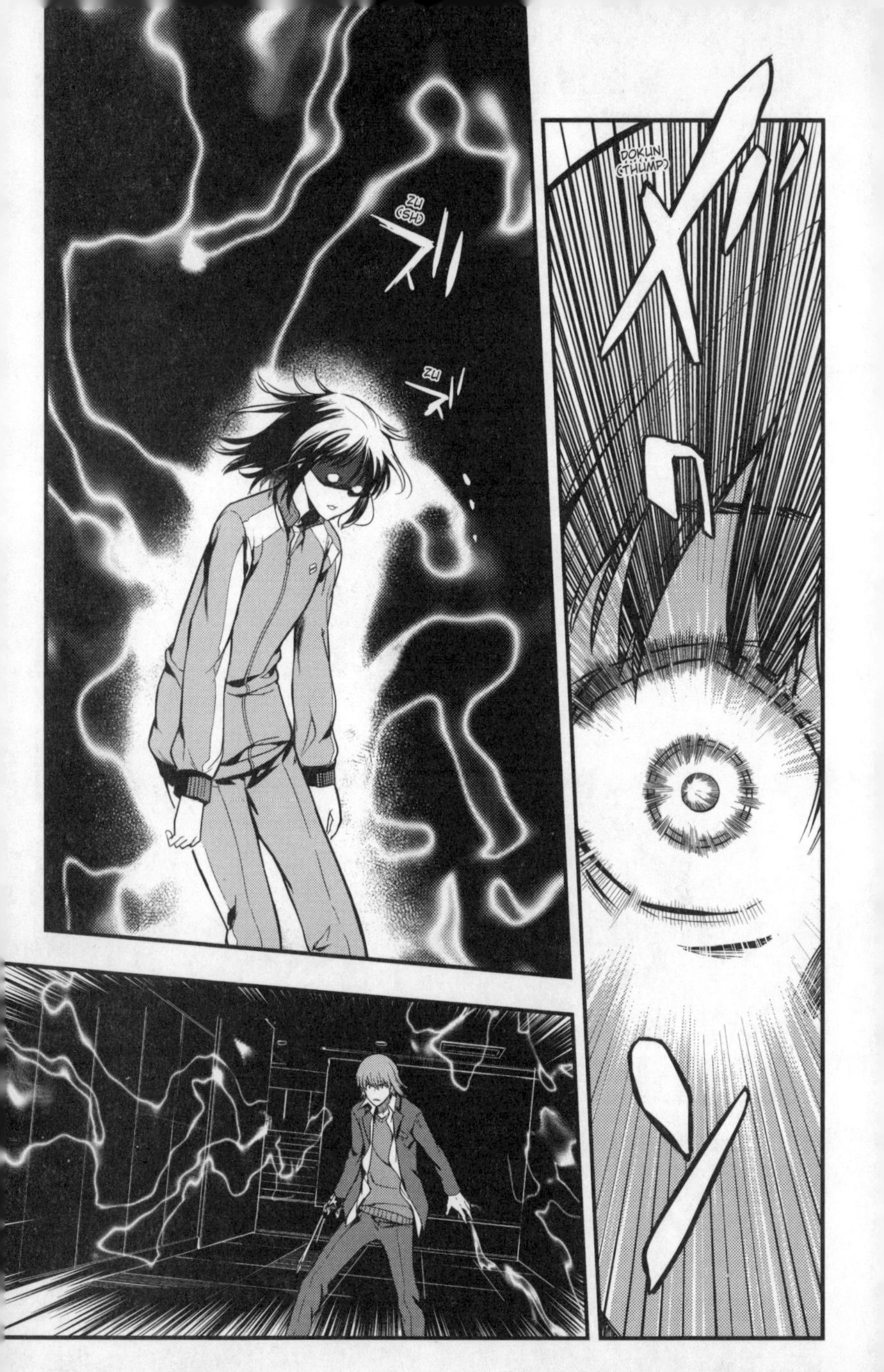
DOKUN (THUMP)
ZU (SH)
ZU

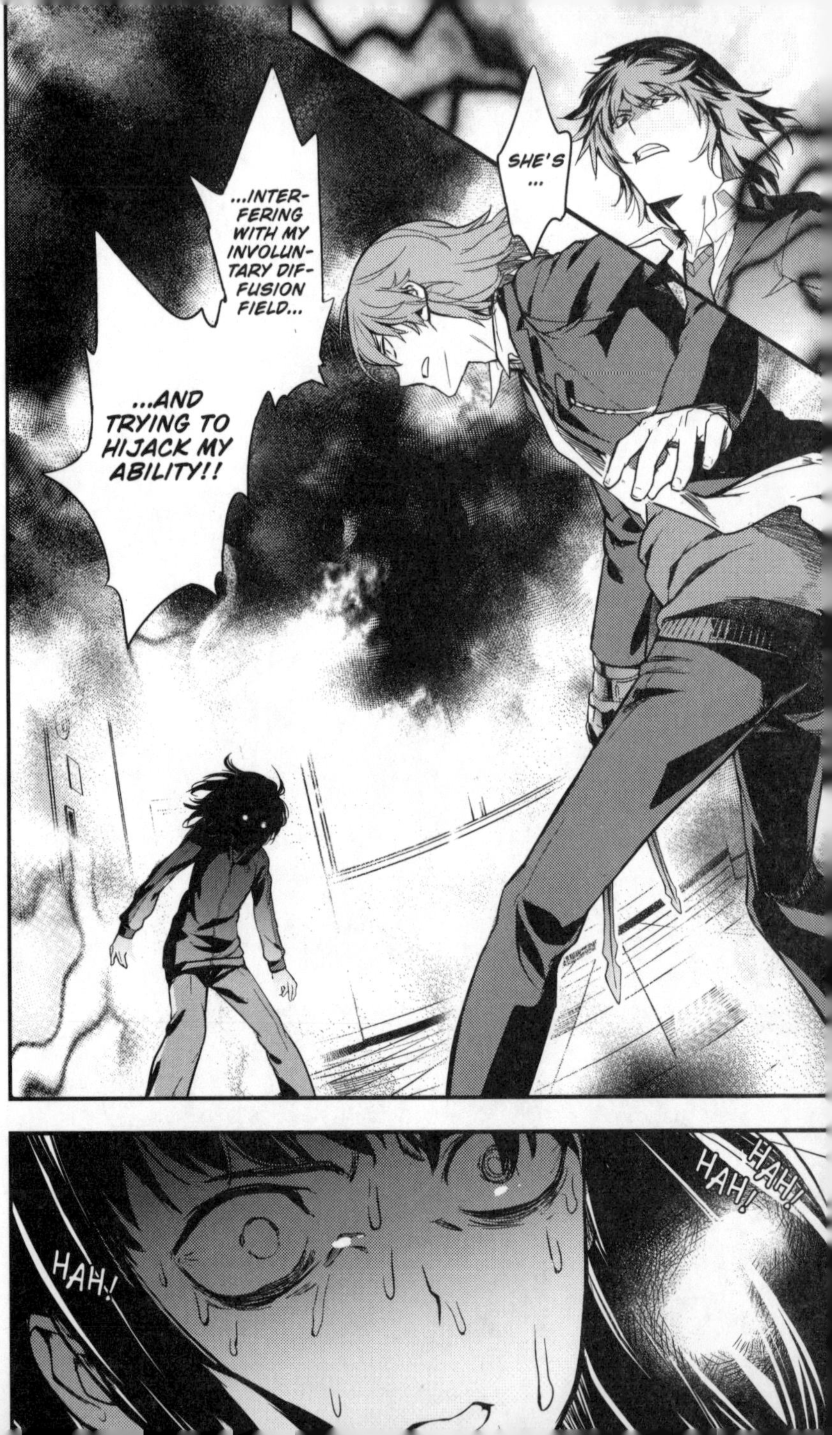
SHE'S ...
...INTERFERING WITH MY INVOLUNTARY DIFFUSION FIELD...
...AND TRYING TO HIJACK MY ABILITY!!
HAH! HAH!
HAH!

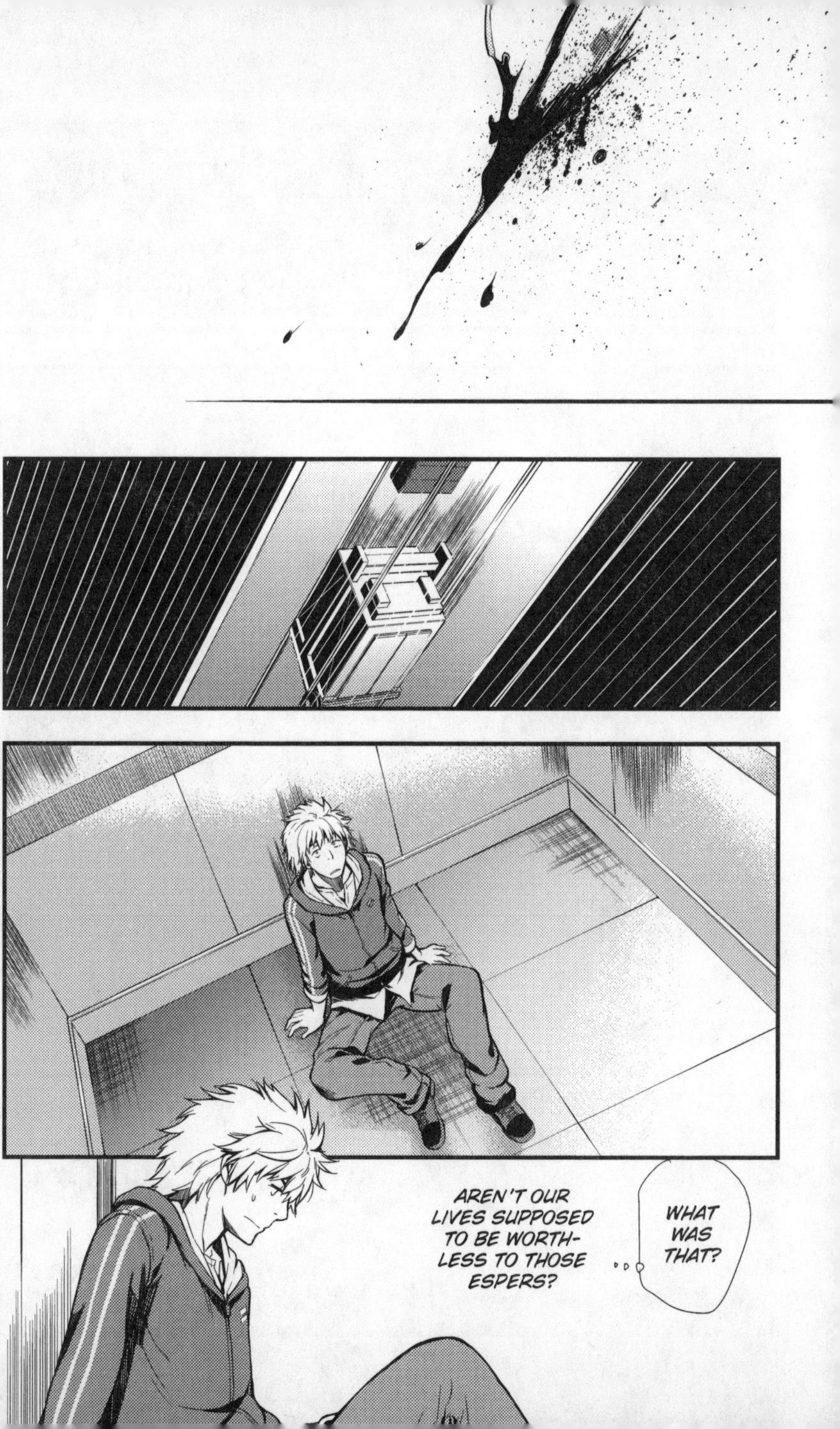
WHAT WAS THAT?
AREN'T OUR LIVES SUPPOSED TO BE WORTH-LESS TO THOSE ESPERS?

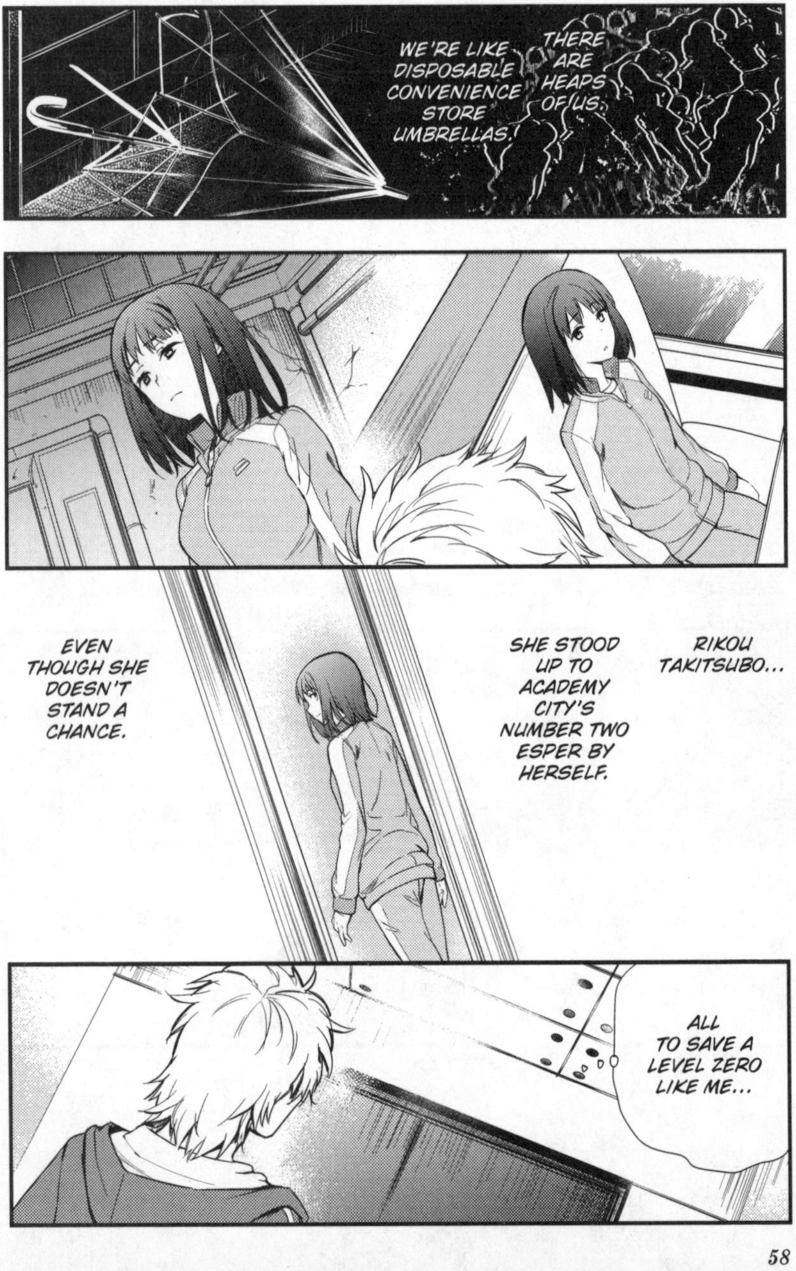
THERE ARE HEAPS OF US.
WE'RE LIKE DISPOSABLE CONVENIENCE STORE UMBRELLAS.
RIKOU TAKITSUBO...
SHE STOOD UP TO ACADEMY CITY'S NUMBER TWO ESPER BY HERSELF.
EVEN THOUGH SHE DOESN'T STAND A CHANCE.
ALL TO SAVE A LEVEL ZERO LIKE ME...

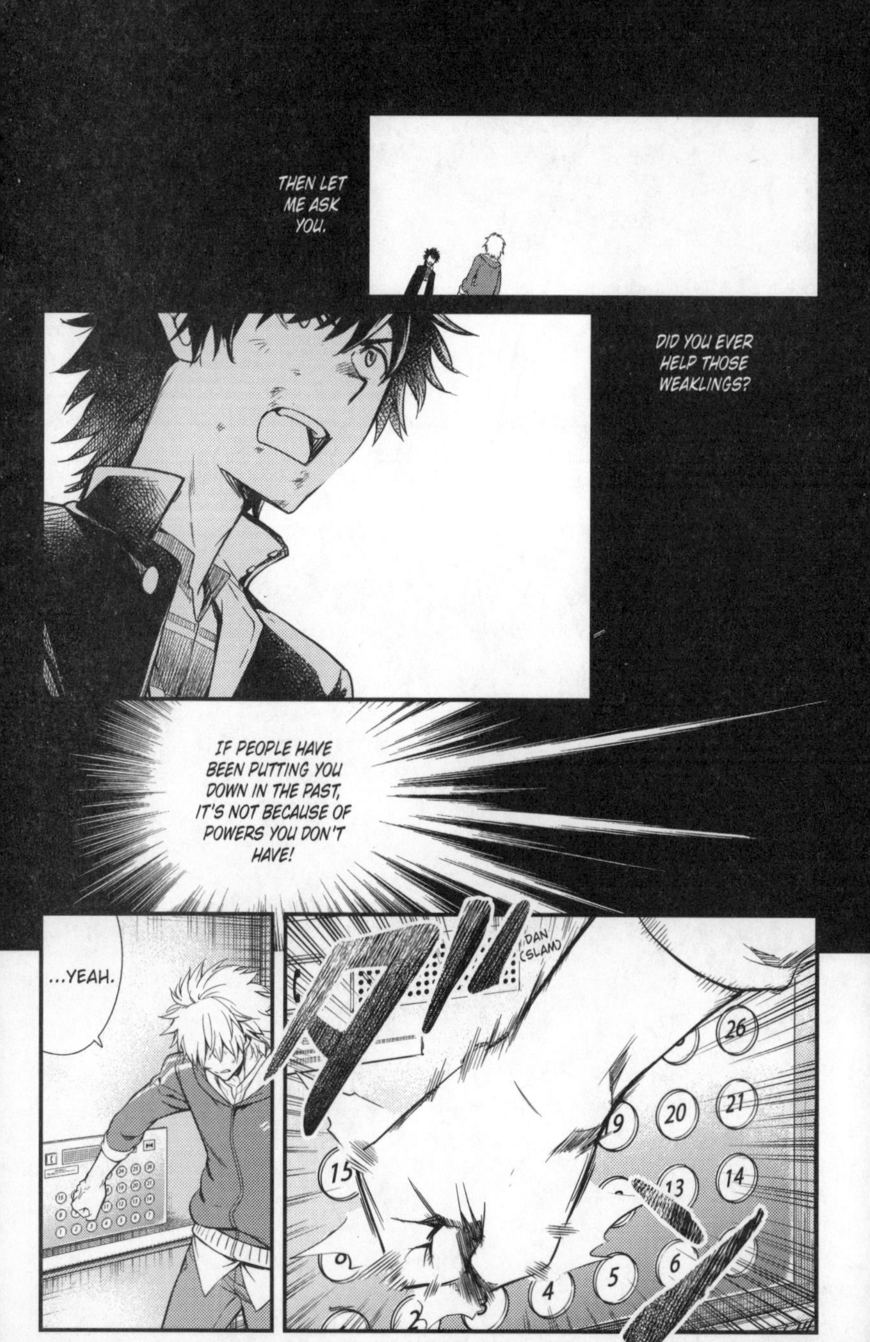
THEN LET ME ASK YOU.
DID YOU EVER HELP THOSE WEAKLINGS?
IF PEOPLE HAVE BEEN PUTTING YOU DOWN IN THE PAST, IT'S NOT BECAUSE OF POWERS YOU DON'T HAVE!
DAN (SLAM)
...YEAH.

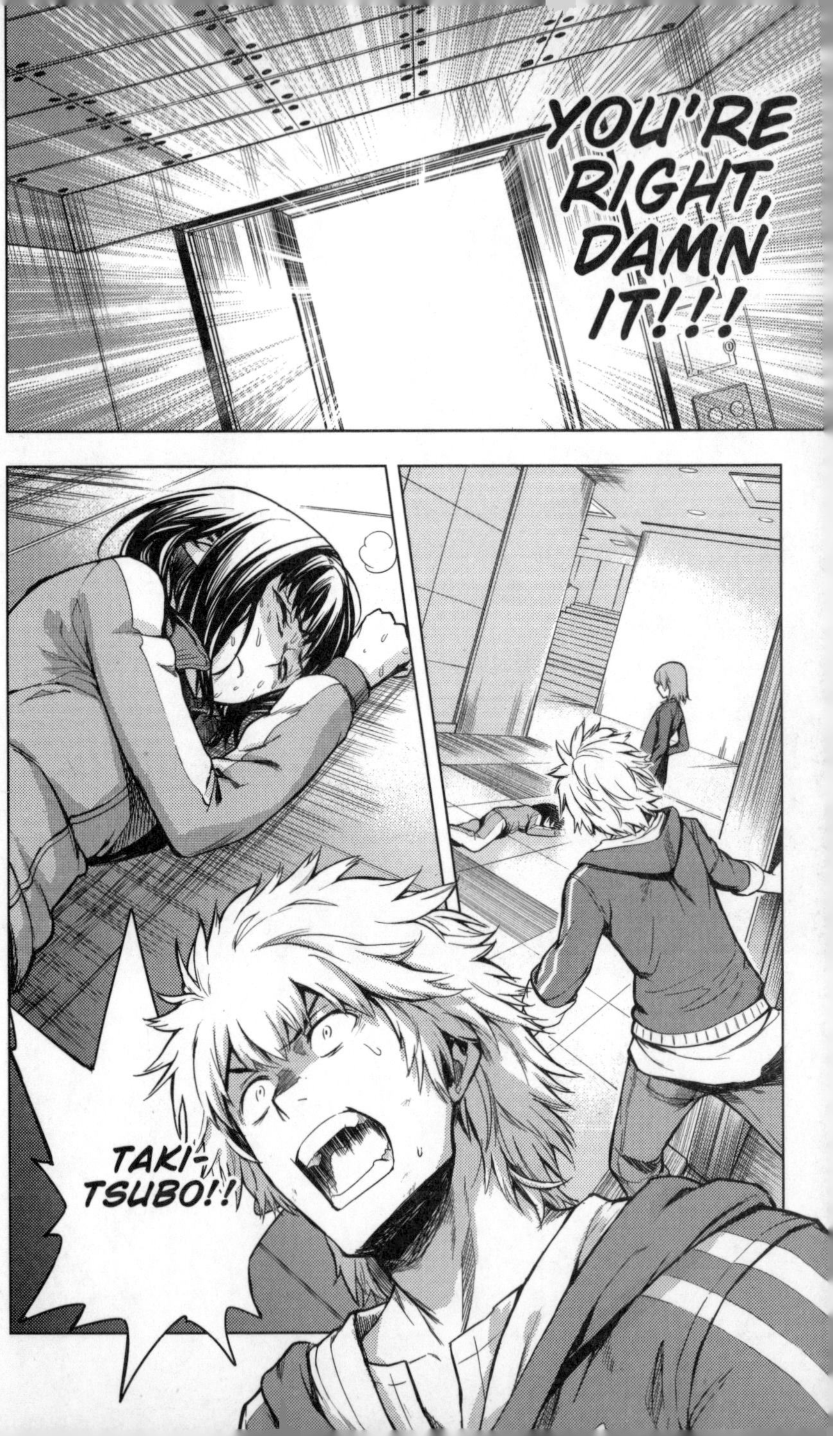
YOU'RE RIGHT, DAMN IT!!!
TAKI-TSUBO!!

Transmission data from "UNDER_LINE"

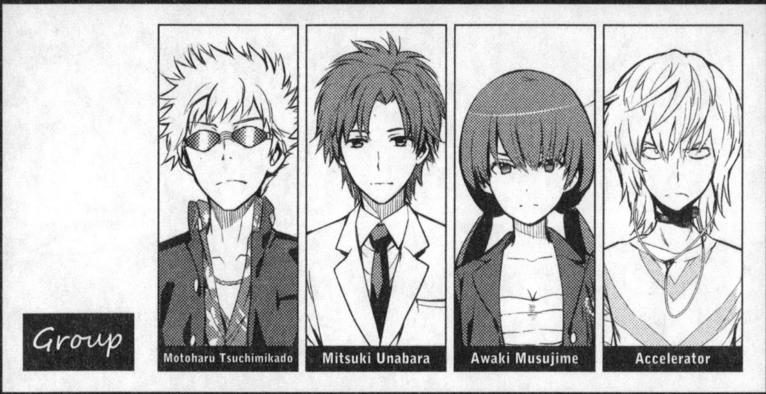
Group
Motoharu Tsuchimikado
Mitsuki Unabara
Awaki Musujime
Accelerator

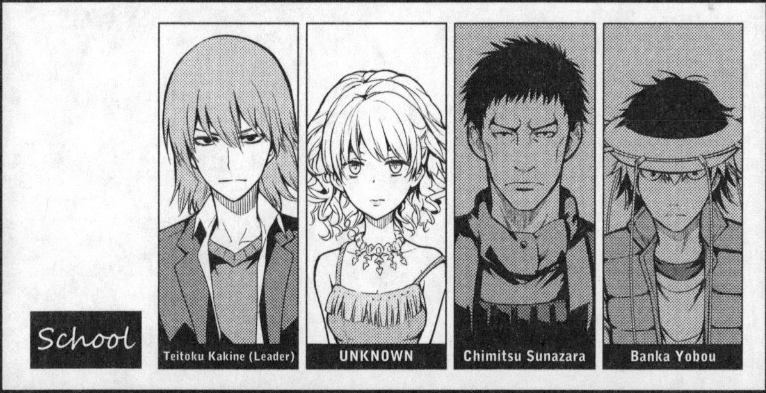
School
Teitoku Kakine (Leader)
UNKNOWN
Chimitsu Sunazara
Banka Yobou

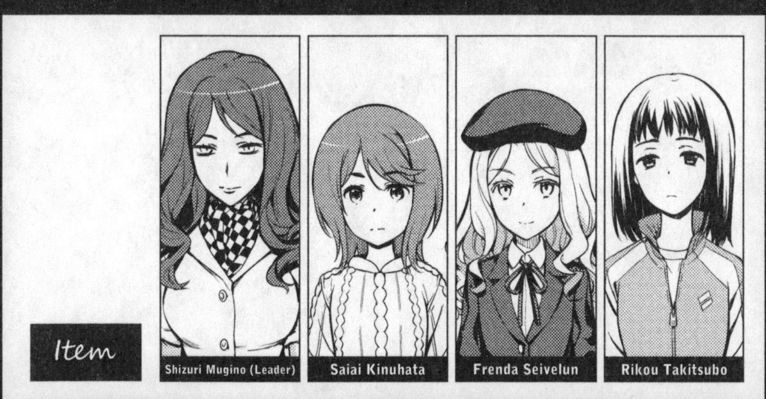
Item
Shizuri Mugino (Leader)
Saiai Kinuhata
Frenda Seivelun
Rikou Takitsubo

A Certain Magical Index

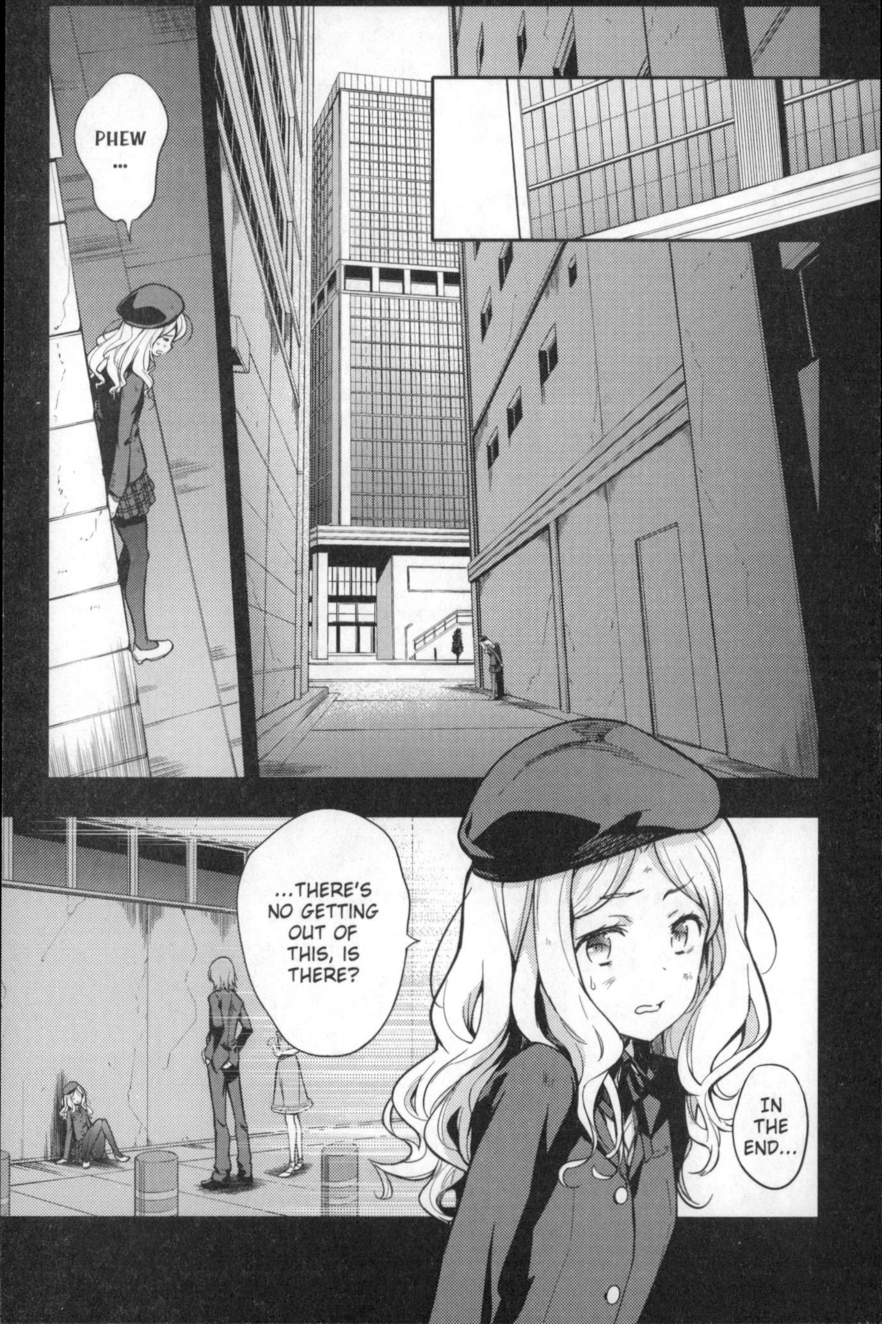
PHEW ...
IN THE END...
...THERE'S NO GETTING OUT OF THIS, IS THERE?

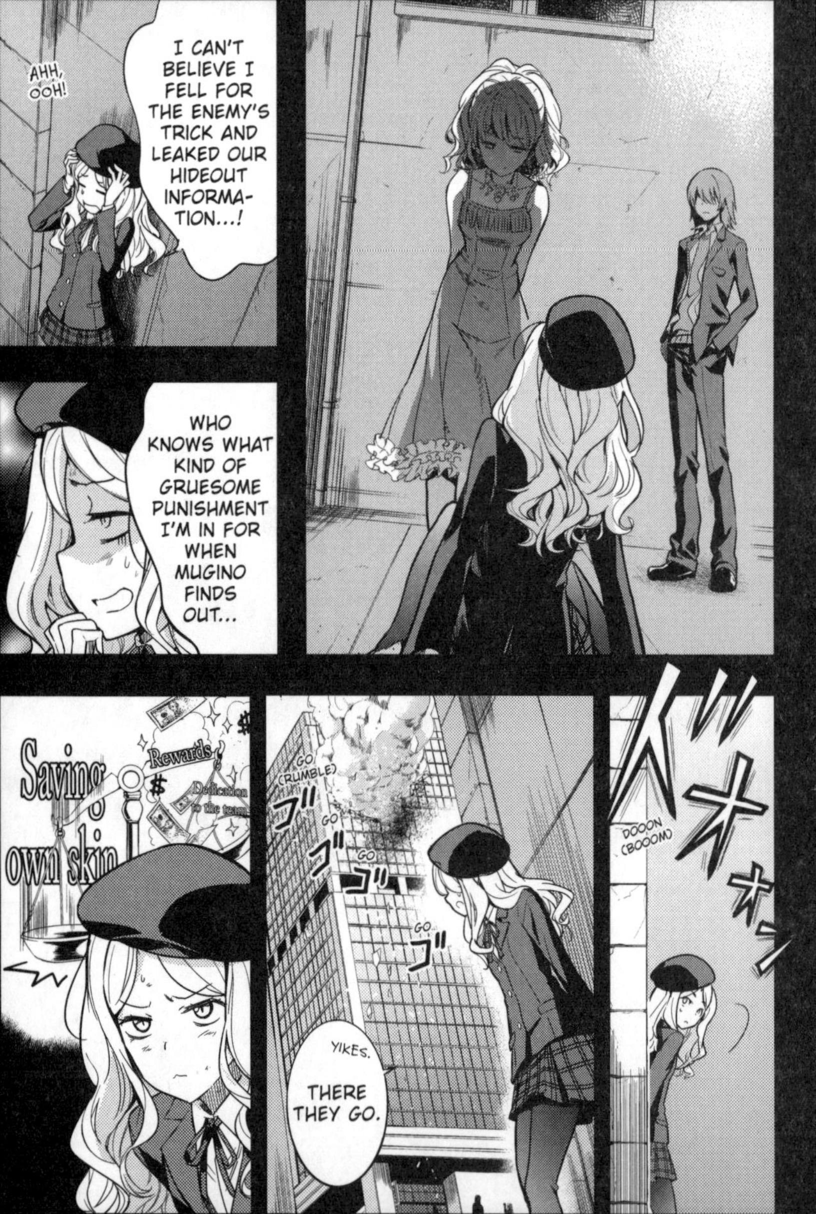
AHH, OOH!
I CAN'T BELIEVE I FELL FOR THE ENEMY'S TRICK AND LEAKED OUR HIDEOUT INFORMATION...!
WHO KNOWS WHAT KIND OF GRUESOME PUNISHMENT I'M IN FOR WHEN MUGINO FINDS OUT...
DOOON (BOOOM)
GO (RUMBLE)
GO
GO
GO
YIKES.
THERE THEY GO.
Saving own skin
Rewards
Dedication to the team

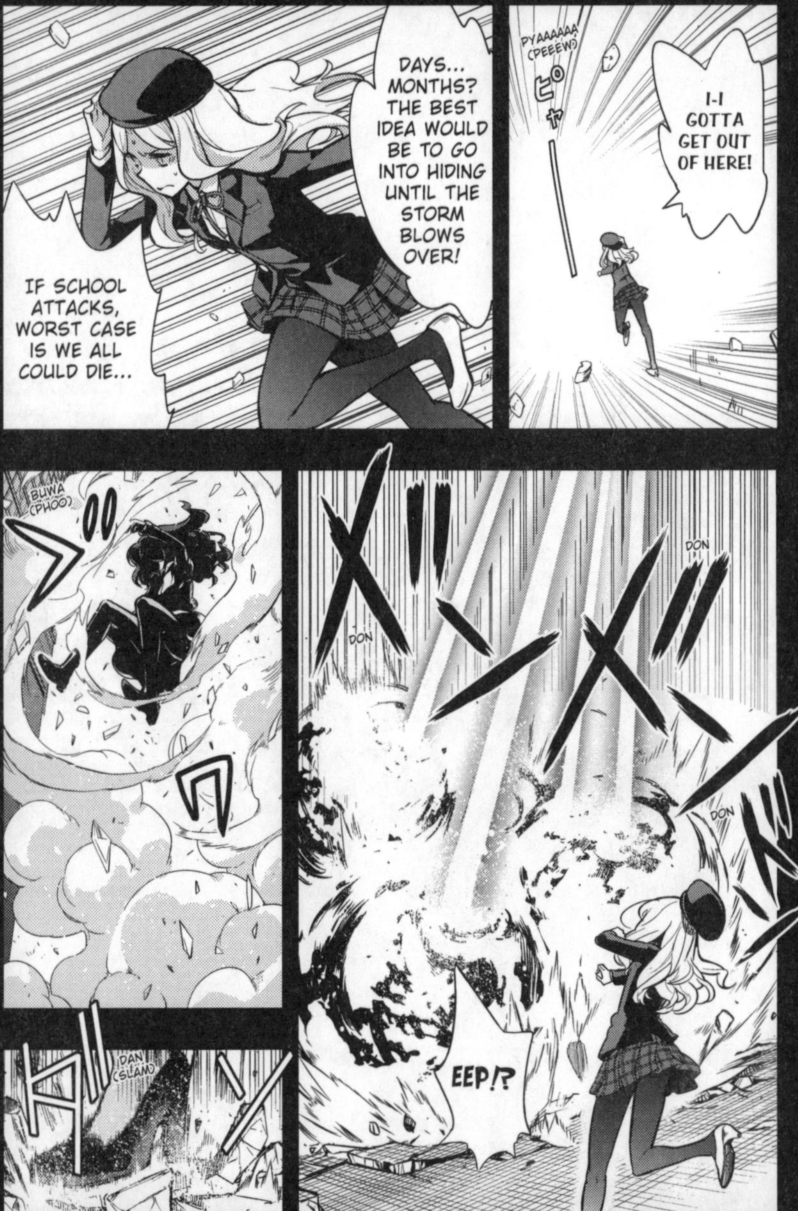
PYAAAAAA (PEEEEW)
I-I GOTTA GET OUT OF HERE!
DAYS... MONTHS? THE BEST IDEA WOULD BE TO GO INTO HIDING UNTIL THE STORM BLOWS OVER!
IF SCHOOL ATTACKS, WORST CASE IS WE ALL COULD DIE...
DON
DON
DON
EEP!?
BUWA (PHOO)
DAN (SLAM)

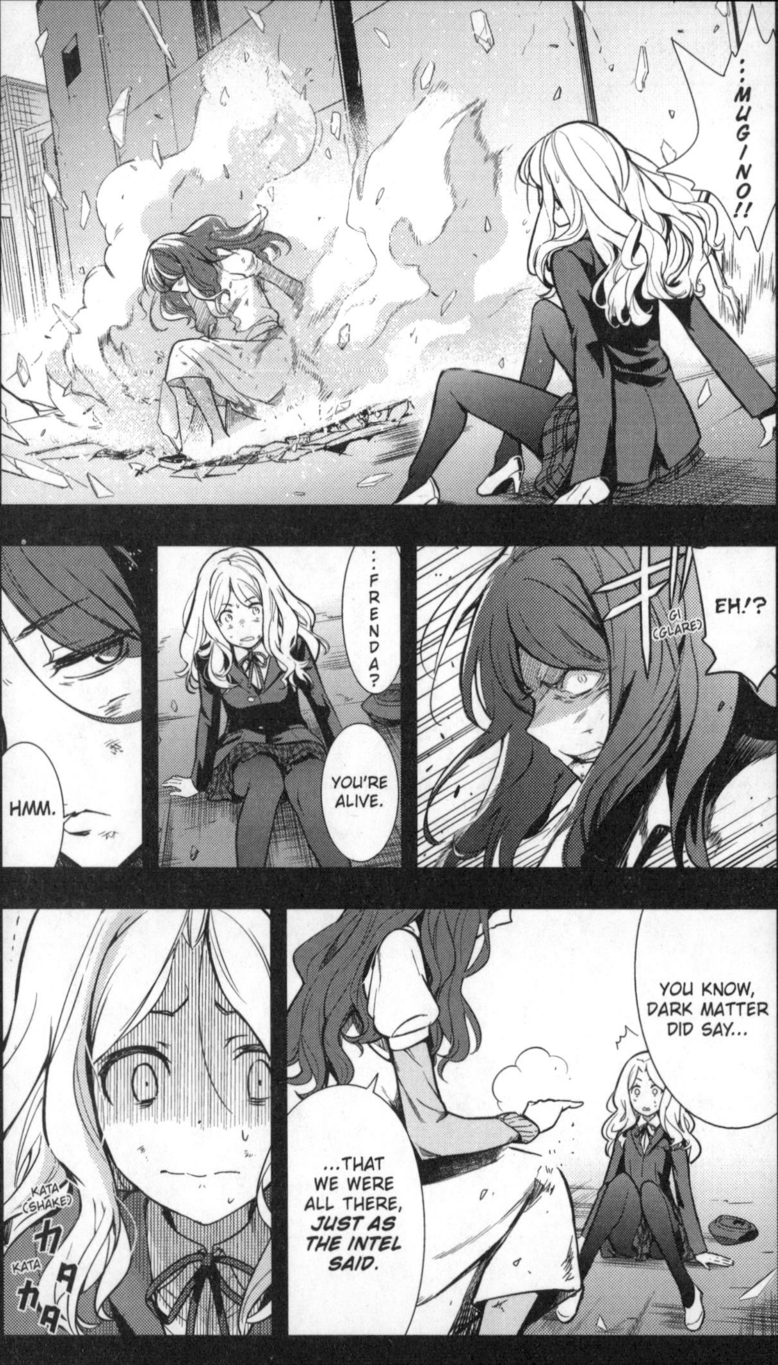

...MUGINO!!
EH!?
GI (GLARE)
...FRENDA?
YOU'RE ALIVE.
HMM.
YOU KNOW, DARK MATTER DID SAY...
...THAT WE WERE ALL THERE, JUST AS THE INTEL SAID.
KATA (SHAKE)
KATA

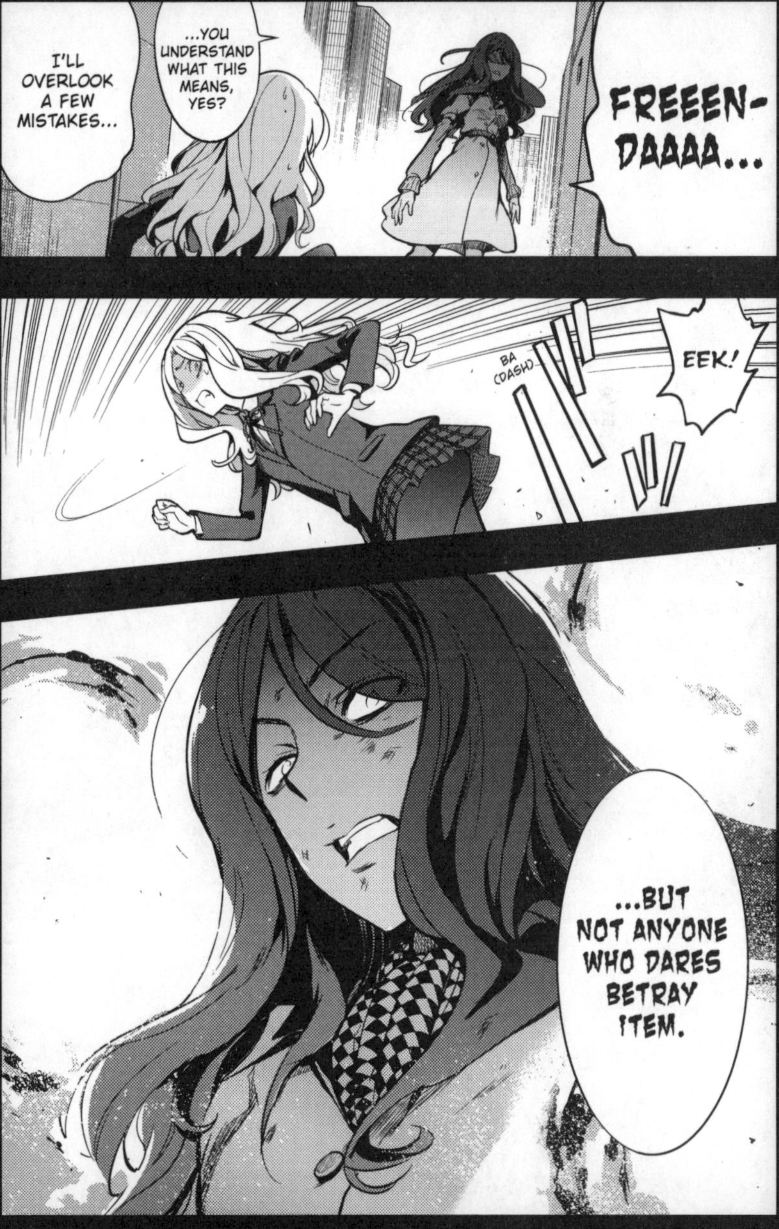
FREEEN-DAAAA...
...YOU UNDERSTAND WHAT THIS MEANS, YES?
I'LL OVERLOOK A FEW MISTAKES...
EEK!
BA (DASH)
...BUT NOT ANYONE WHO DARES BETRAY ITEM.

#144 DISTRICT 3 "HIDEOUT" ③

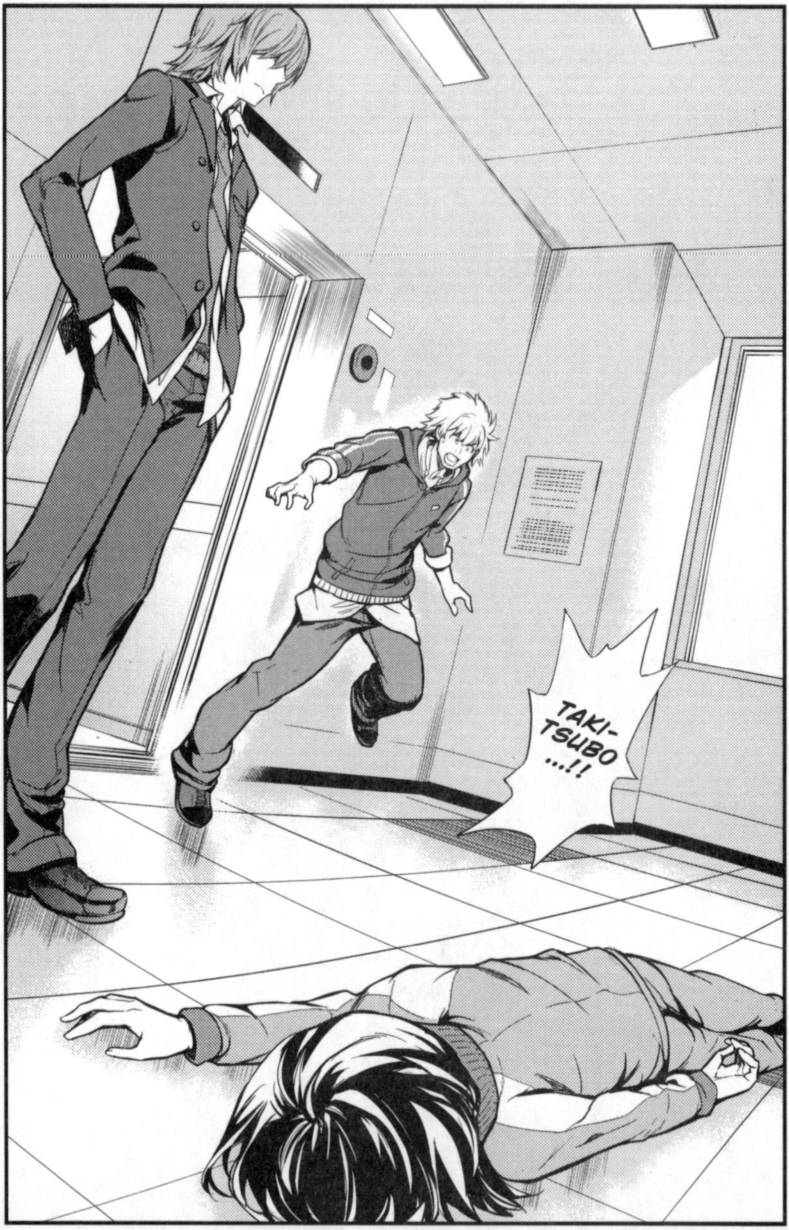
TAKI-TSUBO ...!!

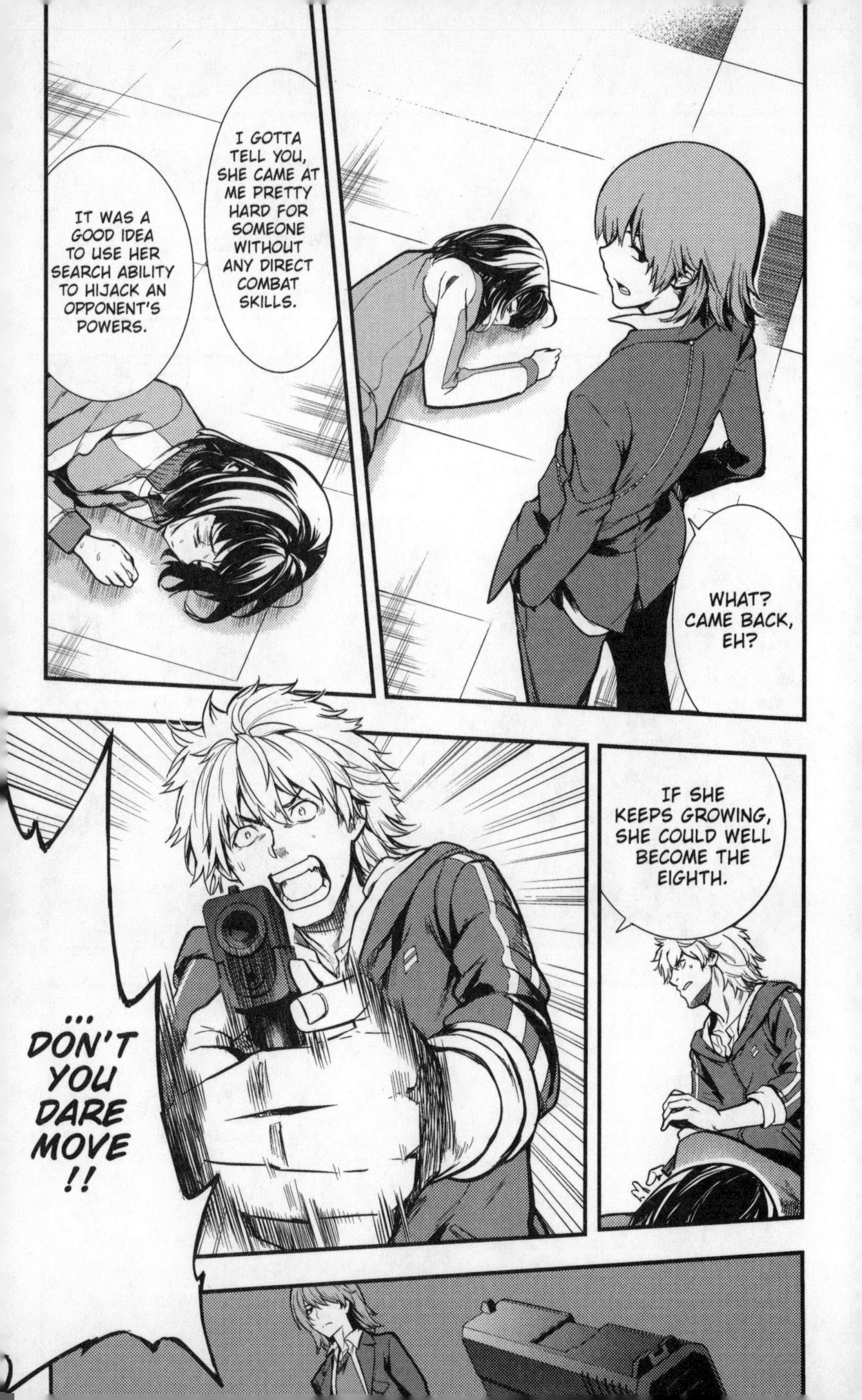
WHAT? CAME BACK, EH?
I GOTTA TELL YOU, SHE CAME AT ME PRETTY HARD FOR SOMEONE WITHOUT ANY DIRECT COMBAT SKILLS.
IT WAS A GOOD IDEA TO USE HER SEARCH ABILITY TO HIJACK AN OPPONENT'S POWERS.
IF SHE KEEPS GROWING, SHE COULD WELL BECOME THE EIGHTH.
...DON'T YOU DARE MOVE!!

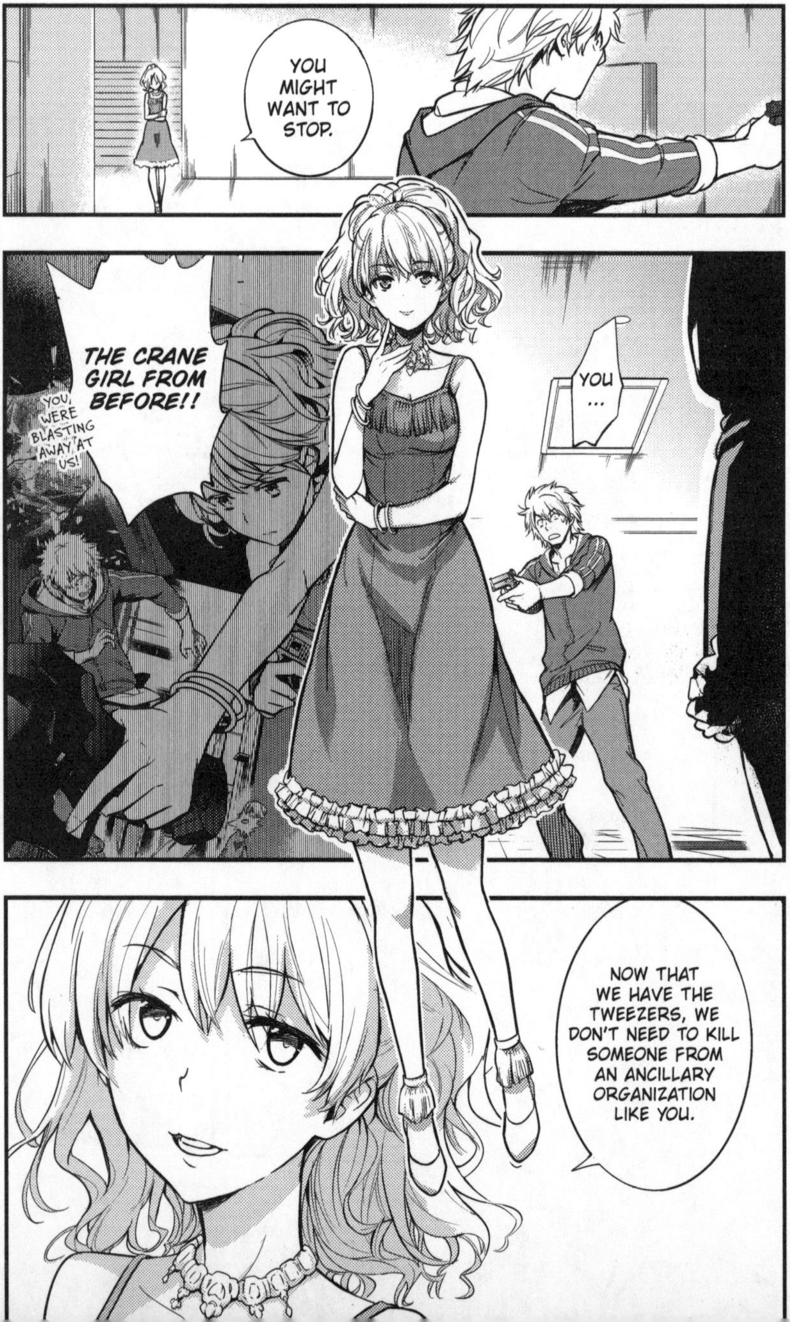
YOU MIGHT WANT TO STOP.
YOU ...
THE CRANE GIRL FROM BEFORE!!
YOU WERE BLASTING AWAY AT US!
NOW THAT WE HAVE THE TWEEZERS, WE DON'T NEED TO KILL SOMEONE FROM AN ANCILLARY ORGANIZATION LIKE YOU.

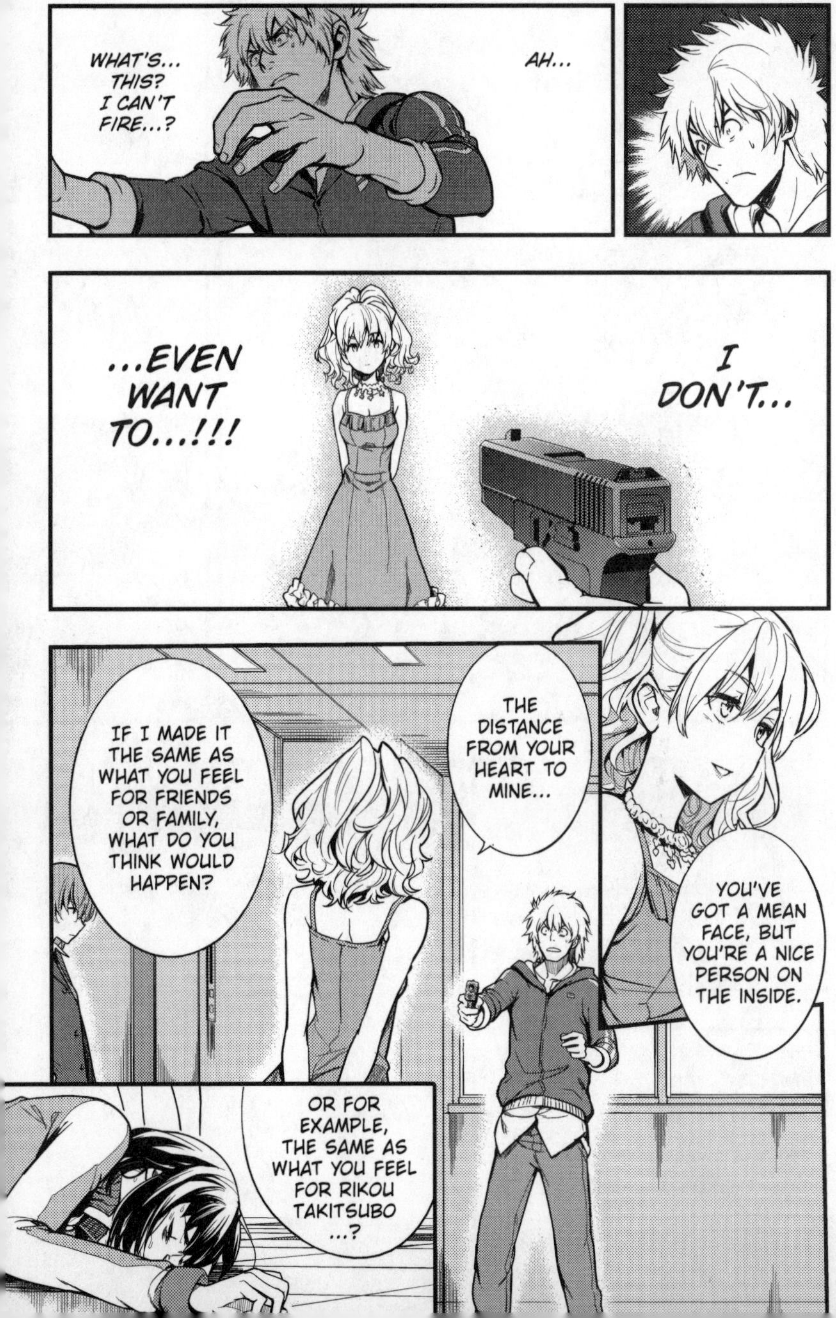
AH...
WHAT'S... THIS? I CAN'T FIRE...?
I DON'T...
...EVEN WANT TO...!!!
YOU'VE GOT A MEAN FACE, BUT YOU'RE A NICE PERSON ON THE INSIDE.
THE DISTANCE FROM YOUR HEART TO MINE...
IF I MADE IT THE SAME AS WHAT YOU FEEL FOR FRIENDS OR FAMILY, WHAT DO YOU THINK WOULD HAPPEN?
OR FOR EXAMPLE, THE SAME AS WHAT YOU FEEL FOR RIKOU TAKITSUBO ...?

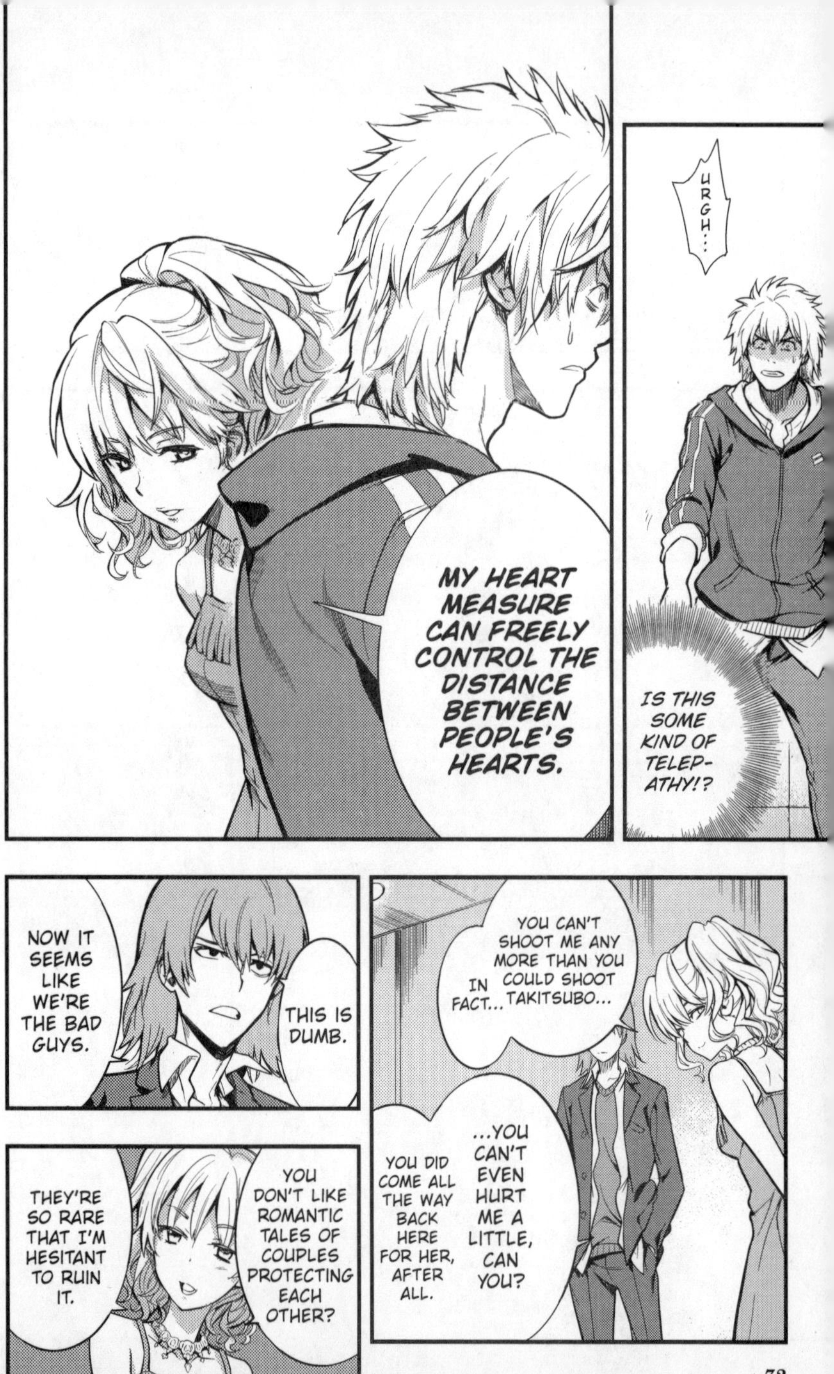
URGH...
IS THIS SOME KIND OF TELEPATHY!?
MY HEART MEASURE CAN FREELY CONTROL THE DISTANCE BETWEEN PEOPLE'S HEARTS.
YOU CAN'T SHOOT ME ANY MORE THAN YOU COULD SHOOT TAKITSUBO...
IN FACT...
...YOU CAN'T EVEN HURT ME A LITTLE, CAN YOU?
YOU DID COME ALL THE WAY BACK HERE FOR HER, AFTER ALL.
THIS IS DUMB.
NOW IT SEEMS LIKE WE'RE THE BAD GUYS.
YOU DON'T LIKE ROMANTIC TALES OF COUPLES PROTECTING EACH OTHER?
THEY'RE SO RARE THAT I'M HESITANT TO RUIN IT.

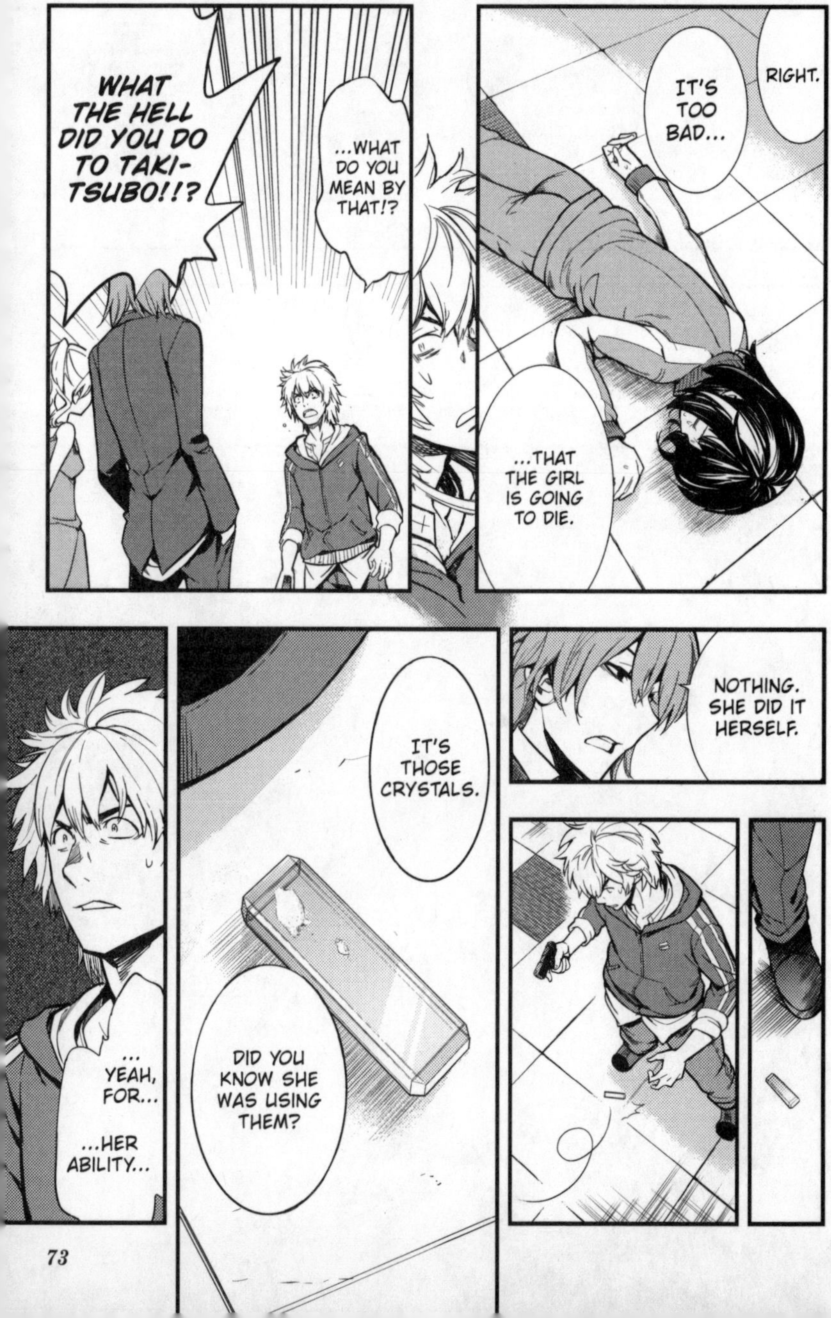
RIGHT.
IT'S TOO BAD...
...THAT THE GIRL IS GOING TO DIE.
...WHAT DO YOU MEAN BY THAT!?
WHAT THE HELL DID YOU DO TO TAKI-TSUBO!!?
NOTHING. SHE DID IT HERSELF.
IT'S THOSE CRYSTALS.
DID YOU KNOW SHE WAS USING THEM?
...YEAH, FOR...
...HER ABILITY...

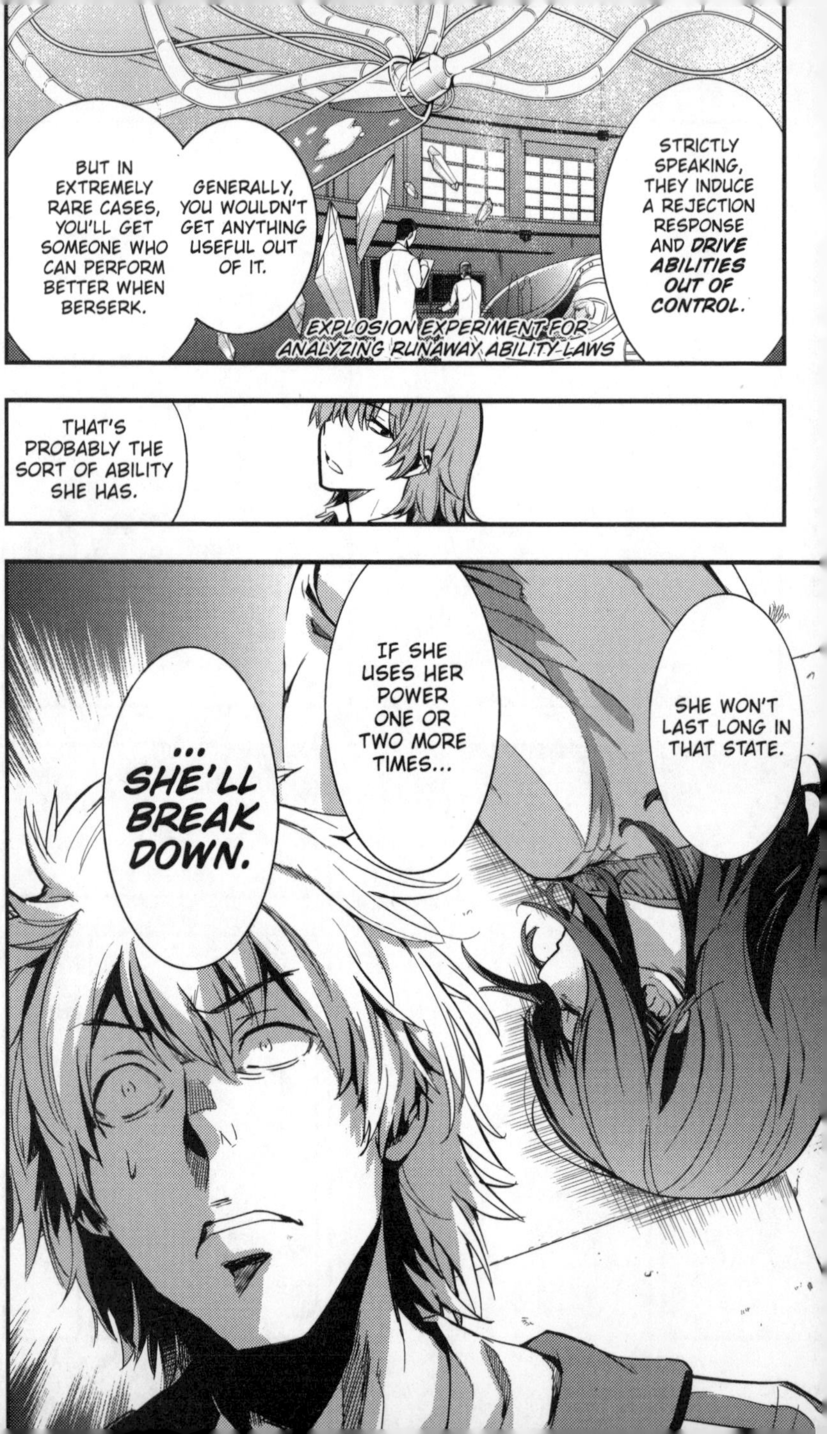
STRICTLY SPEAKING, THEY INDUCE A REJECTION RESPONSE AND ***DRIVE ABILITIES OUT OF CONTROL***.
GENERALLY, YOU WOULDN'T GET ANYTHING USEFUL OUT OF IT.
BUT IN EXTREMELY RARE CASES, YOU'LL GET SOMEONE WHO CAN PERFORM BETTER WHEN BERSERK.
EXPLOSION EXPERIMENT FOR ANALYZING RUNAWAY ABILITY LAWS
THAT'S PROBABLY THE SORT OF ABILITY SHE HAS.
SHE WON'T LAST LONG IN THAT STATE.
IF SHE USES HER POWER ONE OR TWO MORE TIMES...
...***SHE'LL BREAK DOWN.***

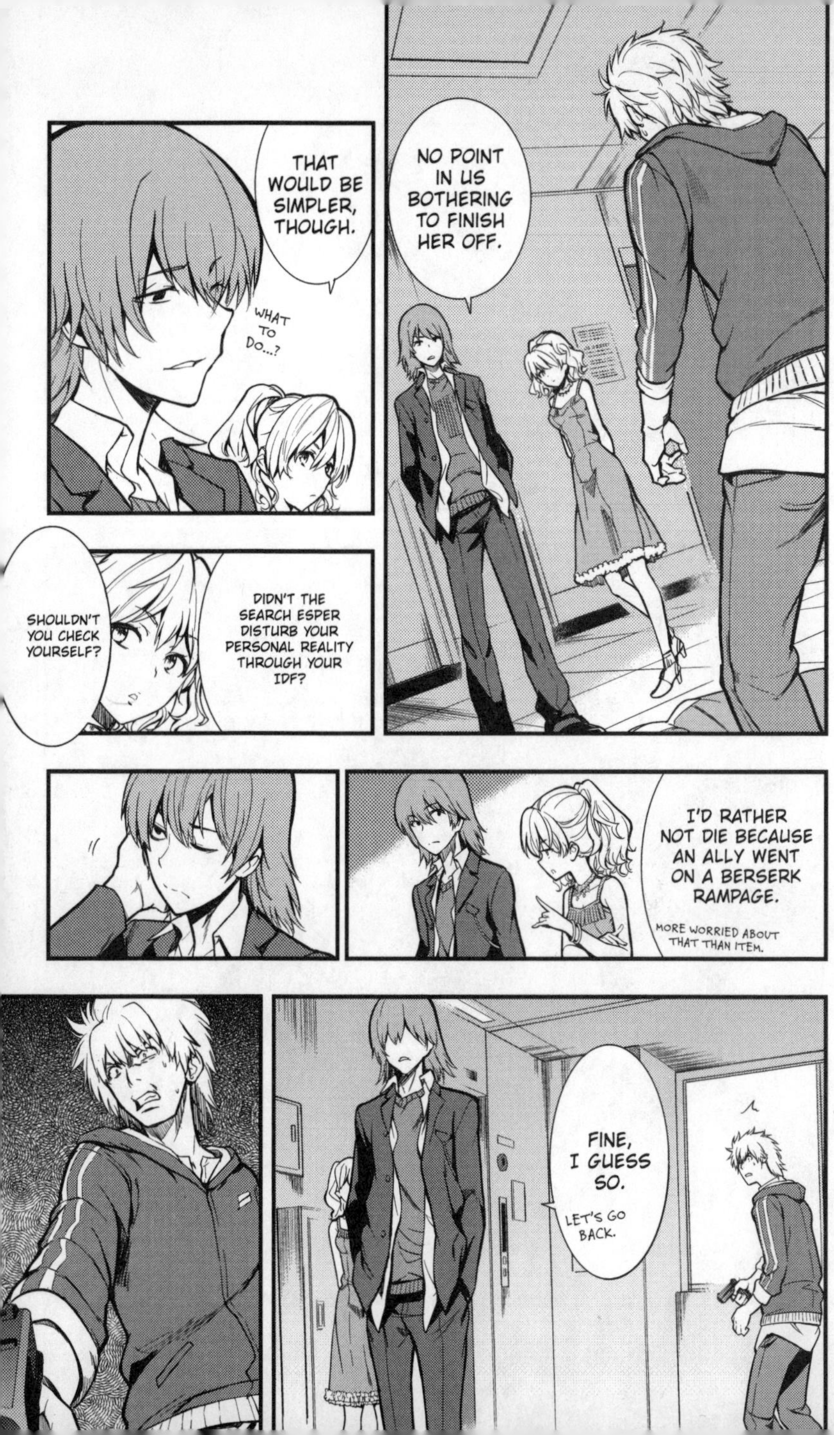
NO POINT IN US BOTHERING TO FINISH HER OFF.
THAT WOULD BE SIMPLER, THOUGH.
WHAT TO DO...?
DIDN'T THE SEARCH ESPER DISTURB YOUR PERSONAL REALITY THROUGH YOUR IDF?
SHOULDN'T YOU CHECK YOURSELF?
I'D RATHER NOT DIE BECAUSE AN ALLY WENT ON A BERSERK RAMPAGE.
MORE WORRIED ABOUT THAT THAN ITEM.
FINE, I GUESS SO.
LET'S GO BACK.

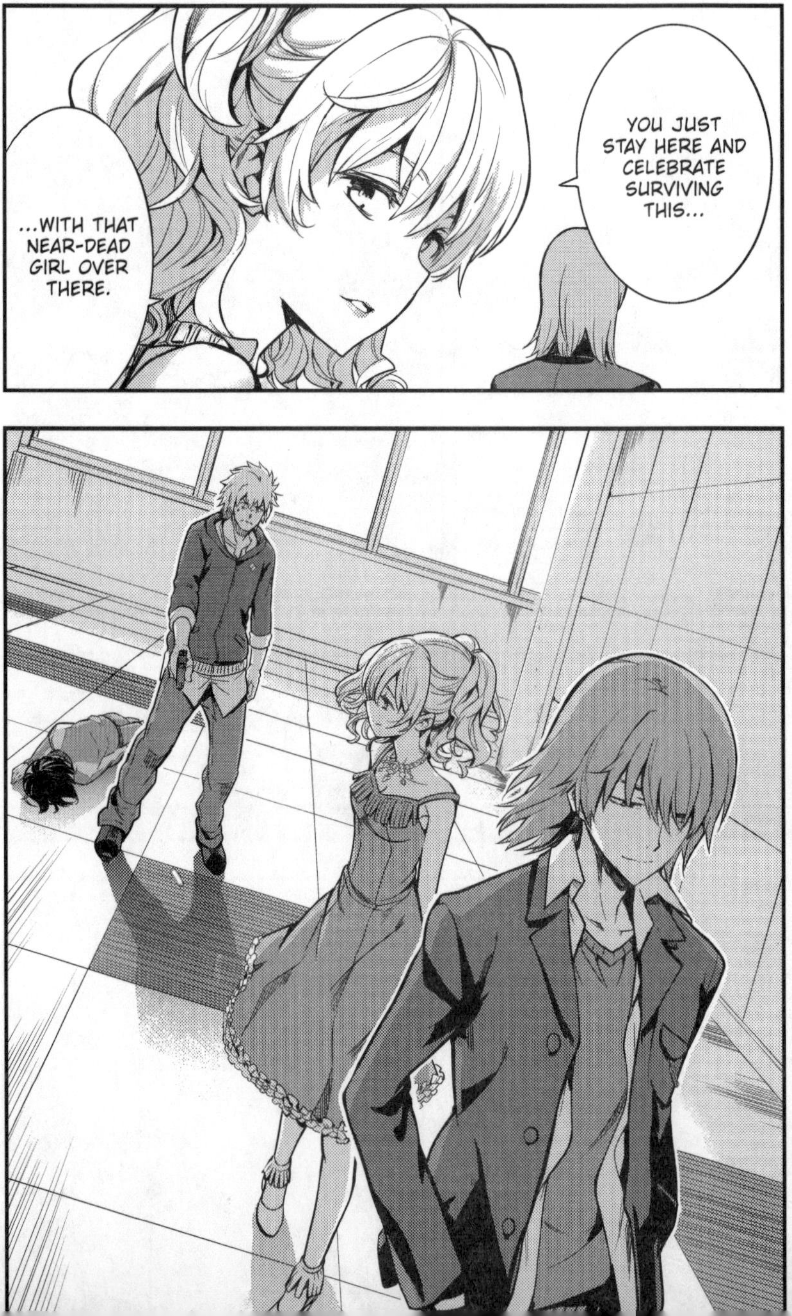
YOU JUST STAY HERE AND CELEBRATE SURVIVING THIS...
...WITH THAT NEAR-DEAD GIRL OVER THERE.

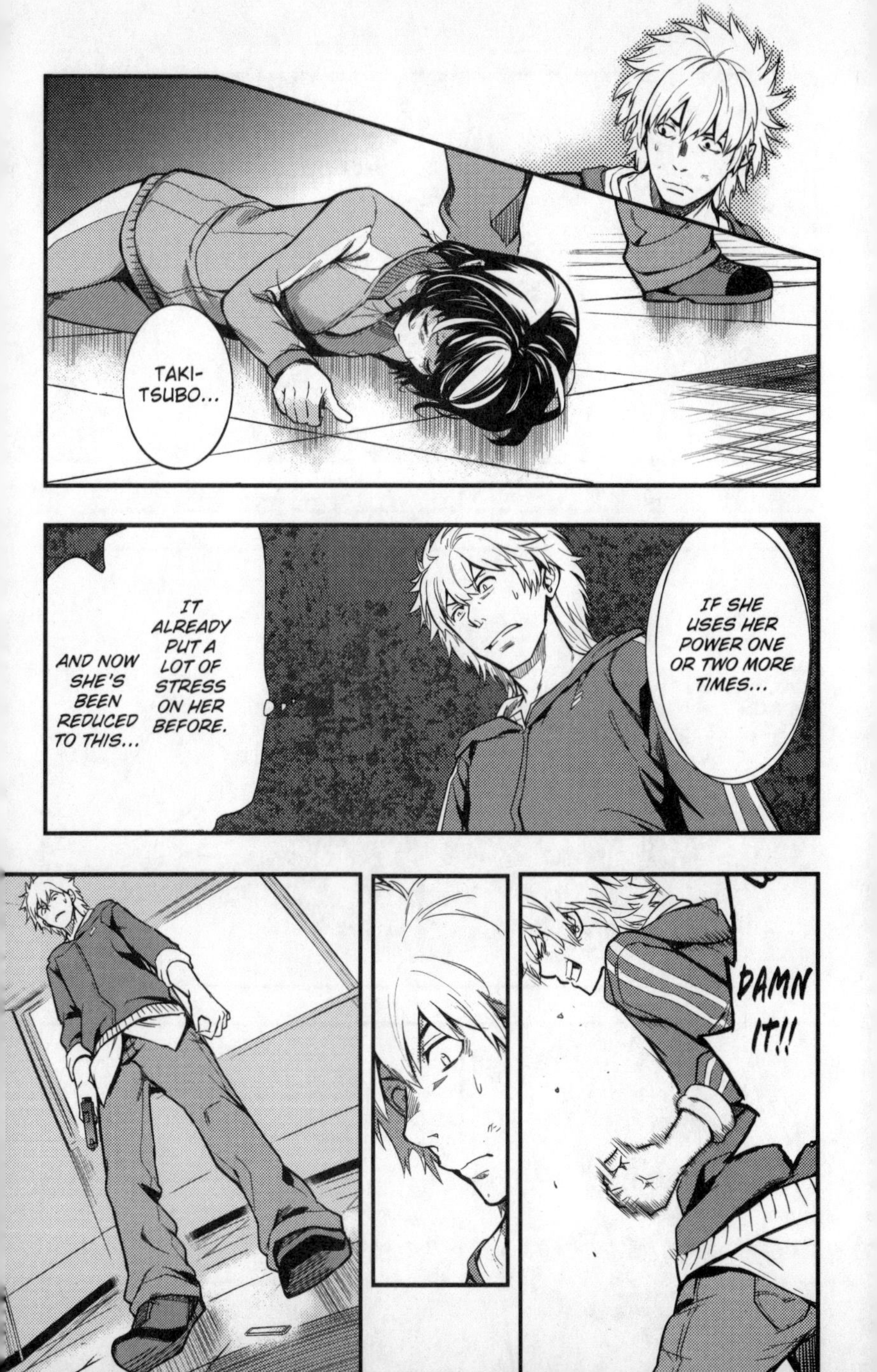

TAKI-TSUBO...
IF SHE USES HER POWER ONE OR TWO MORE TIMES...
IT ALREADY PUT A LOT OF STRESS ON HER BEFORE.
AND NOW SHE'S BEEN REDUCED TO THIS...
DAMN IT!!

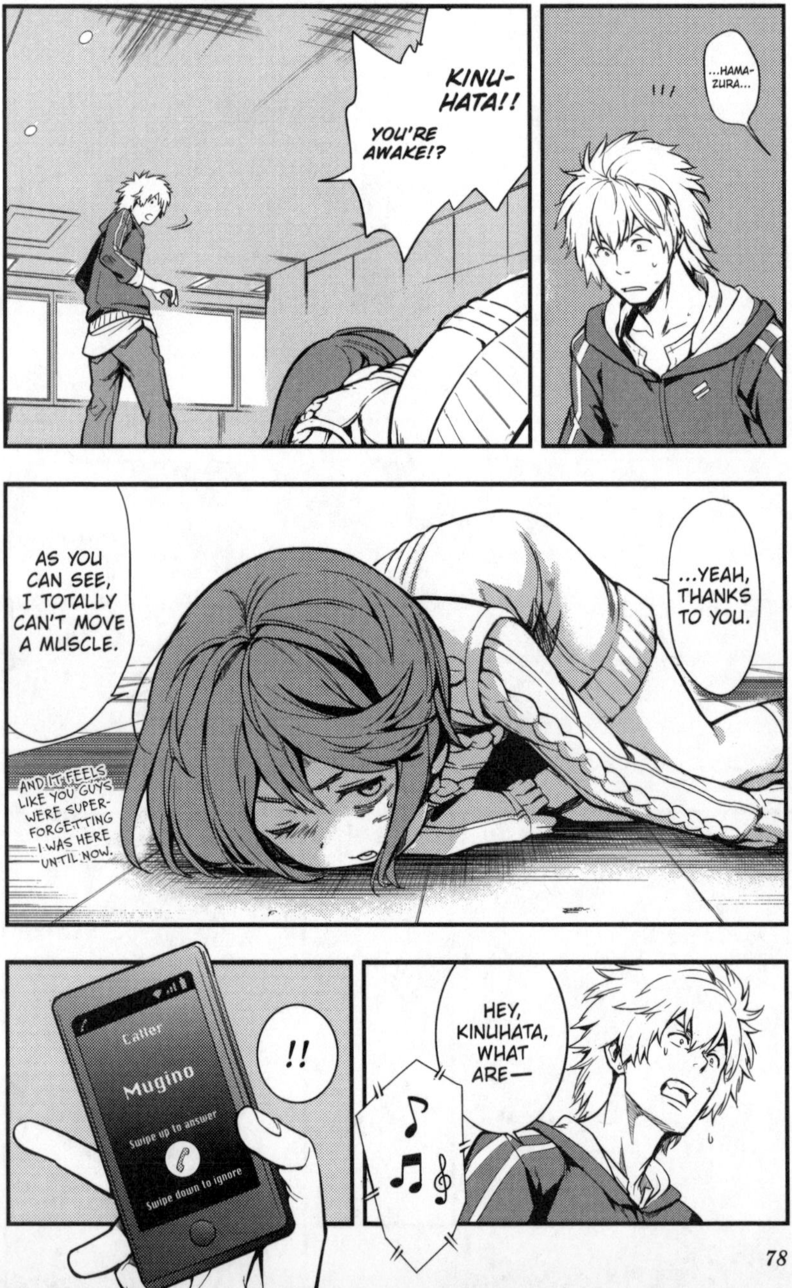

...HAMA-ZURA...
!!/
KINU-HATA!!
YOU'RE AWAKE!?
...YEAH, THANKS TO YOU.
AS YOU CAN SEE, I TOTALLY CAN'T MOVE A MUSCLE.
AND IT FEELS LIKE YOU GUYS WERE SUPER-FORGETTING I WAS HERE UNTIL NOW.
HEY, KINUHATA, WHAT ARE—
!!
Caller
Mugino
Swipe up to answer
Swipe down to ignore

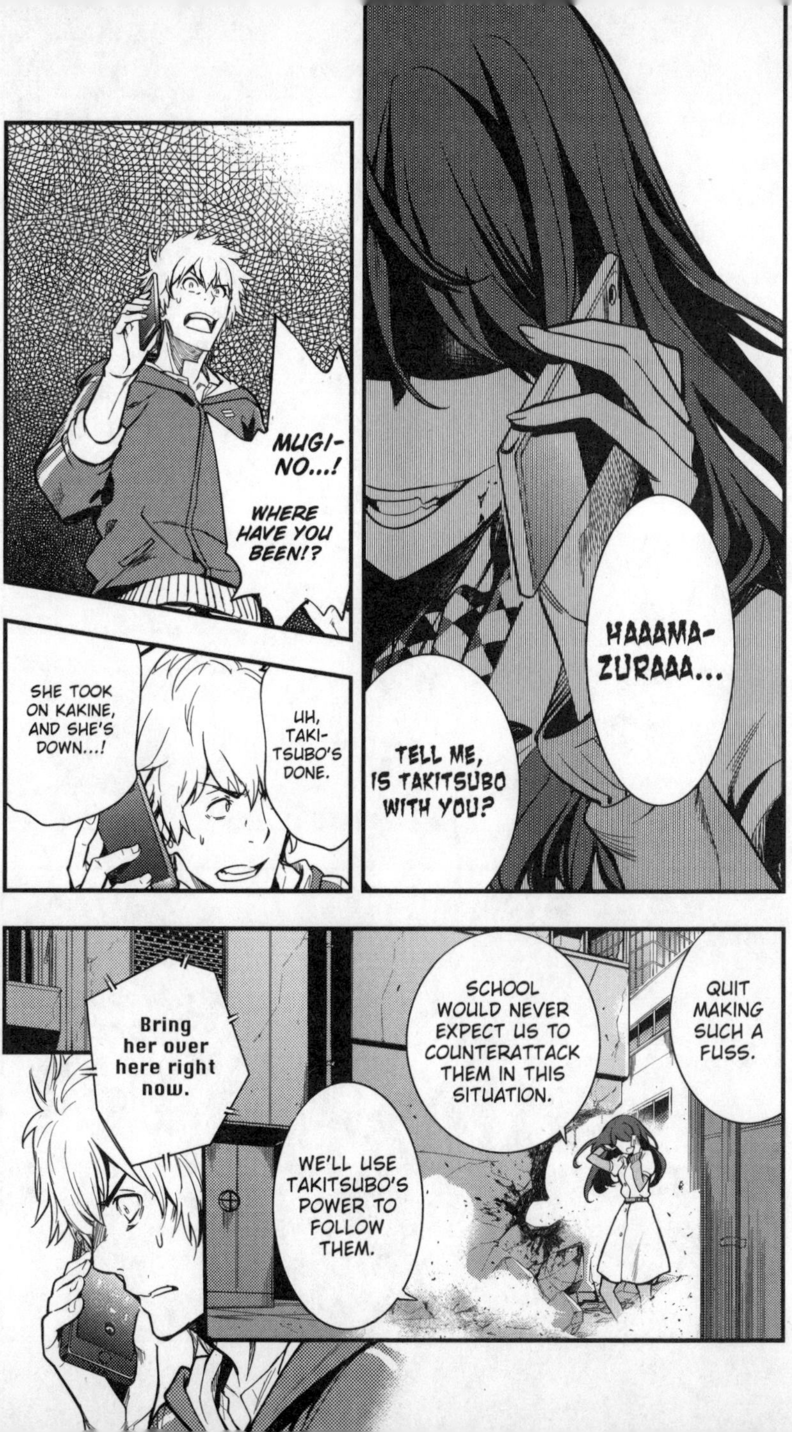
HAAAMA-ZURAAA...
TELL ME, IS TAKITSUBO WITH YOU?
MUGI-NO...!
WHERE HAVE YOU BEEN!?
UH, TAKI-TSUBO'S DONE.
SHE TOOK ON KAKINE, AND SHE'S DOWN...!
QUIT MAKING SUCH A FUSS.
SCHOOL WOULD NEVER EXPECT US TO COUNTERATTACK THEM IN THIS SITUATION.
WE'LL USE TAKITSUBO'S POWER TO FOLLOW THEM.
Bring her over here right now.

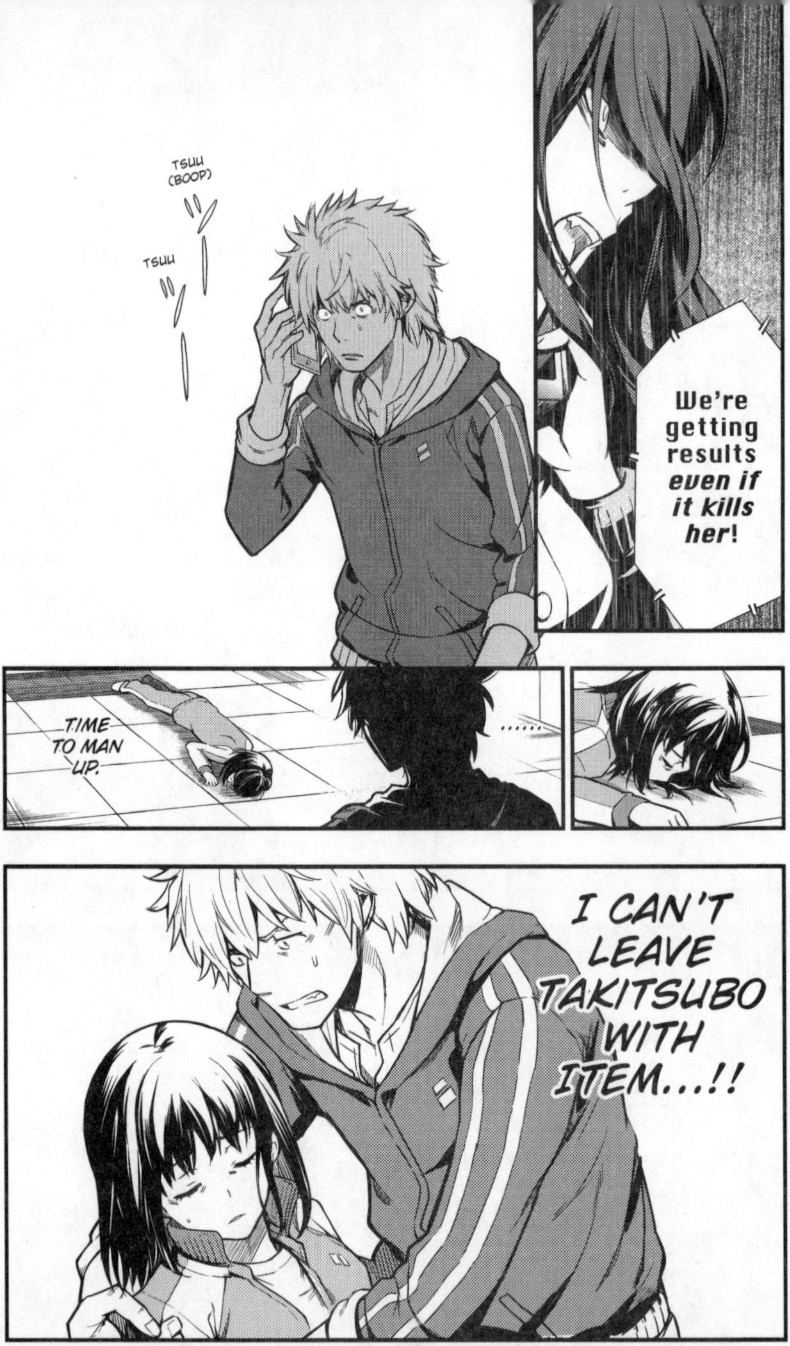
We're getting results *even if* it kills her!
TSUU (BOOP)
TSUU
......
TIME TO MAN UP.
I CAN'T LEAVE TAKITSUBO WITH ITEM...!!

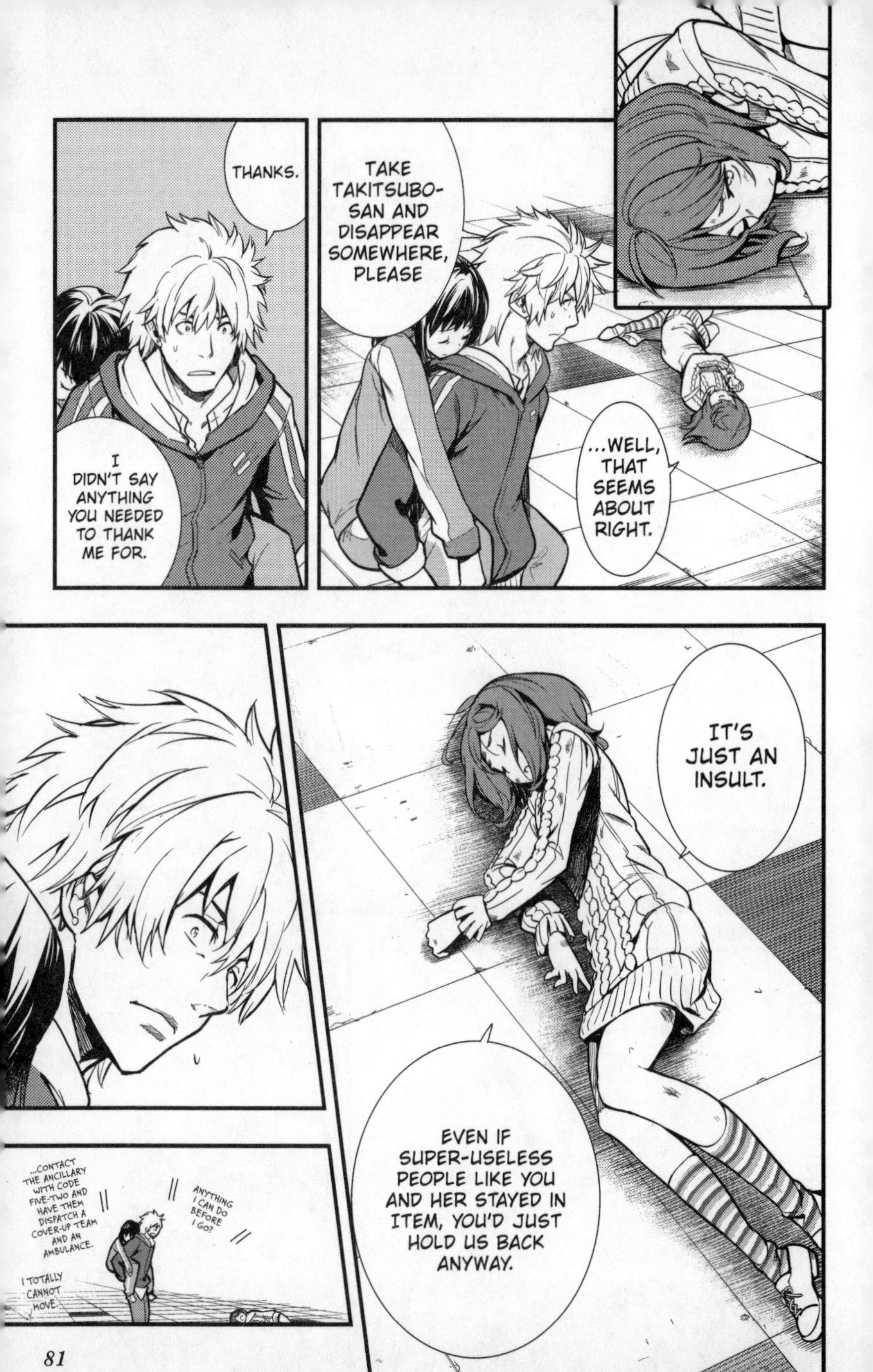
TAKE TAKITSUBO-SAN AND DISAPPEAR SOMEWHERE, PLEASE
...WELL, THAT SEEMS ABOUT RIGHT.
THANKS.
I DIDN'T SAY ANYTHING YOU NEEDED TO THANK ME FOR.
IT'S JUST AN INSULT.
EVEN IF SUPER-USELESS PEOPLE LIKE YOU AND HER STAYED IN ITEM, YOU'D JUST HOLD US BACK ANYWAY.
ANYTHING I CAN DO BEFORE I GO?
...CONTACT THE ANCILLARY WITH CODE FIVE-TWO AND HAVE THEM DISPATCH A COVER-UP TEAM AND AN AMBULANCE.
I TOTALLY CANNOT MOVE.

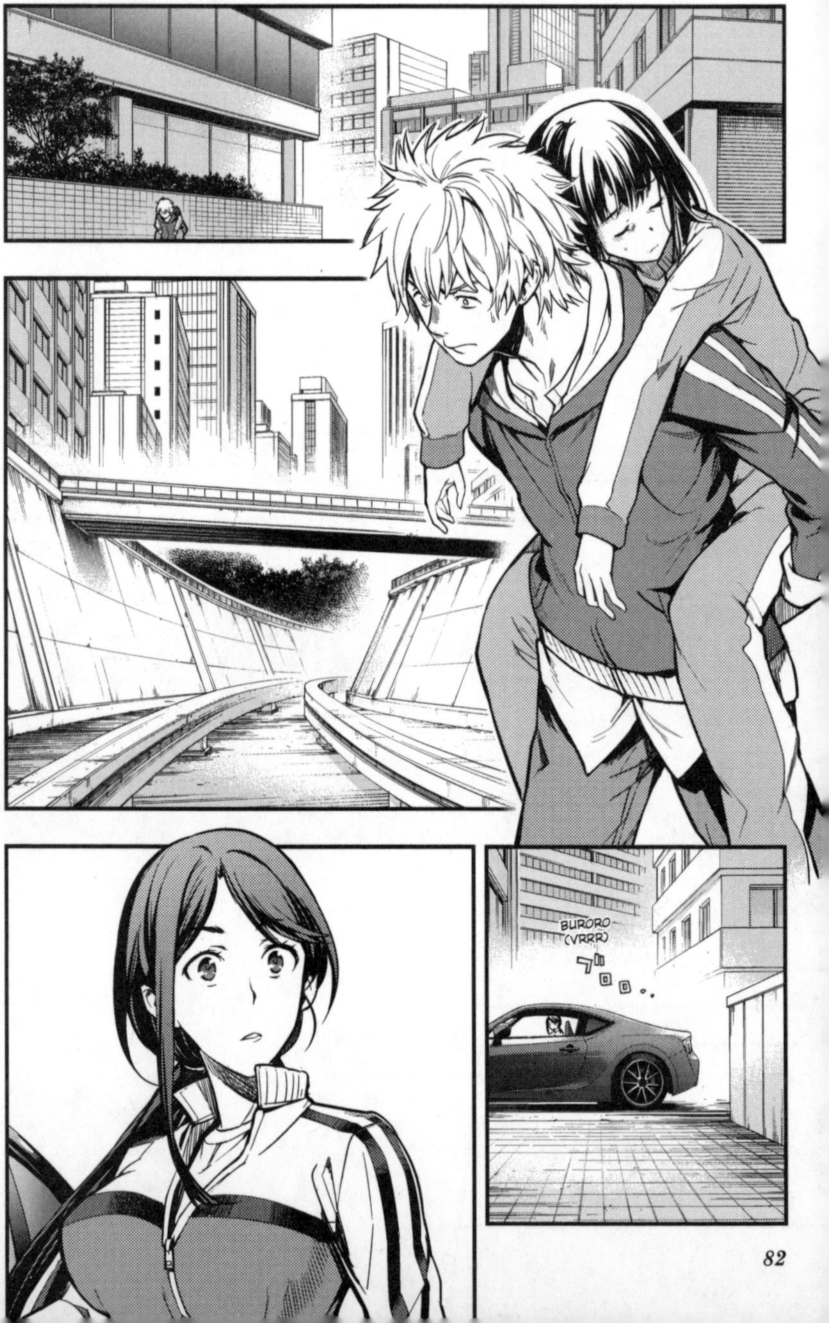
BURORO
(VRRR)
ブロロ。。

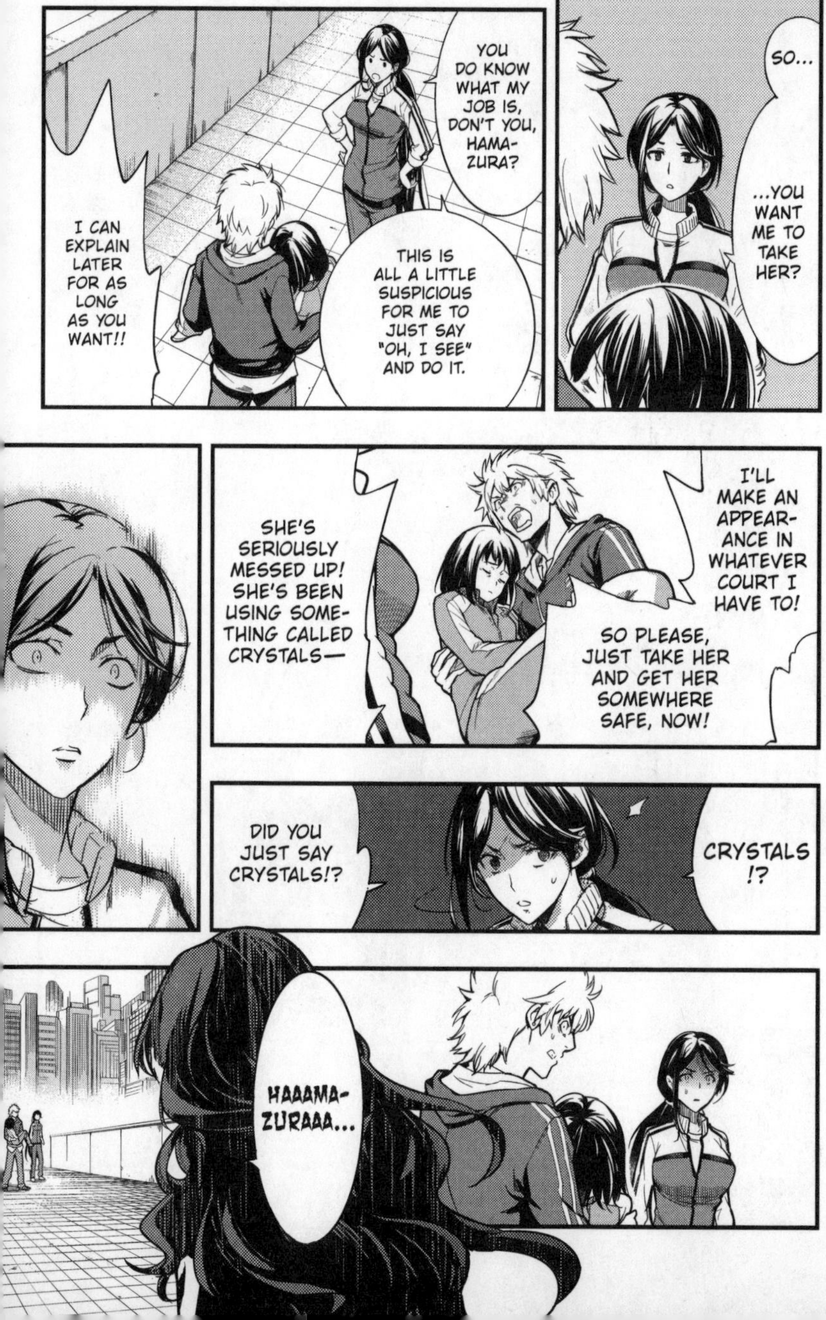
SO...
...YOU WANT ME TO TAKE HER?
YOU DO KNOW WHAT MY JOB IS, DON'T YOU, HAMA-ZURA?
THIS IS ALL A LITTLE SUSPICIOUS FOR ME TO JUST SAY "OH, I SEE" AND DO IT.
I CAN EXPLAIN LATER FOR AS LONG AS YOU WANT!!
I'LL MAKE AN APPEAR-ANCE IN WHATEVER COURT I HAVE TO!
SO PLEASE, JUST TAKE HER AND GET HER SOMEWHERE SAFE, NOW!
SHE'S SERIOUSLY MESSED UP! SHE'S BEEN USING SOME-THING CALLED CRYSTALS—
CRYSTALS!?
DID YOU JUST SAY CRYSTALS!?
HAAAMA-ZURAAA...

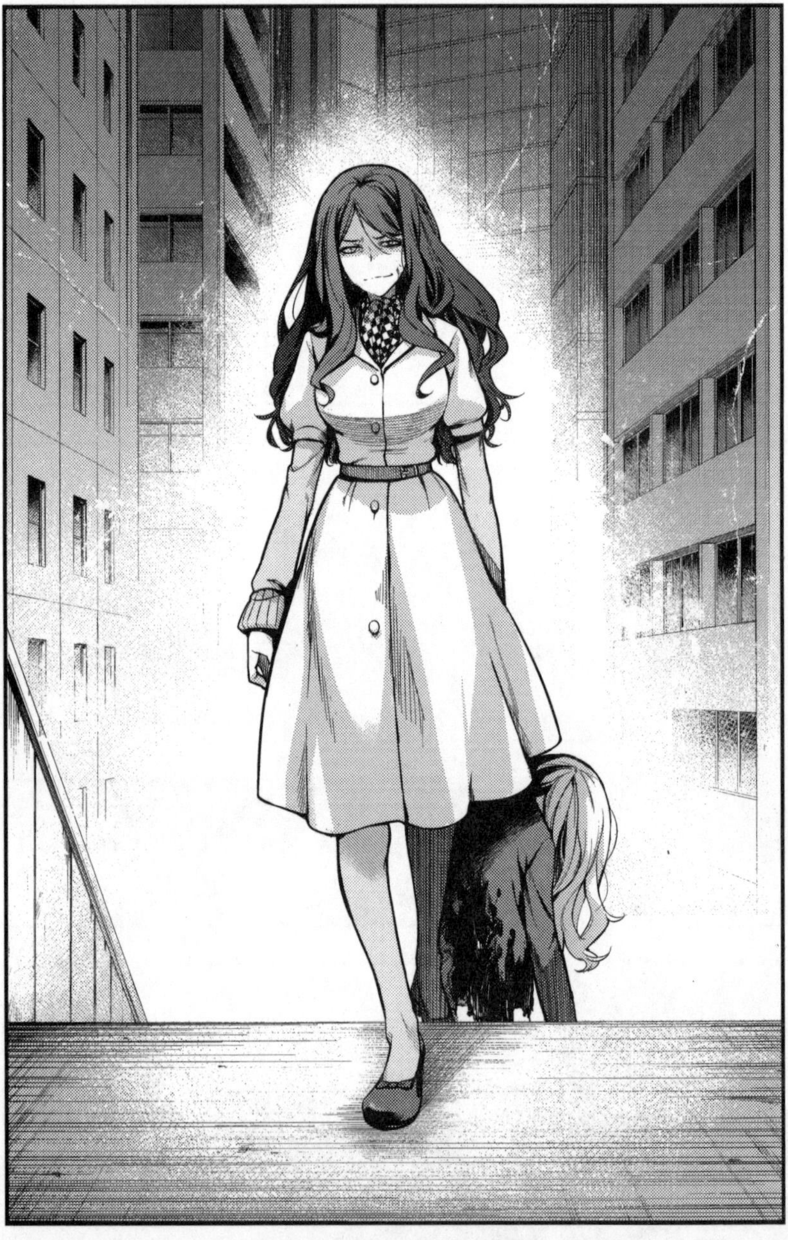

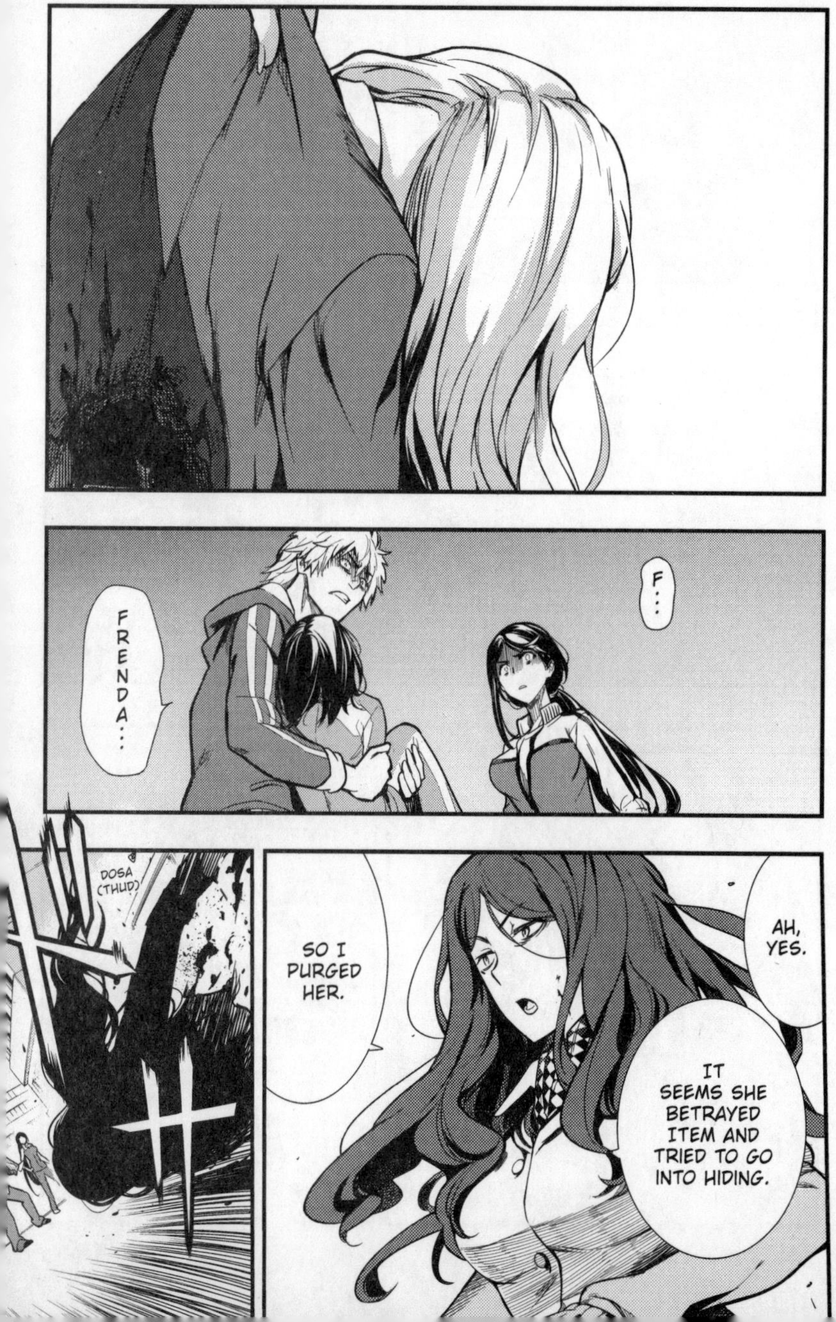
F...
FRENDA...
AH, YES.
IT SEEMS SHE BETRAYED ITEM AND TRIED TO GO INTO HIDING.
SO I PURGED HER.
DOSA (THUD)

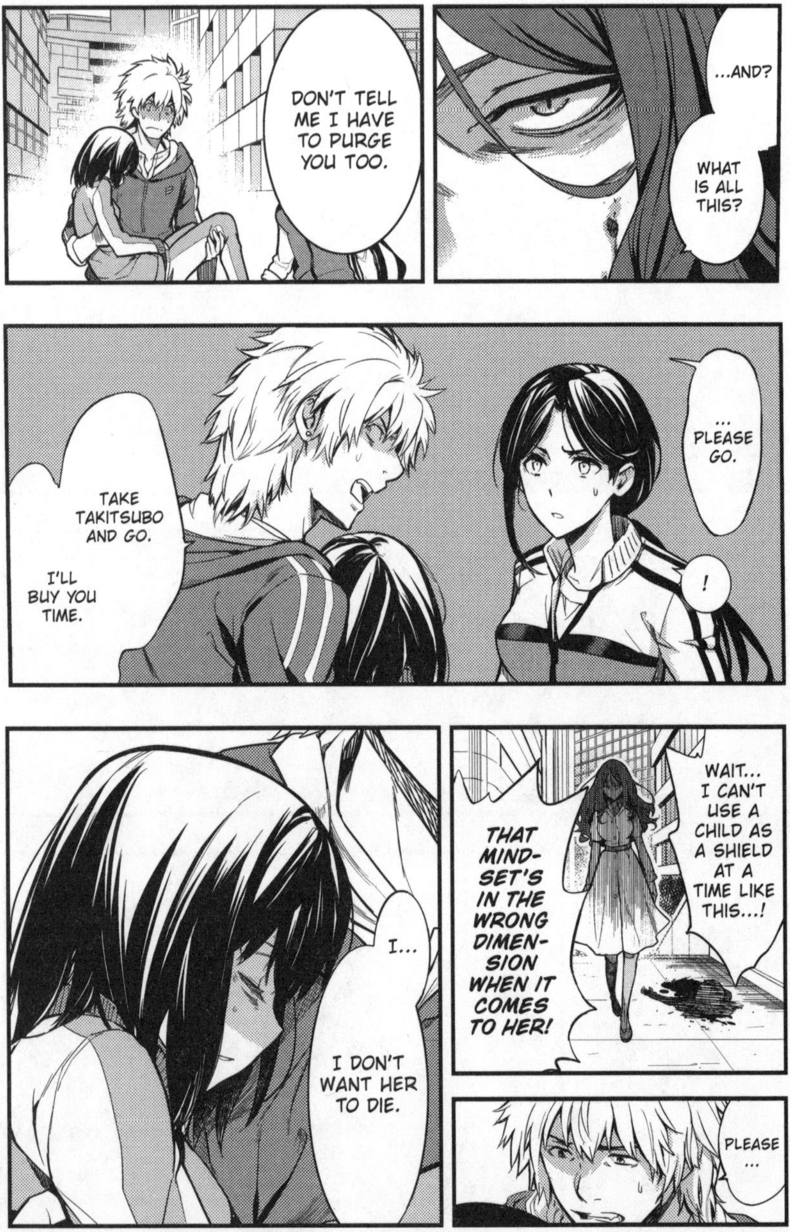
...AND?
WHAT IS ALL THIS?
DON'T TELL ME I HAVE TO PURGE YOU TOO.
... PLEASE GO.
!
TAKE TAKITSUBO AND GO.
I'LL BUY YOU TIME.
WAIT... I CAN'T USE A CHILD AS A SHIELD AT A TIME LIKE THIS...!
THAT MIND-SET'S IN THE WRONG DIMEN-SION WHEN IT COMES TO HER!
PLEASE ...
I...
I DON'T WANT HER TO DIE.

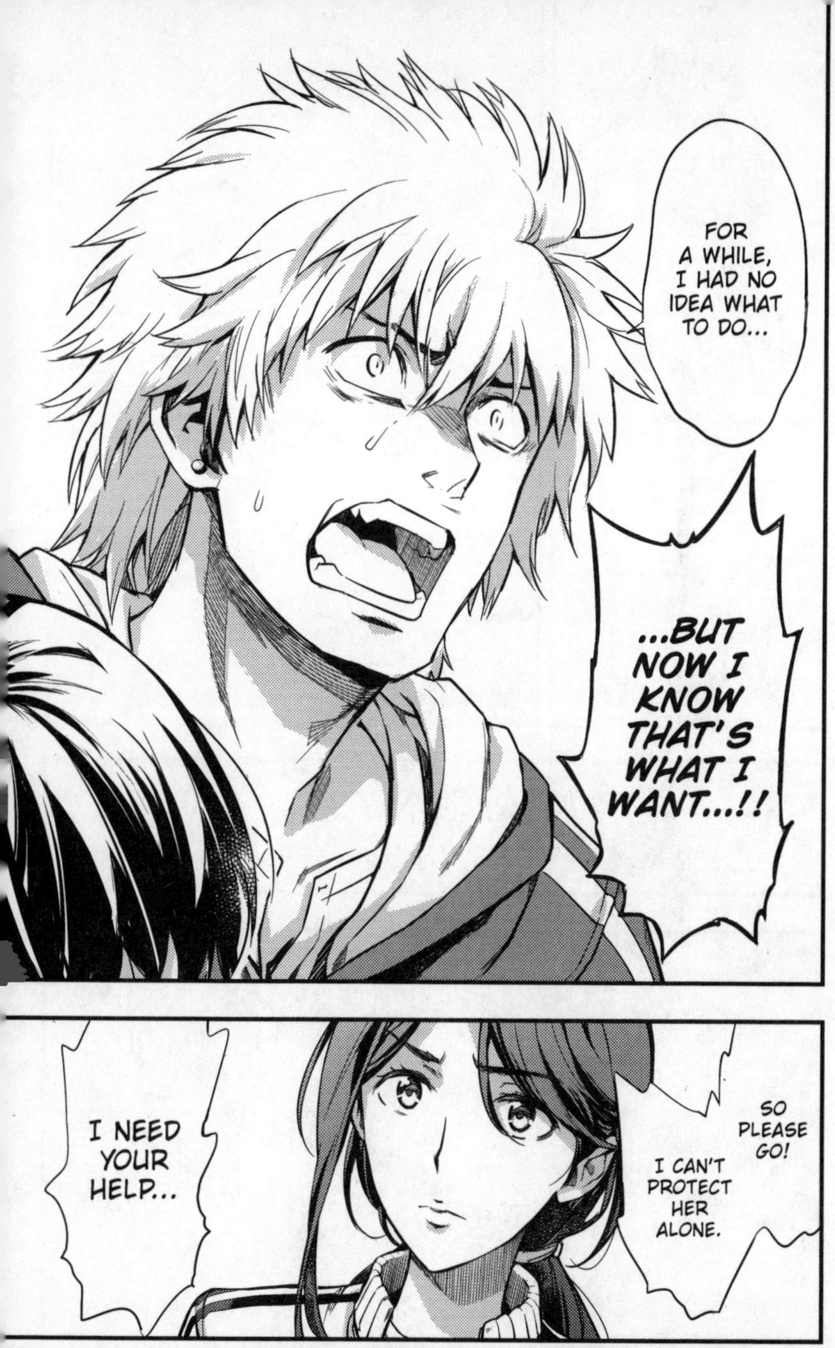
FOR A WHILE, I HAD NO IDEA WHAT TO DO...
...BUT NOW I KNOW THAT'S WHAT I WANT...!!
SO PLEASE GO!
I CAN'T PROTECT HER ALONE.
I NEED YOUR HELP...

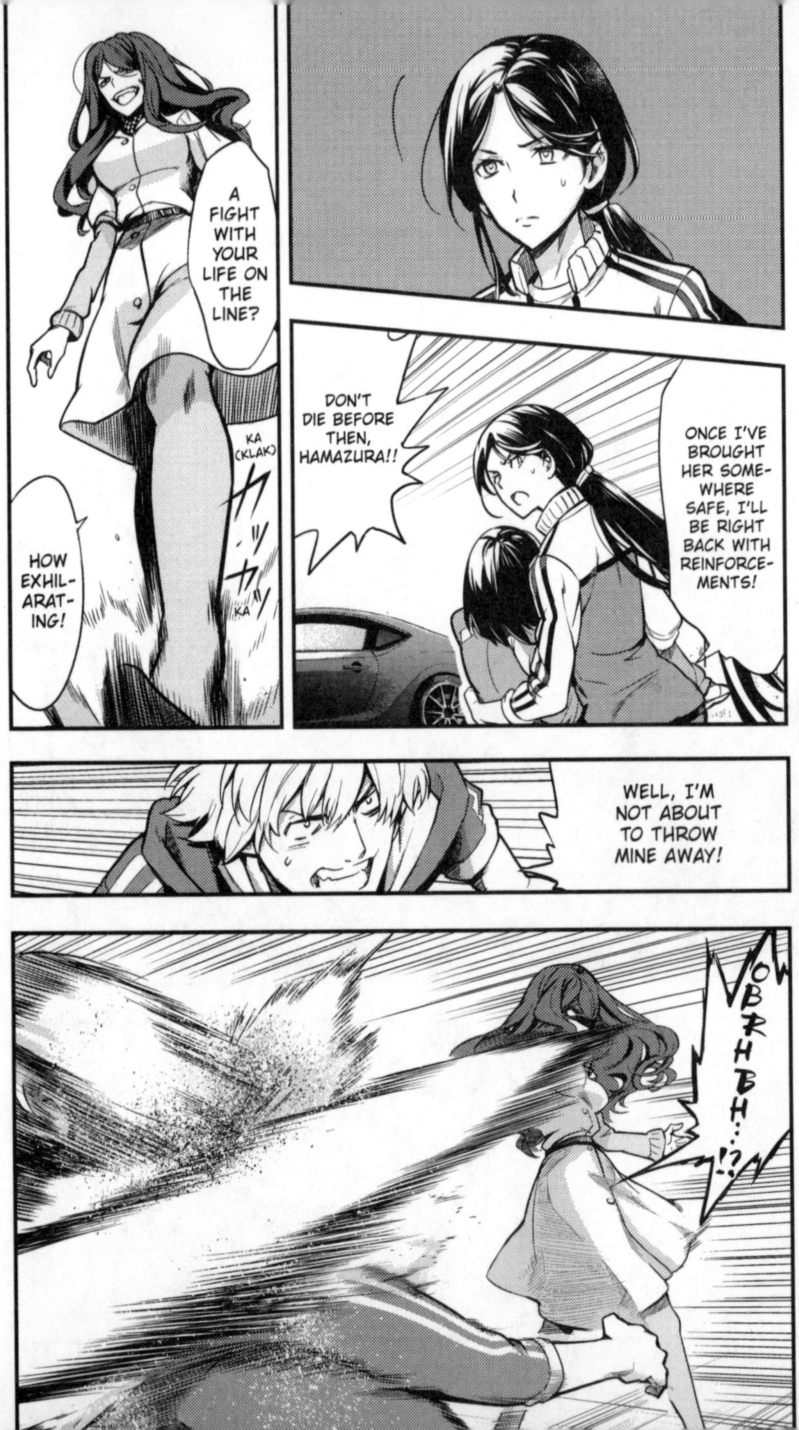
ONCE I'VE BROUGHT HER SOME-WHERE SAFE, I'LL BE RIGHT BACK WITH REINFORCE-MENTS!
DON'T DIE BEFORE THEN, HAMAZURA!!
A FIGHT WITH YOUR LIFE ON THE LINE?
KA (KLAK)
KA
HOW EXHIL-ARAT-ING!
WELL, I'M NOT ABOUT TO THROW MINE AWAY!
OBRHBH...!?

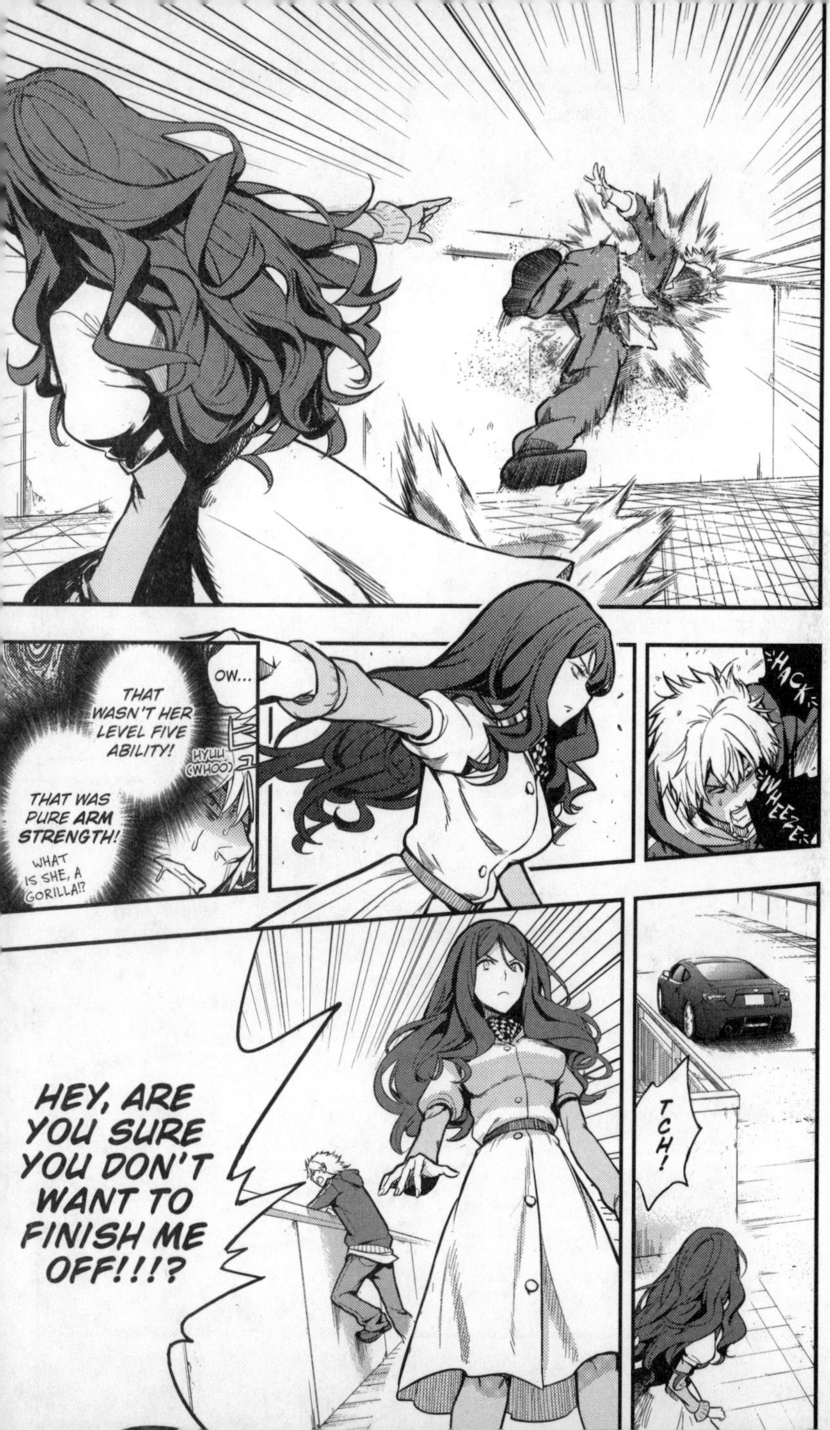
HACK
WHEEZE
OW...
THAT WASN'T HER LEVEL FIVE ABILITY!
HYUU (WHOO)
THAT WAS PURE ARM STRENGTH!
WHAT IS SHE, A GORILLA!?
TCH!
HEY, ARE YOU SURE YOU DON'T WANT TO FINISH ME OFF!!!?

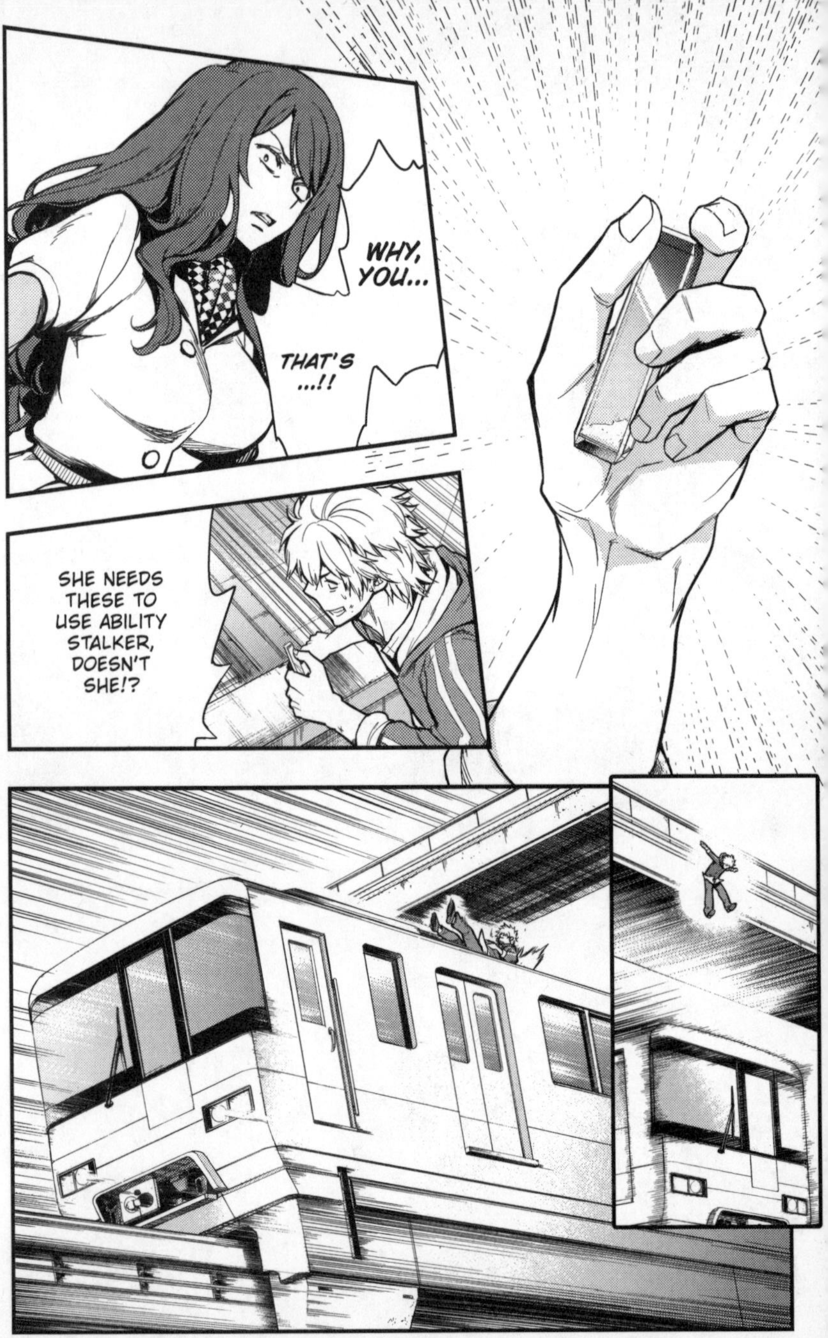
WHY, YOU...
THAT'S ...!!
SHE NEEDS THESE TO USE ABILITY STALKER, DOESN'T SHE!?

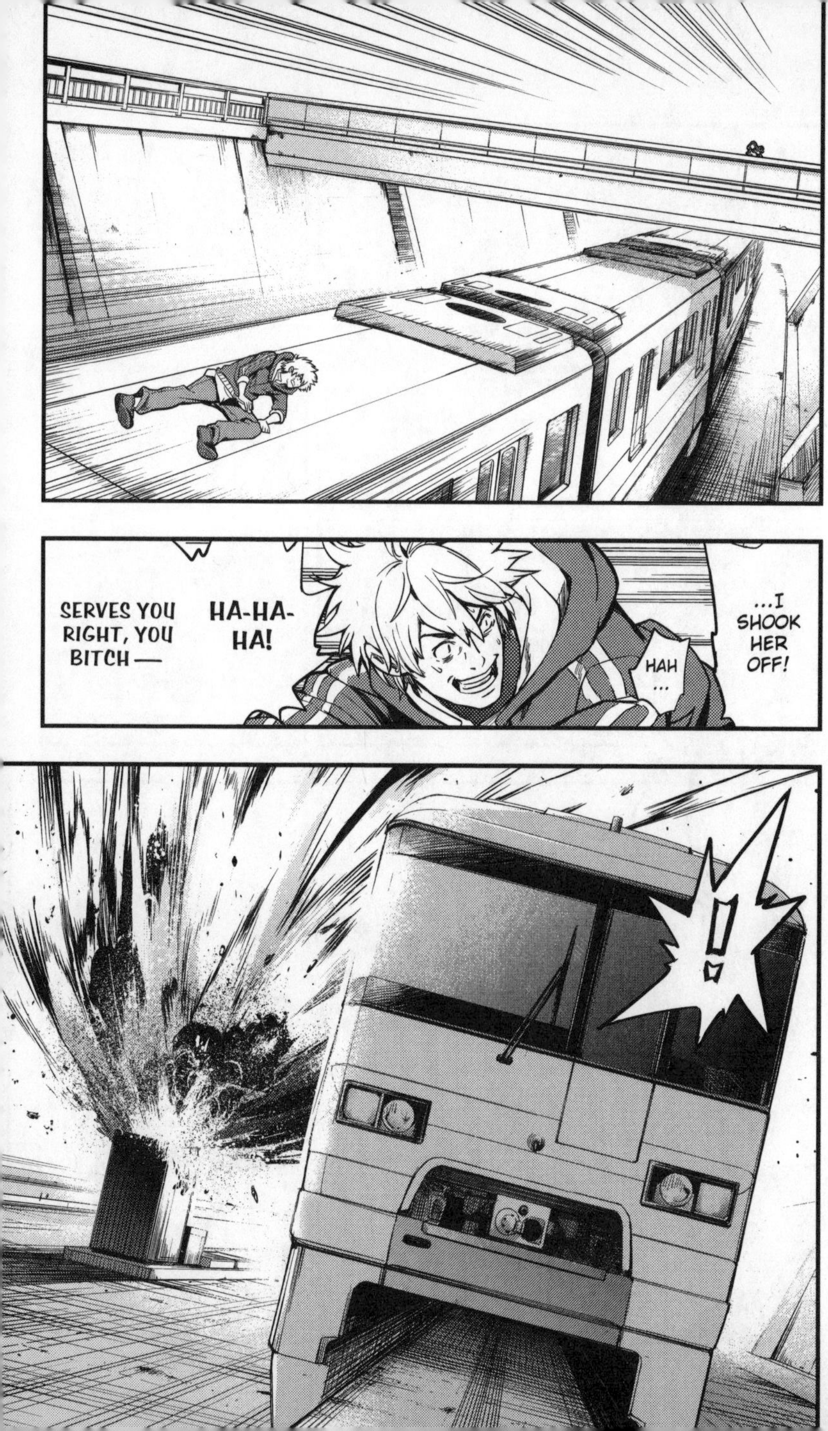
...I SHOOK HER OFF!
HAH ...
HA-HA-HA!
SERVES YOU RIGHT, YOU BITCH—
!

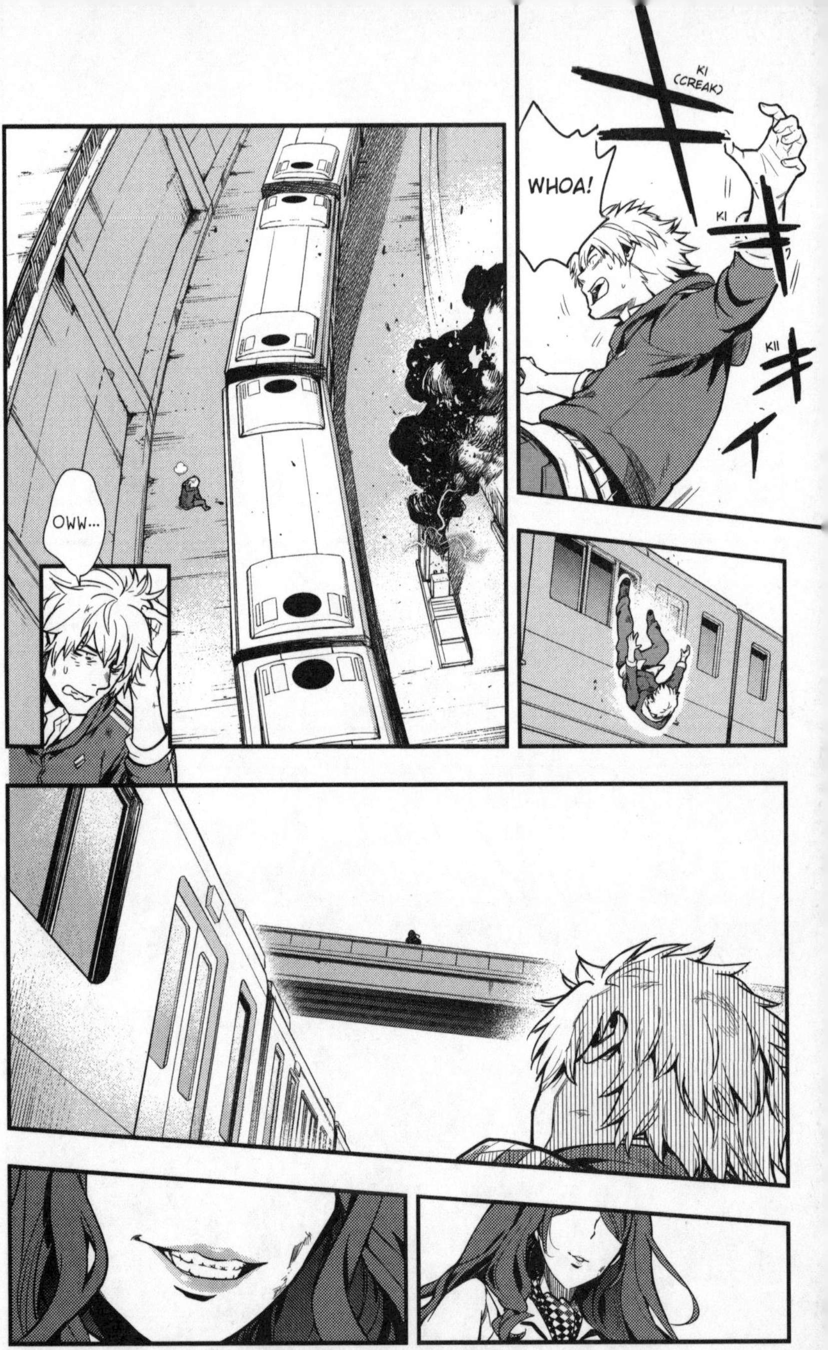
KI (CREAK)
WHOA!
KI
KII
OWW...

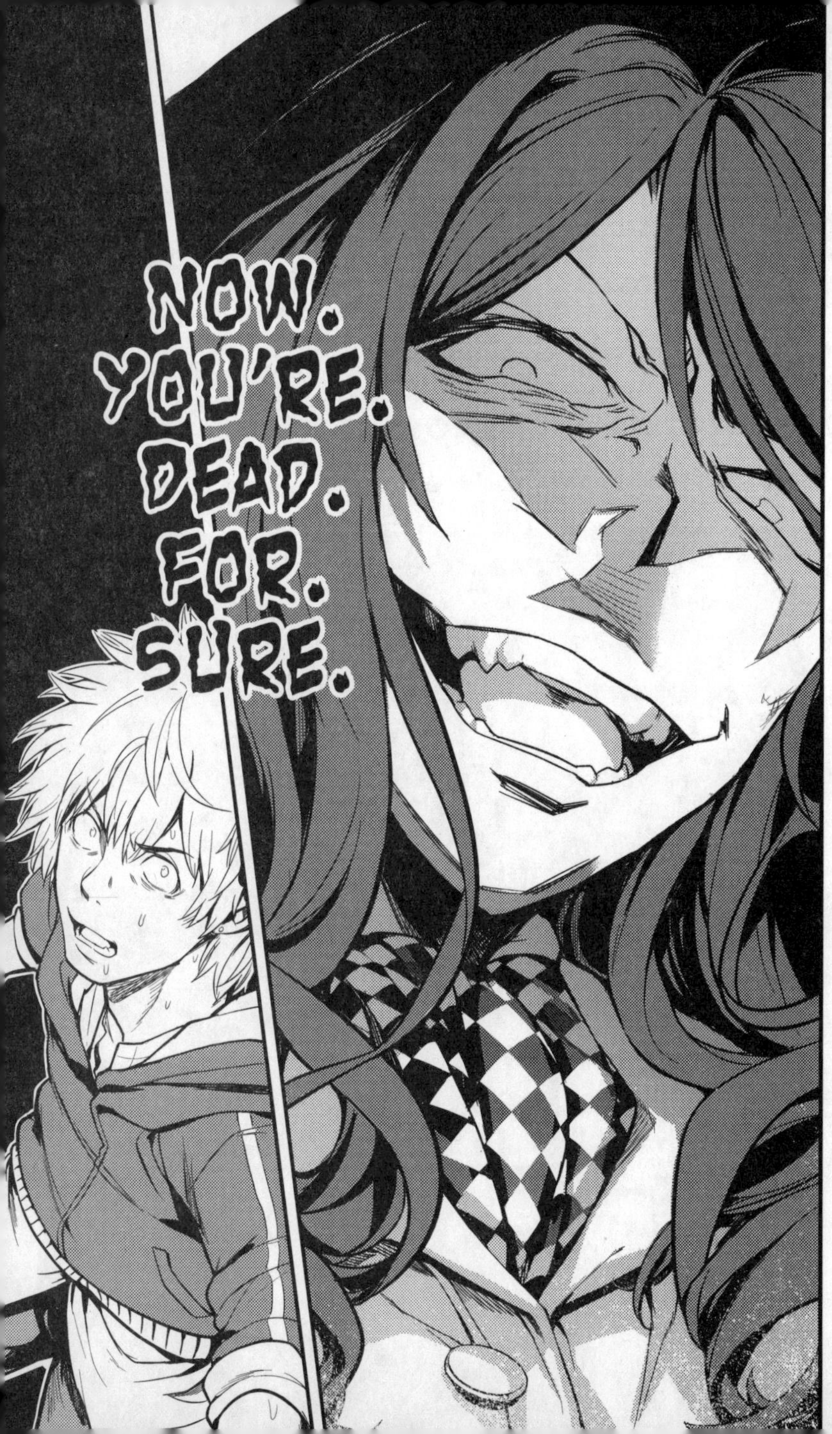
NOW. YOU'RE. DEAD. FOR. SURE.

A Certain Magical Index

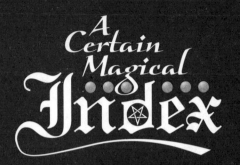

#145 DISTRICT 3 REFINERY ①

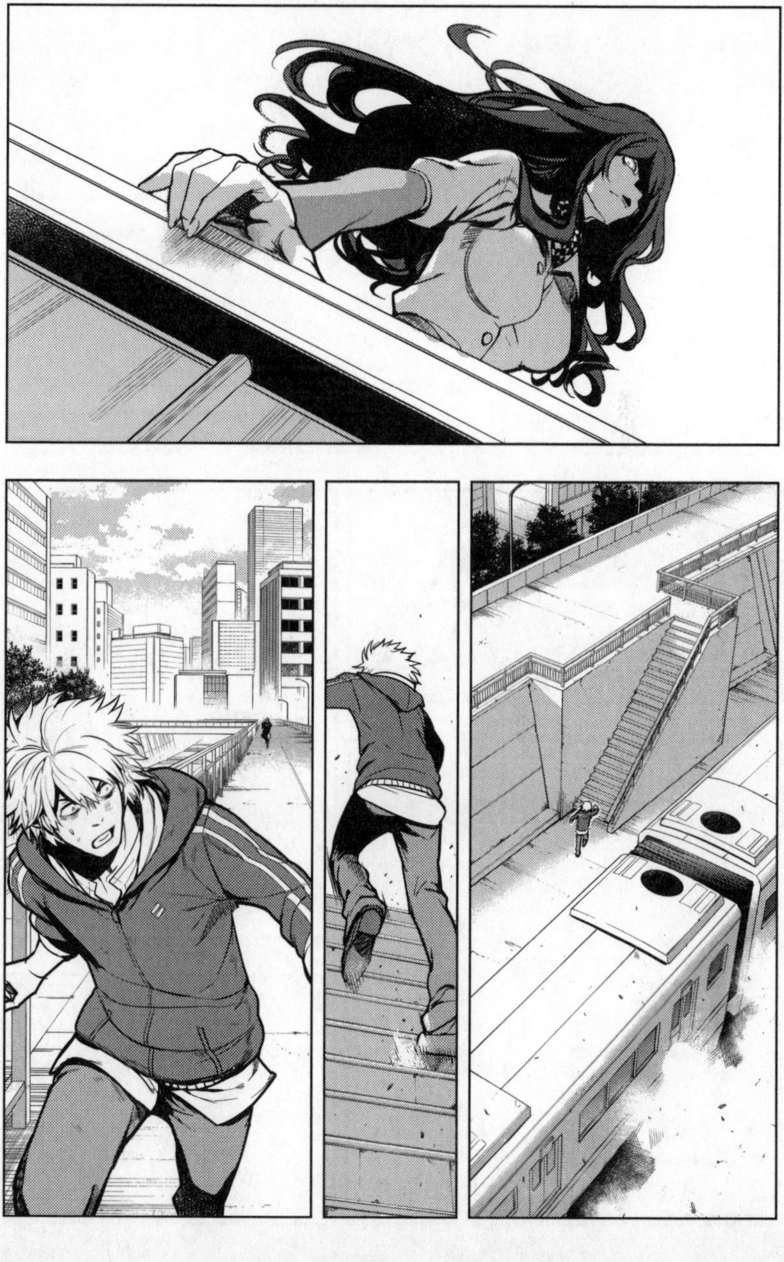

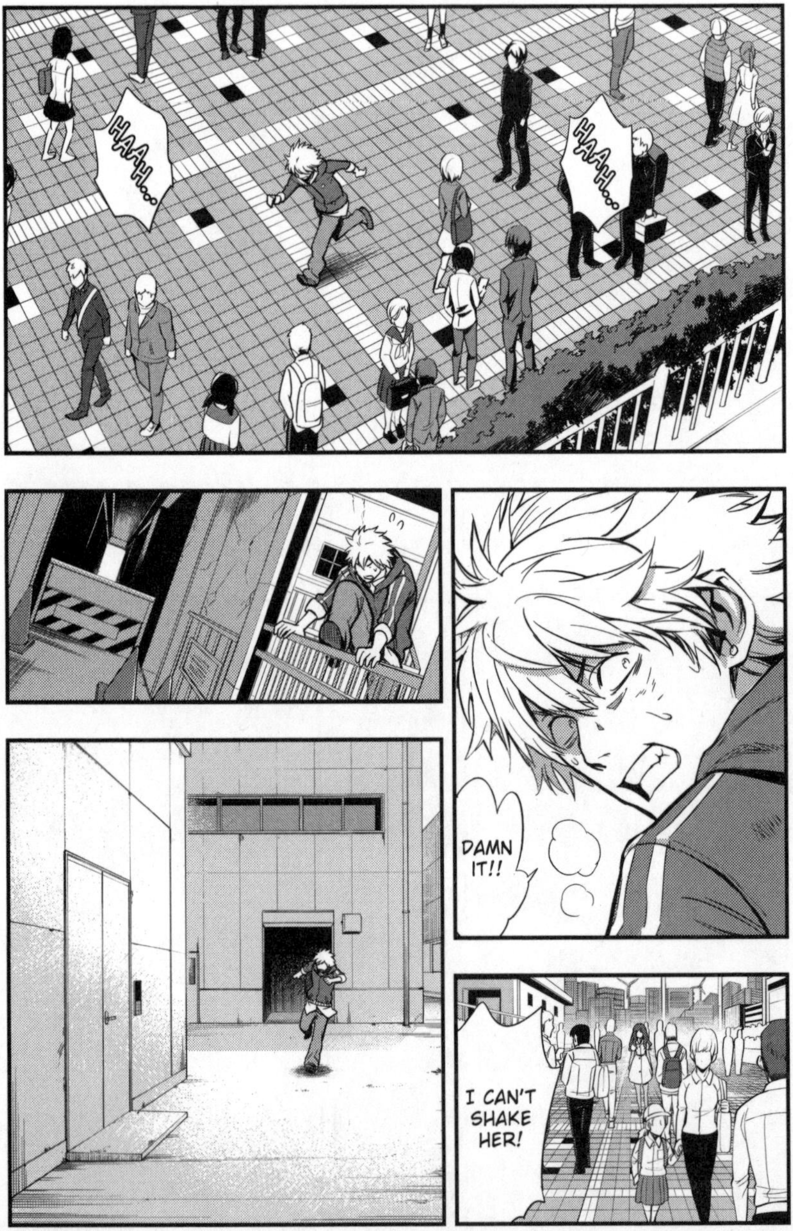
HAAAH...
HAAAH...
DAMN IT!!
I CAN'T SHAKE HER!

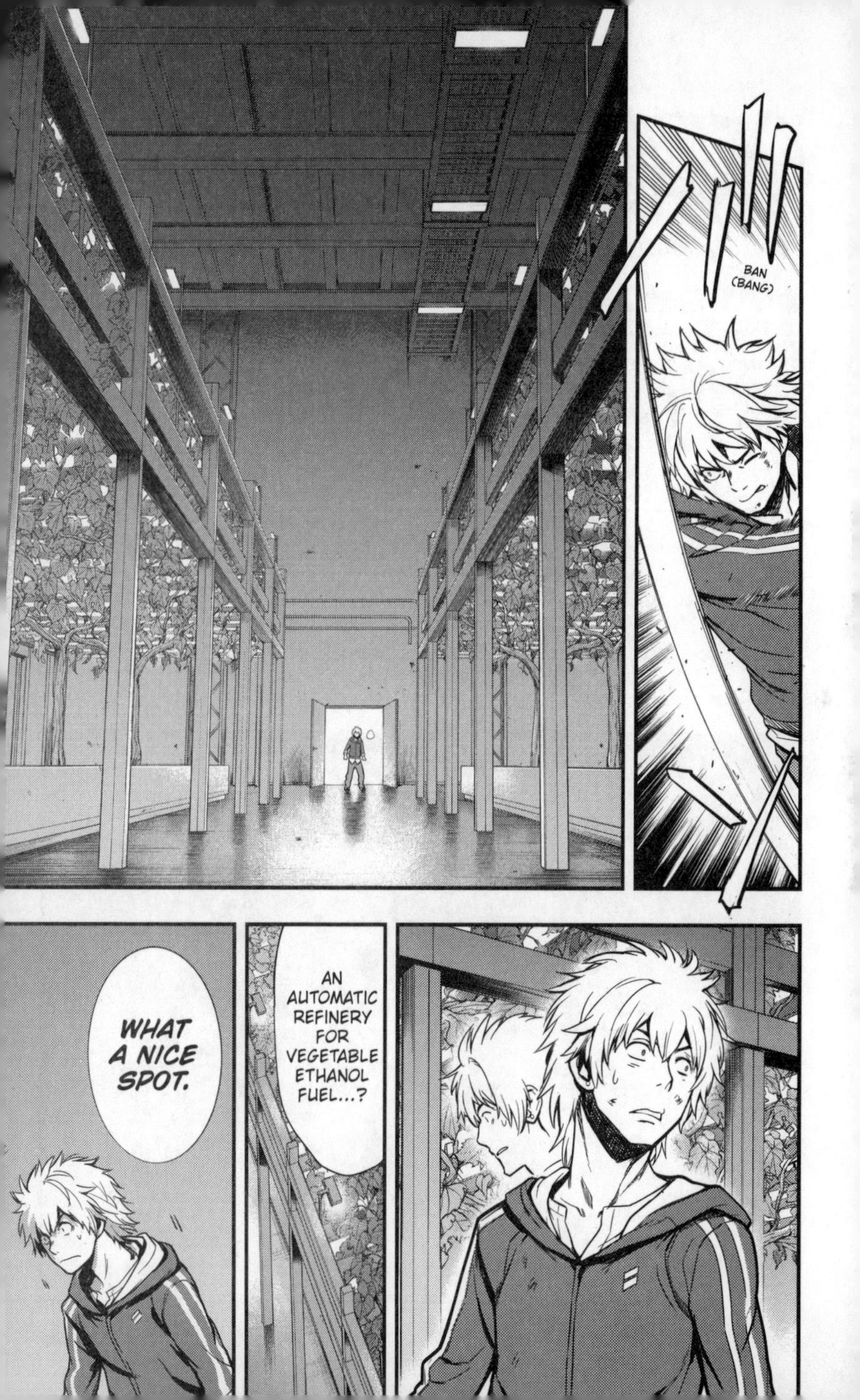
BAN (BANG)
AN AUTOMATIC REFINERY FOR VEGETABLE ETHANOL FUEL...?
WHAT A NICE SPOT.

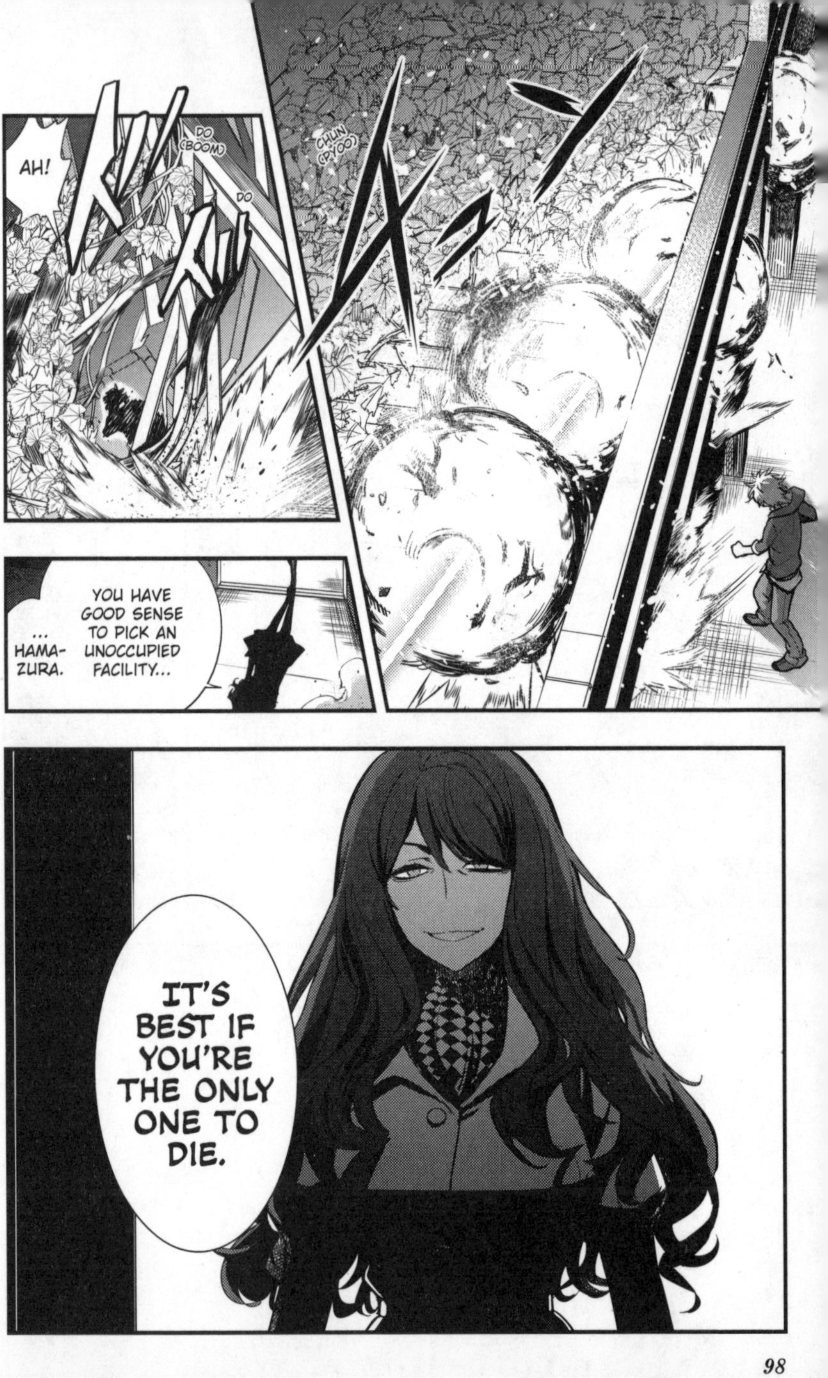
CHUN (PYOO)
DO (BOOM)
DO
AH!
YOU HAVE GOOD SENSE TO PICK AN UNOCCUPIED FACILITY...
...HAMAZURA.
IT'S BEST IF YOU'RE THE ONLY ONE TO DIE.

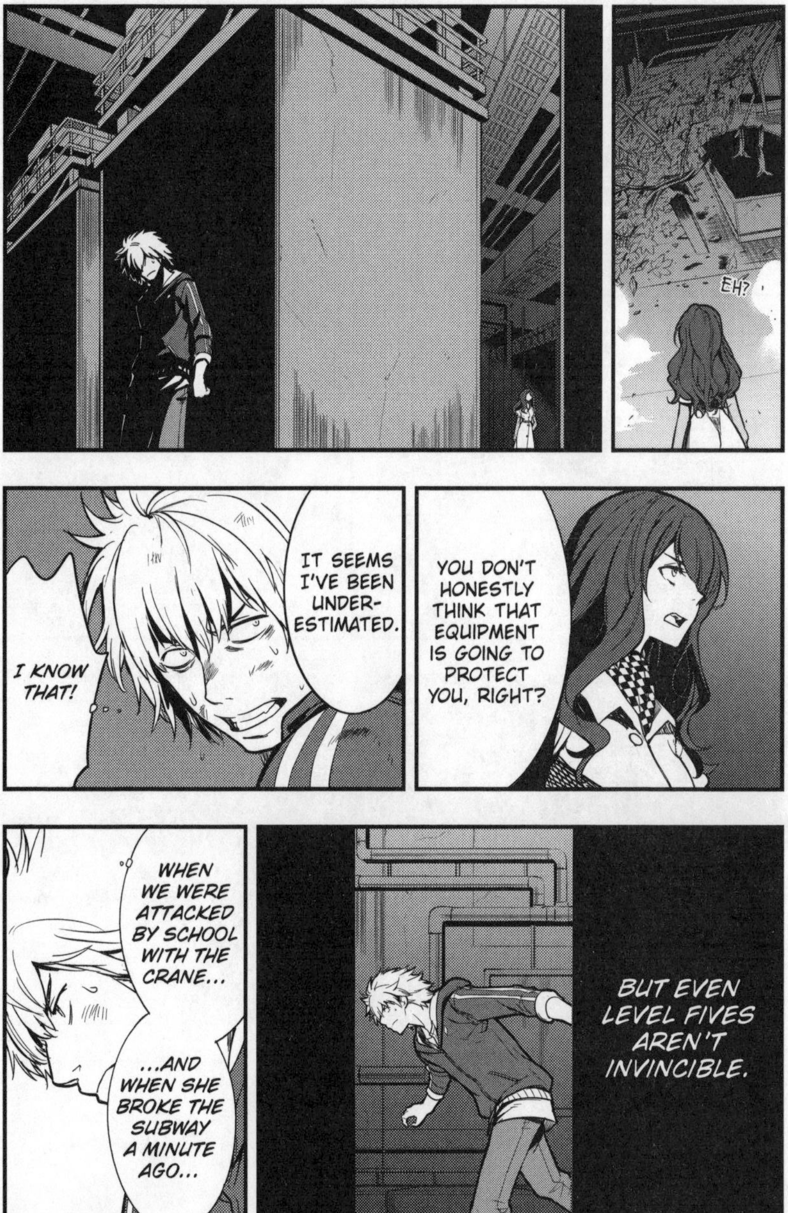
EH?
YOU DON'T HONESTLY THINK THAT EQUIPMENT IS GOING TO PROTECT YOU, RIGHT?
IT SEEMS I'VE BEEN UNDER-ESTIMATED.
I KNOW THAT!
BUT EVEN LEVEL FIVES AREN'T INVINCIBLE.
WHEN WE WERE ATTACKED BY SCHOOL WITH THE CRANE...
...AND WHEN SHE BROKE THE SUBWAY A MINUTE AGO...

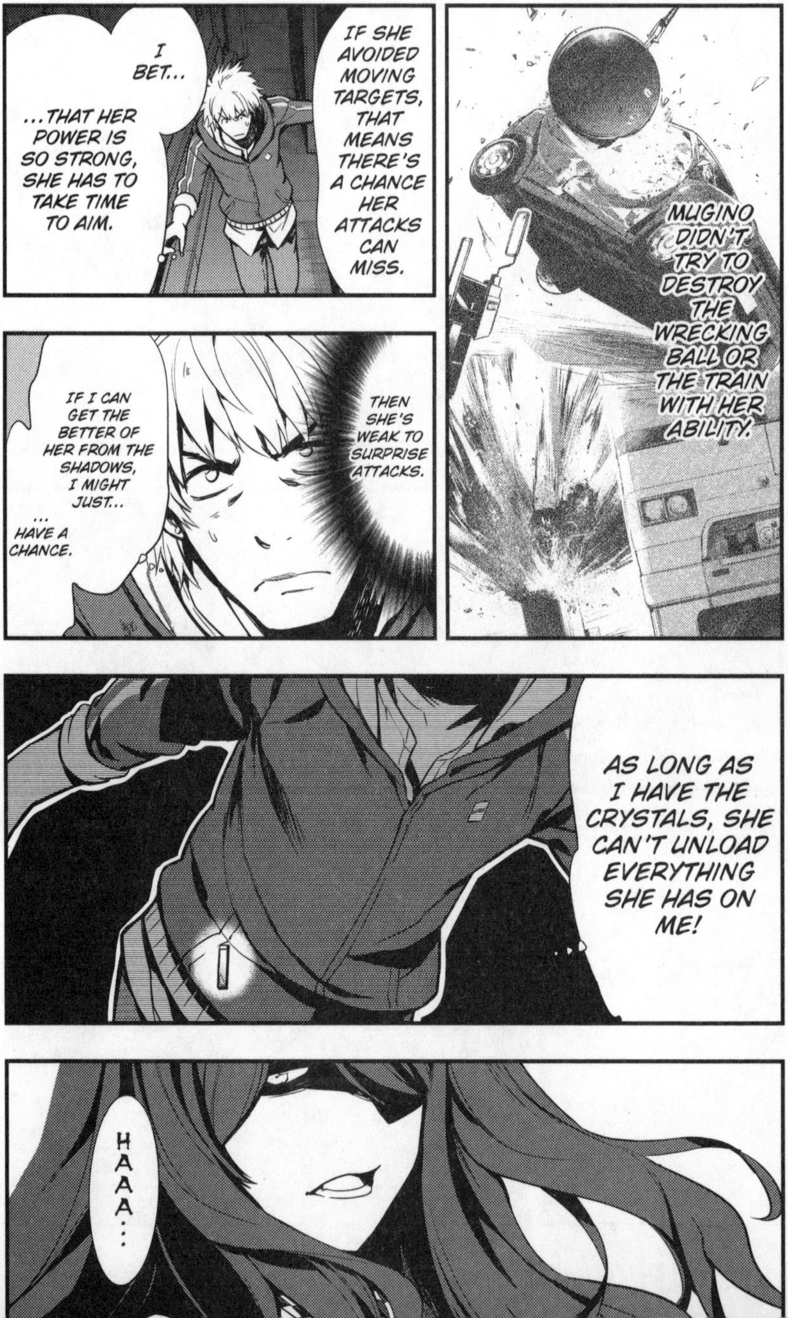
MUGINO DIDN'T TRY TO DESTROY THE WRECKING BALL OR THE TRAIN WITH HER ABILITY.
IF SHE AVOIDED MOVING TARGETS, THAT MEANS THERE'S A CHANCE HER ATTACKS CAN MISS.
I BET...
...THAT HER POWER IS SO STRONG, SHE HAS TO TAKE TIME TO AIM.
THEN SHE'S WEAK TO SURPRISE ATTACKS.
IF I CAN GET THE BETTER OF HER FROM THE SHADOWS, I MIGHT JUST...
...HAVE A CHANCE.
AS LONG AS I HAVE THE CRYSTALS, SHE CAN'T UNLOAD EVERYTHING SHE HAS ON ME!
HAAA...

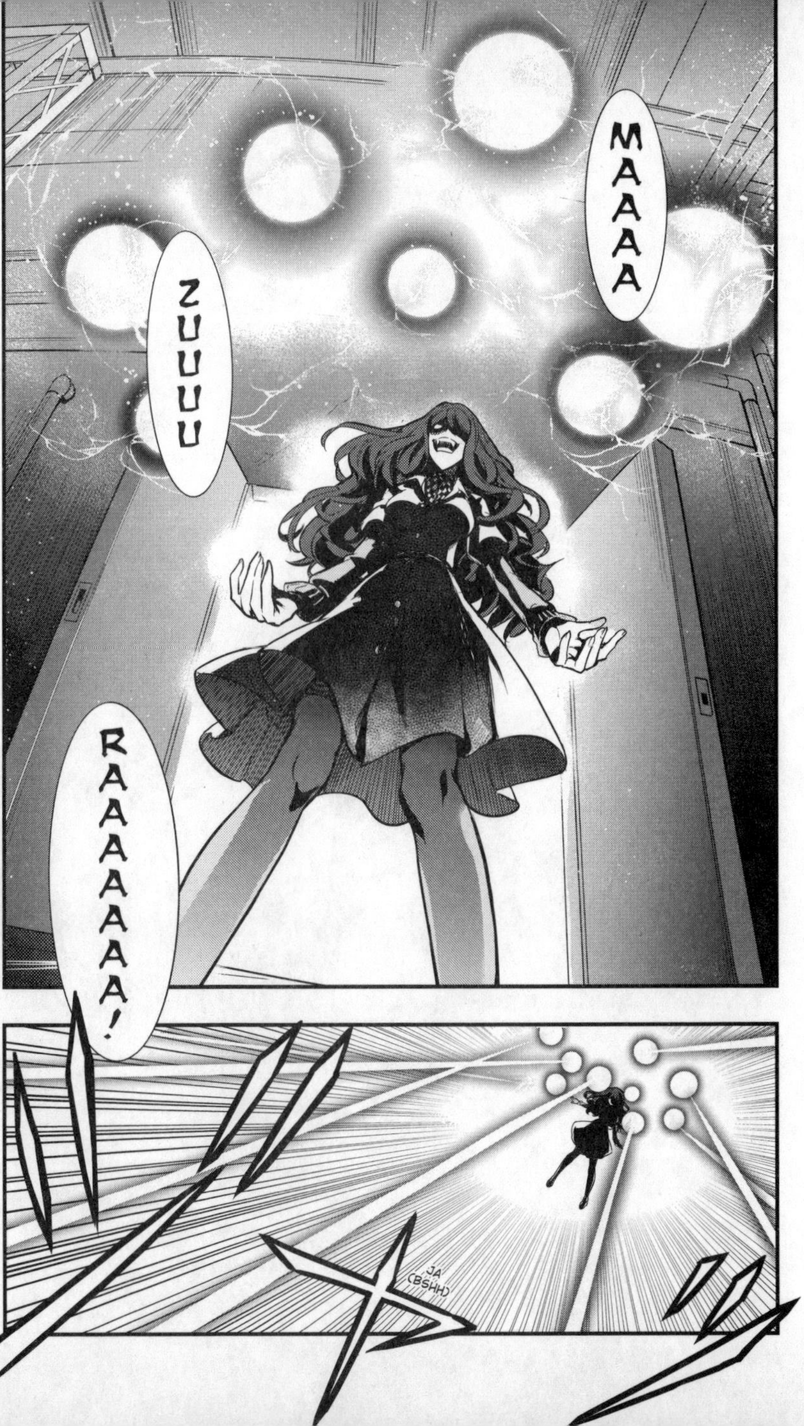
MAAAA
ZUUUU
RAAAAAAA!
JA
(BSHH)

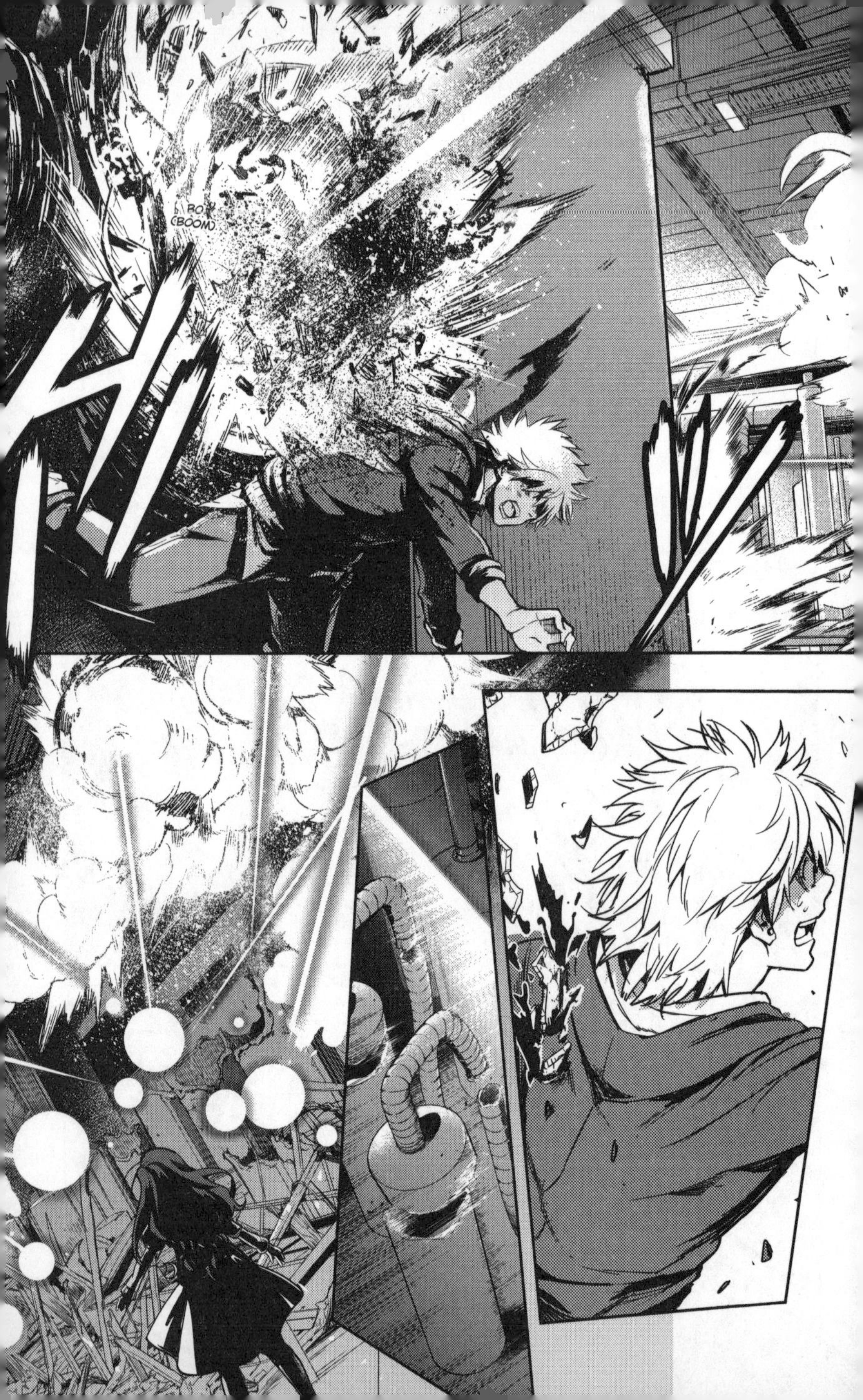
BO
(BOOM)

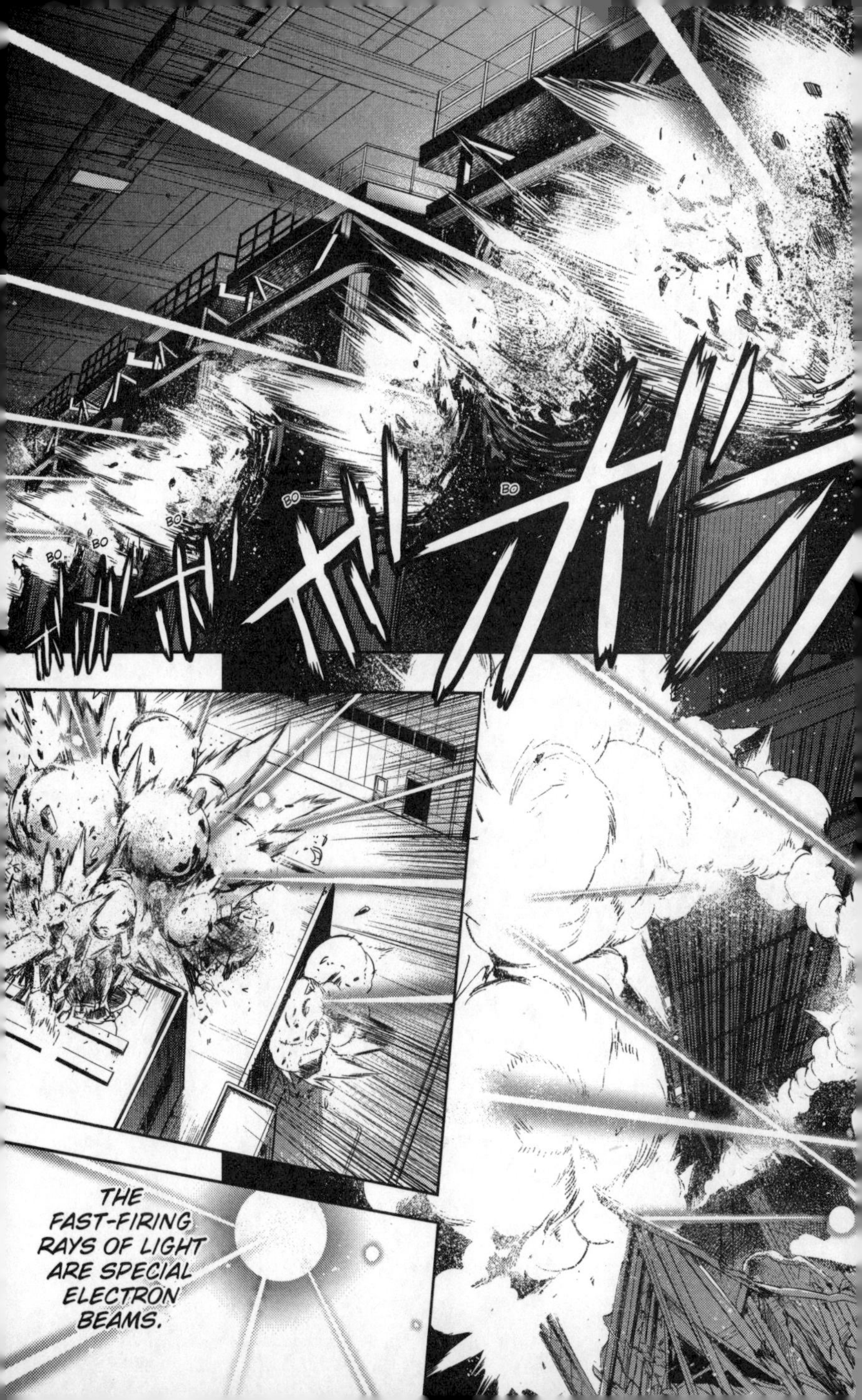
BO
BO
BO
BO
BO
THE FAST-FIRING RAYS OF LIGHT ARE SPECIAL ELECTRON BEAMS.

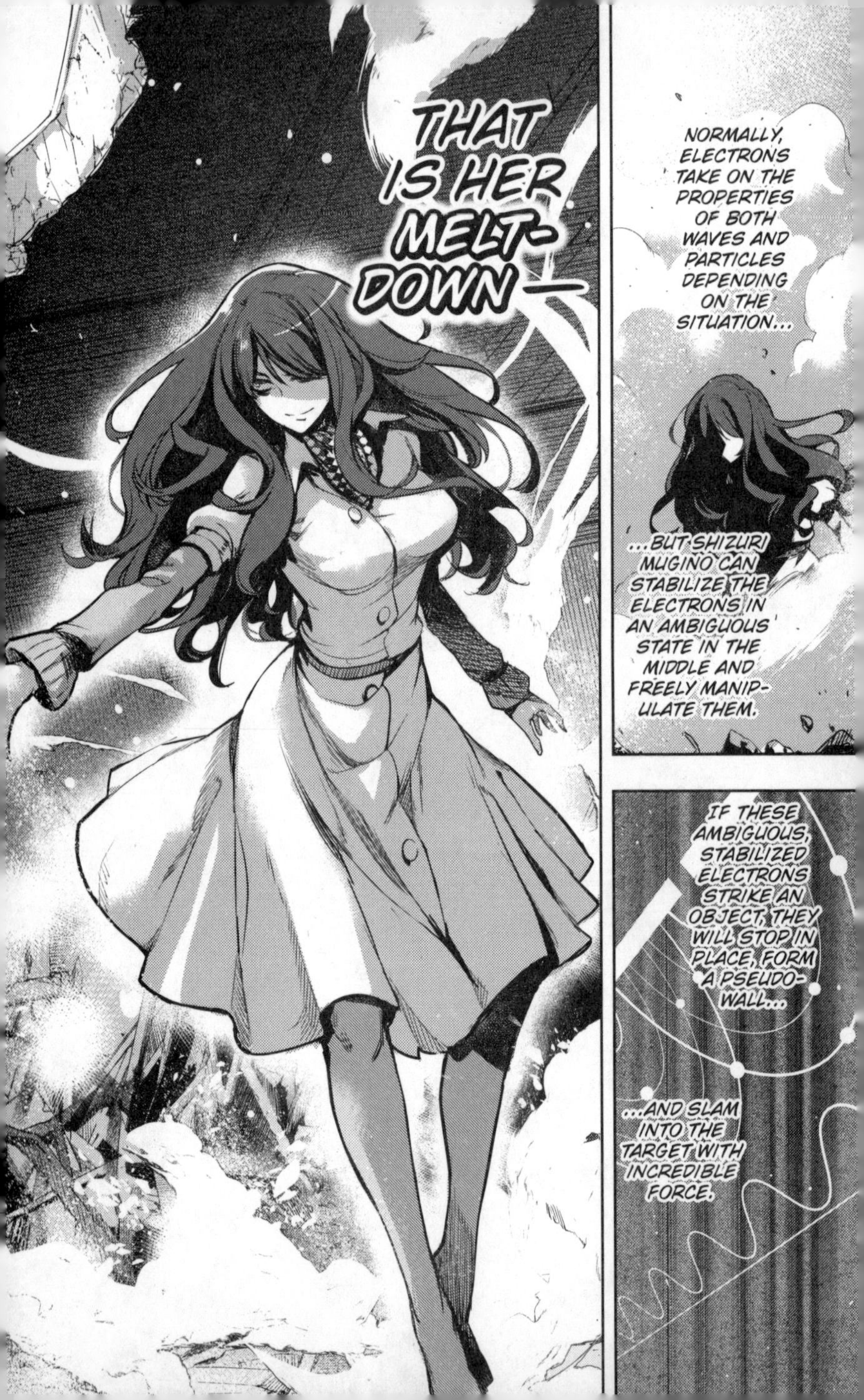
NORMALLY, ELECTRONS TAKE ON THE PROPERTIES OF BOTH WAVES AND PARTICLES DEPENDING ON THE SITUATION...
...BUT SHIZURI MUGINO CAN STABILIZE THE ELECTRONS IN AN AMBIGUOUS STATE IN THE MIDDLE AND FREELY MANIP-ULATE THEM.
IF THESE AMBIGUOUS, STABILIZED ELECTRONS STRIKE AN OBJECT, THEY WILL STOP IN PLACE, FORM A PSEUDO-WALL...
...AND SLAM INTO THE TARGET WITH INCREDIBLE FORCE.
THAT IS HER MELT-DOWN—

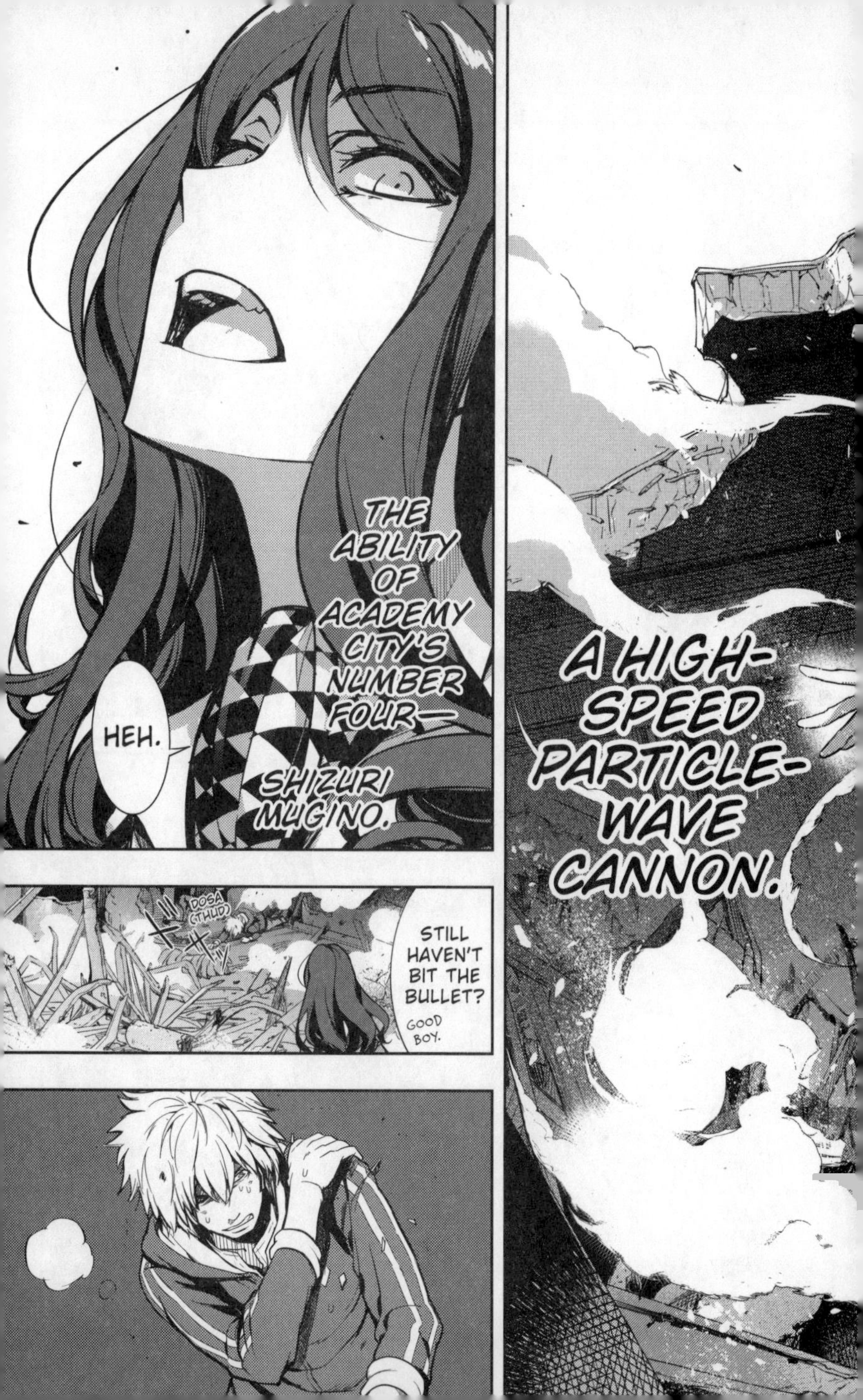
A HIGH-SPEED PARTICLE-WAVE CANNON.
THE ABILITY OF ACADEMY CITY'S NUMBER FOUR—
SHIZURI MUGINO.
HEH.
STILL HAVEN'T BIT THE BULLET?
GOOD BOY.
DOSA (THUD)

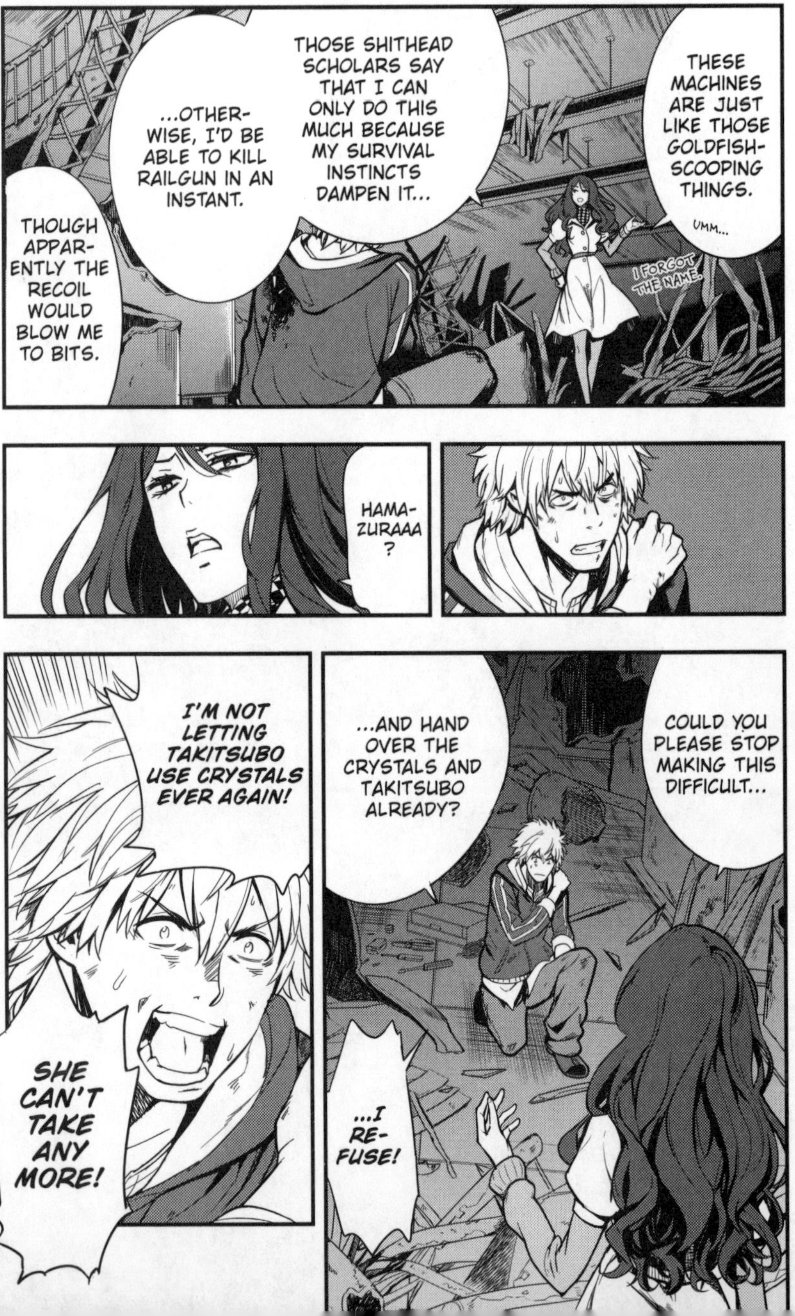
THESE MACHINES ARE JUST LIKE THOSE GOLDFISH-SCOOPING THINGS.
UMM...
I FORGOT THE NAME.
THOSE SHITHEAD SCHOLARS SAY THAT I CAN ONLY DO THIS MUCH BECAUSE MY SURVIVAL INSTINCTS DAMPEN IT...
...OTHER-WISE, I'D BE ABLE TO KILL RAILGUN IN AN INSTANT.
THOUGH APPAR-ENTLY THE RECOIL WOULD BLOW ME TO BITS.
HAMA-ZURAAA?
COULD YOU PLEASE STOP MAKING THIS DIFFICULT...
...AND HAND OVER THE CRYSTALS AND TAKITSUBO ALREADY?
...I RE-FUSE!
I'M NOT LETTING TAKITSUBO USE CRYSTALS EVER AGAIN!
SHE CAN'T TAKE ANY MORE!

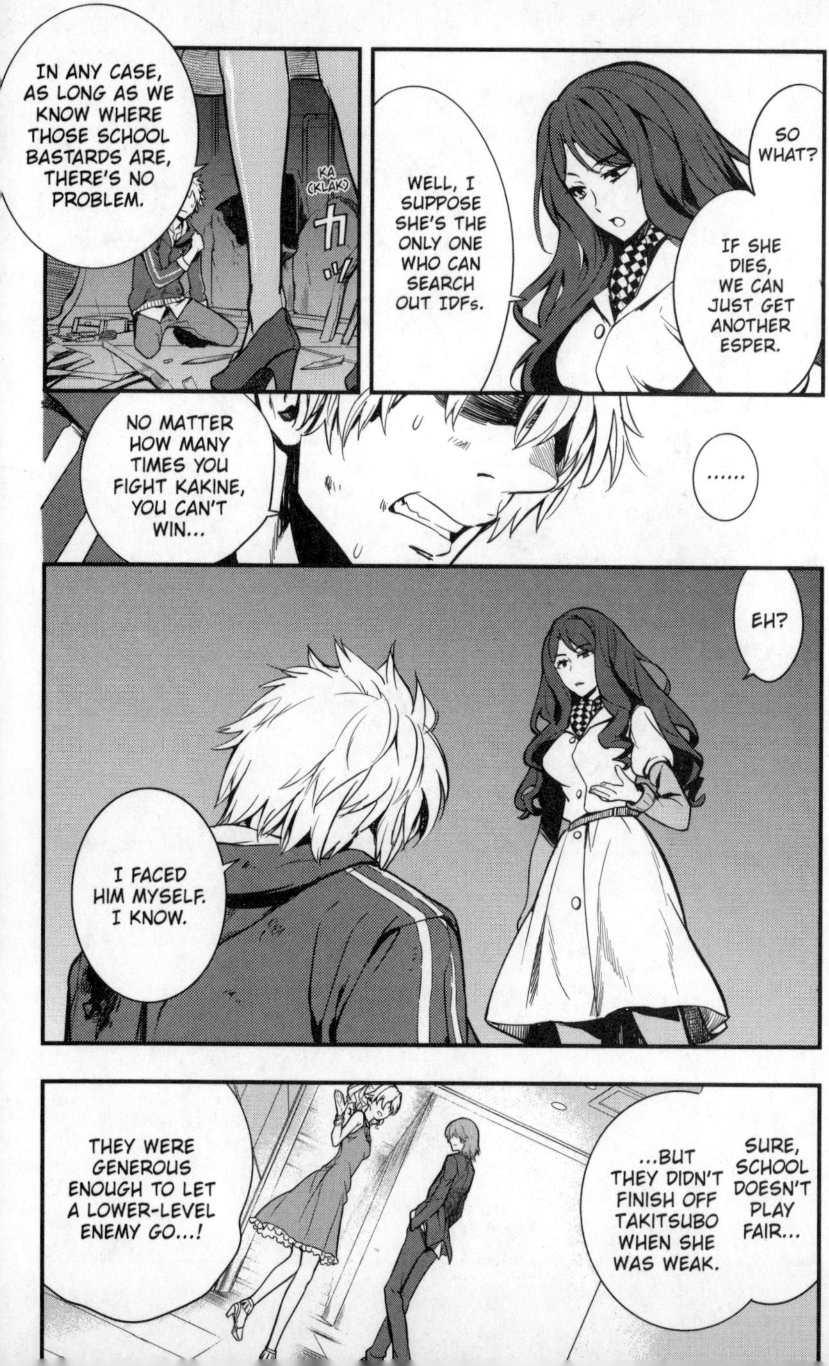
SO WHAT?
IF SHE DIES, WE CAN JUST GET ANOTHER ESPER.
WELL, I SUPPOSE SHE'S THE ONLY ONE WHO CAN SEARCH OUT IDFs.
KA (KLAK)
IN ANY CASE, AS LONG AS WE KNOW WHERE THOSE SCHOOL BASTARDS ARE, THERE'S NO PROBLEM.
......
NO MATTER HOW MANY TIMES YOU FIGHT KAKINE, YOU CAN'T WIN...
EH?
I FACED HIM MYSELF. I KNOW.
SURE, SCHOOL DOESN'T PLAY FAIR...
...BUT THEY DIDN'T FINISH OFF TAKITSUBO WHEN SHE WAS WEAK.
THEY WERE GENEROUS ENOUGH TO LET A LOWER-LEVEL ENEMY GO...!

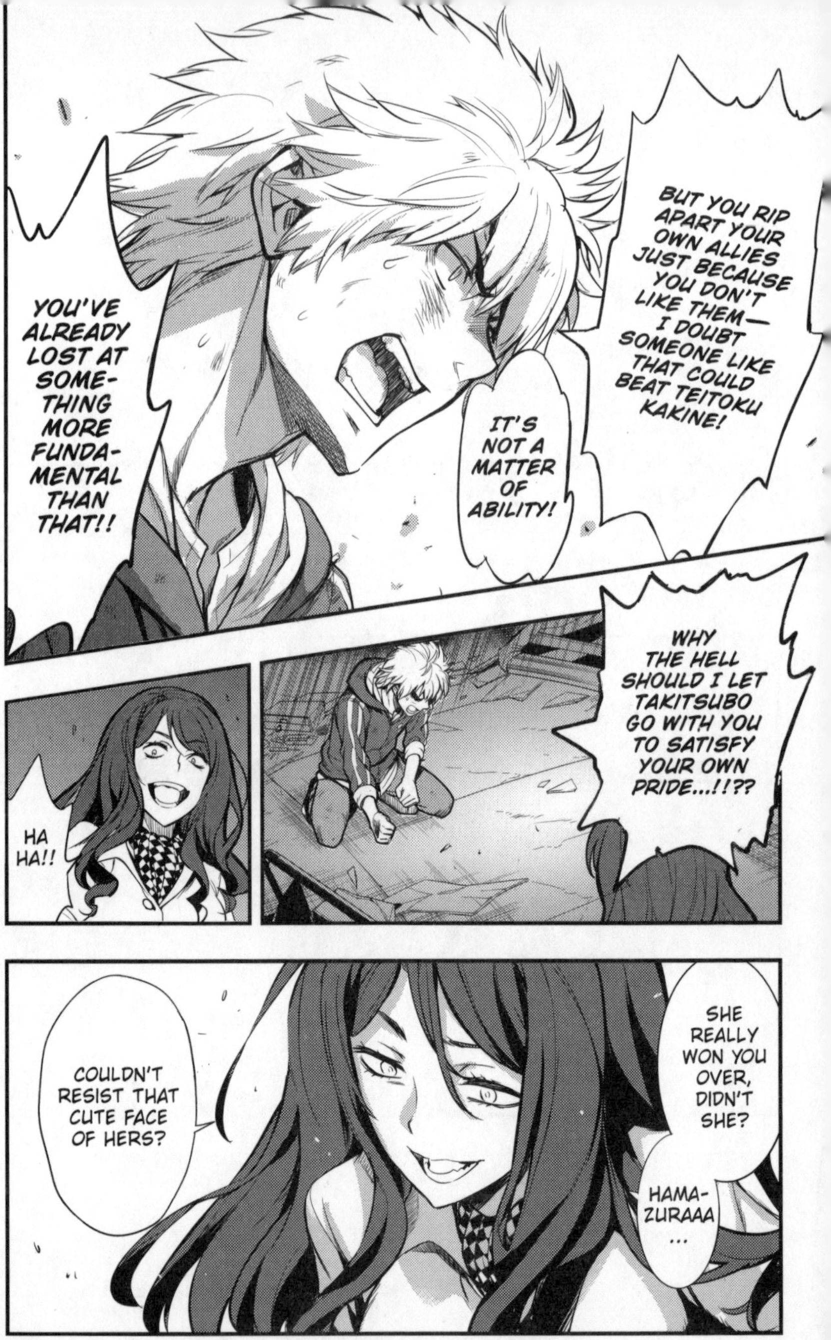
BUT YOU RIP APART YOUR OWN ALLIES JUST BECAUSE YOU DON'T LIKE THEM— I DOUBT SOMEONE LIKE THAT COULD BEAT TEITOKU KAKINE!
IT'S NOT A MATTER OF ABILITY!
YOU'VE ALREADY LOST AT SOME-THING MORE FUNDA-MENTAL THAN THAT!!
WHY THE HELL SHOULD I LET TAKITSUBO GO WITH YOU TO SATISFY YOUR OWN PRIDE...!!??
HA HA!!
SHE REALLY WON YOU OVER, DIDN'T SHE?
HAMA-ZURAAA...
COULDN'T RESIST THAT CUTE FACE OF HERS?

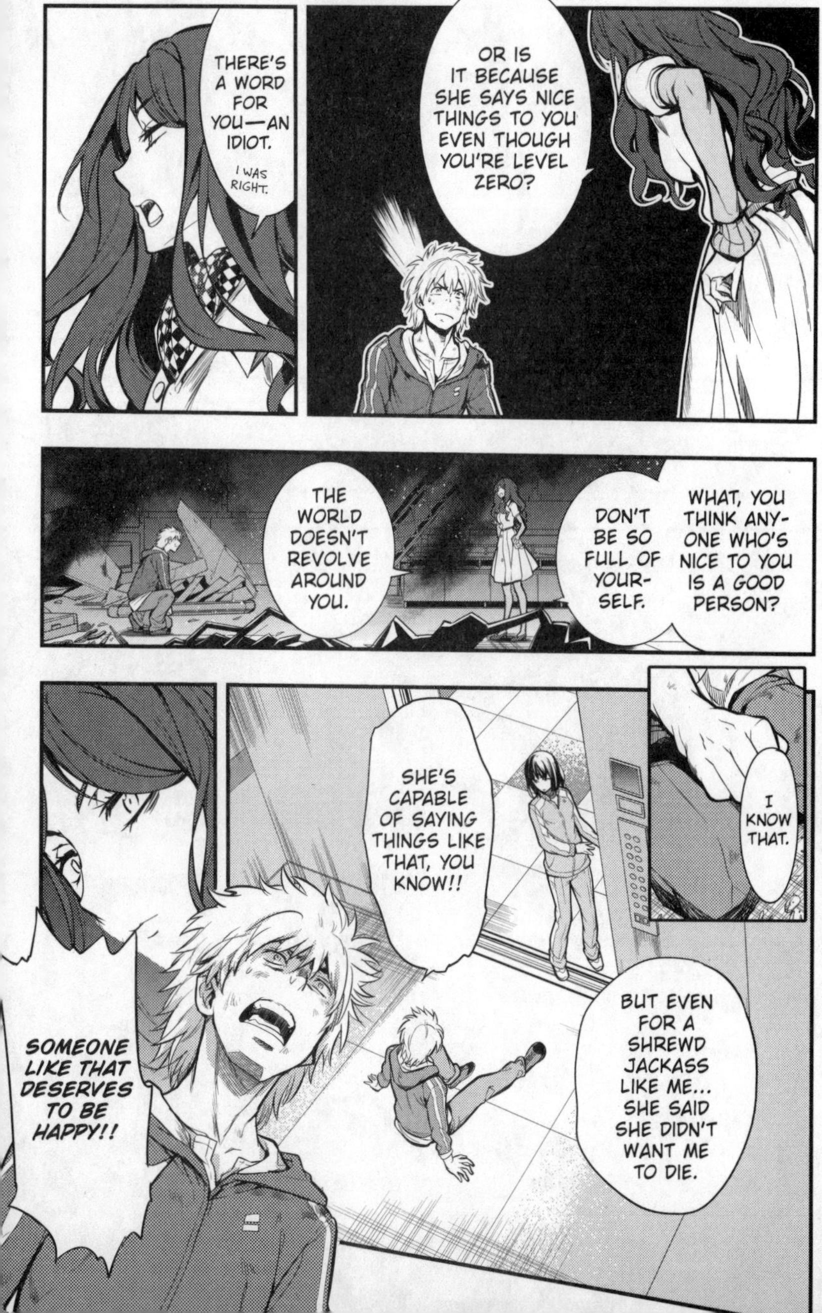
OR IS IT BECAUSE SHE SAYS NICE THINGS TO YOU EVEN THOUGH YOU'RE LEVEL ZERO?
THERE'S A WORD FOR YOU—AN IDIOT.
I WAS RIGHT.
WHAT, YOU THINK ANY-ONE WHO'S NICE TO YOU IS A GOOD PERSON?
DON'T BE SO FULL OF YOUR-SELF.
THE WORLD DOESN'T REVOLVE AROUND YOU.
I KNOW THAT.
BUT EVEN FOR A SHREWD JACKASS LIKE ME... SHE SAID SHE DIDN'T WANT ME TO DIE.
SHE'S CAPABLE OF SAYING THINGS LIKE THAT, YOU KNOW!!
SOMEONE LIKE THAT DESERVES TO BE HAPPY!!

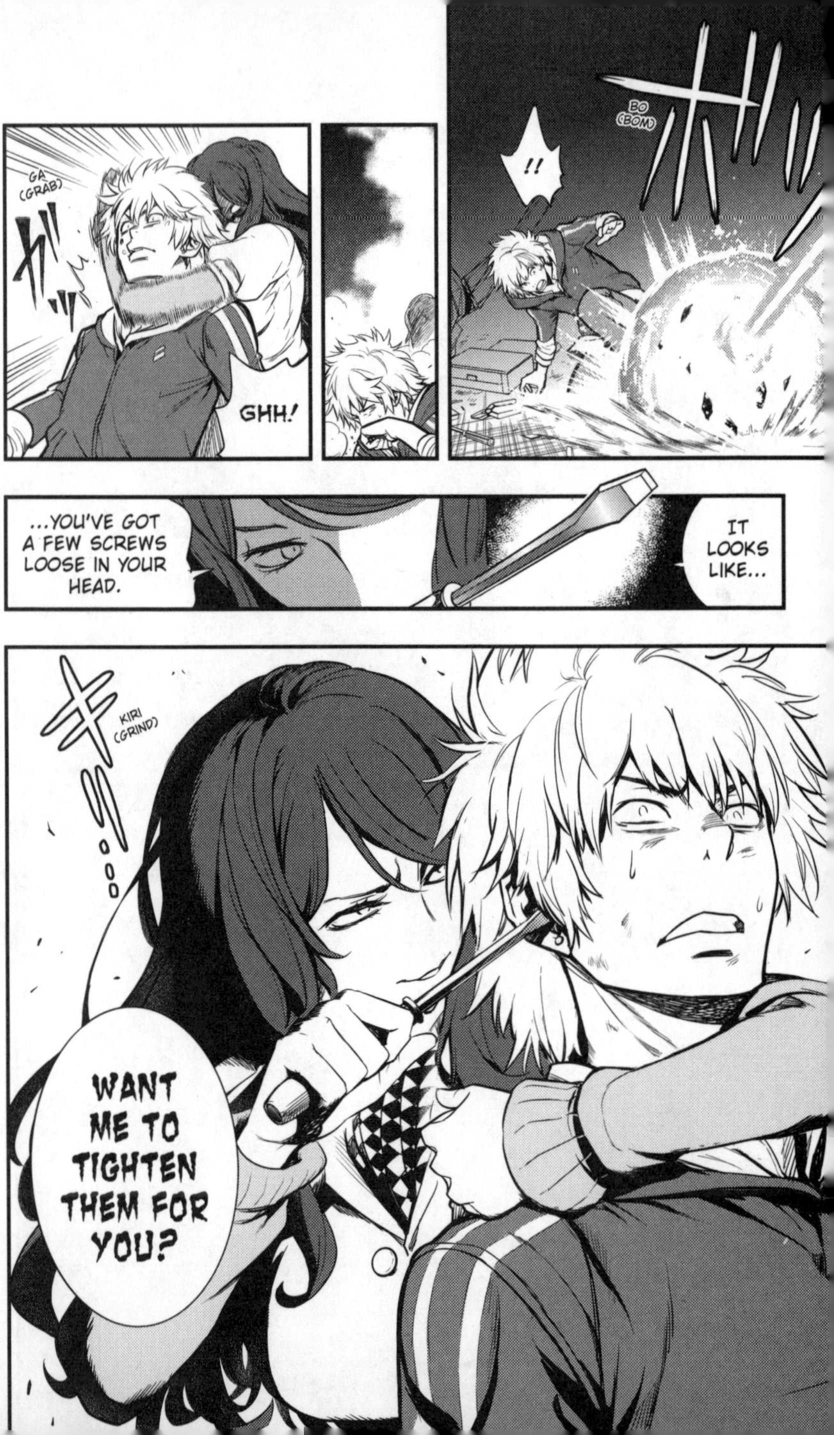
BO (BOM)
!!
GA (GRAB)
GHH!
IT LOOKS LIKE...
...YOU'VE GOT A FEW SCREWS LOOSE IN YOUR HEAD.
KIRI (GRIND)
WANT ME TO TIGHTEN THEM FOR YOU?

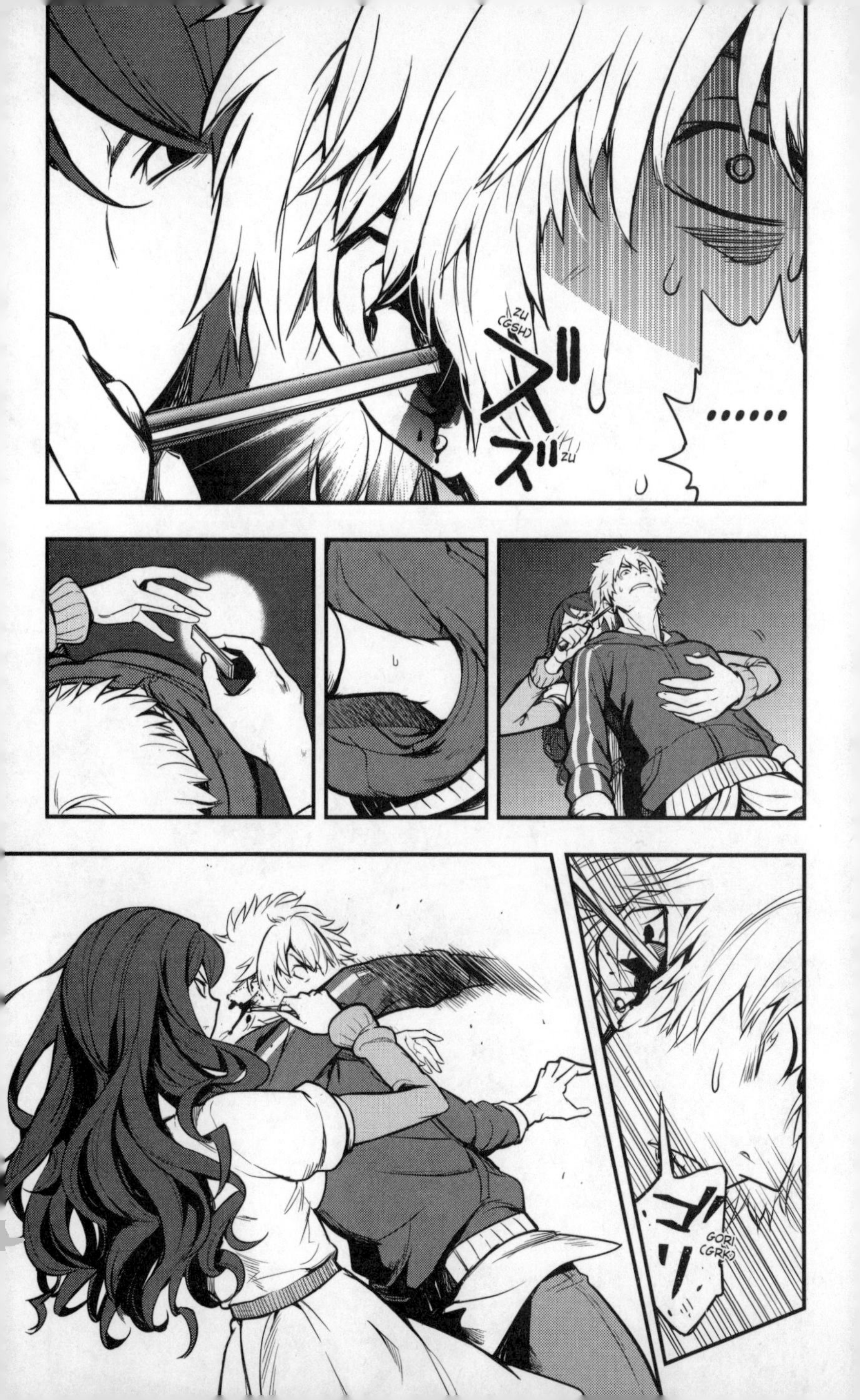
......
ZU (GSH)
ZU
GORI (GRK)

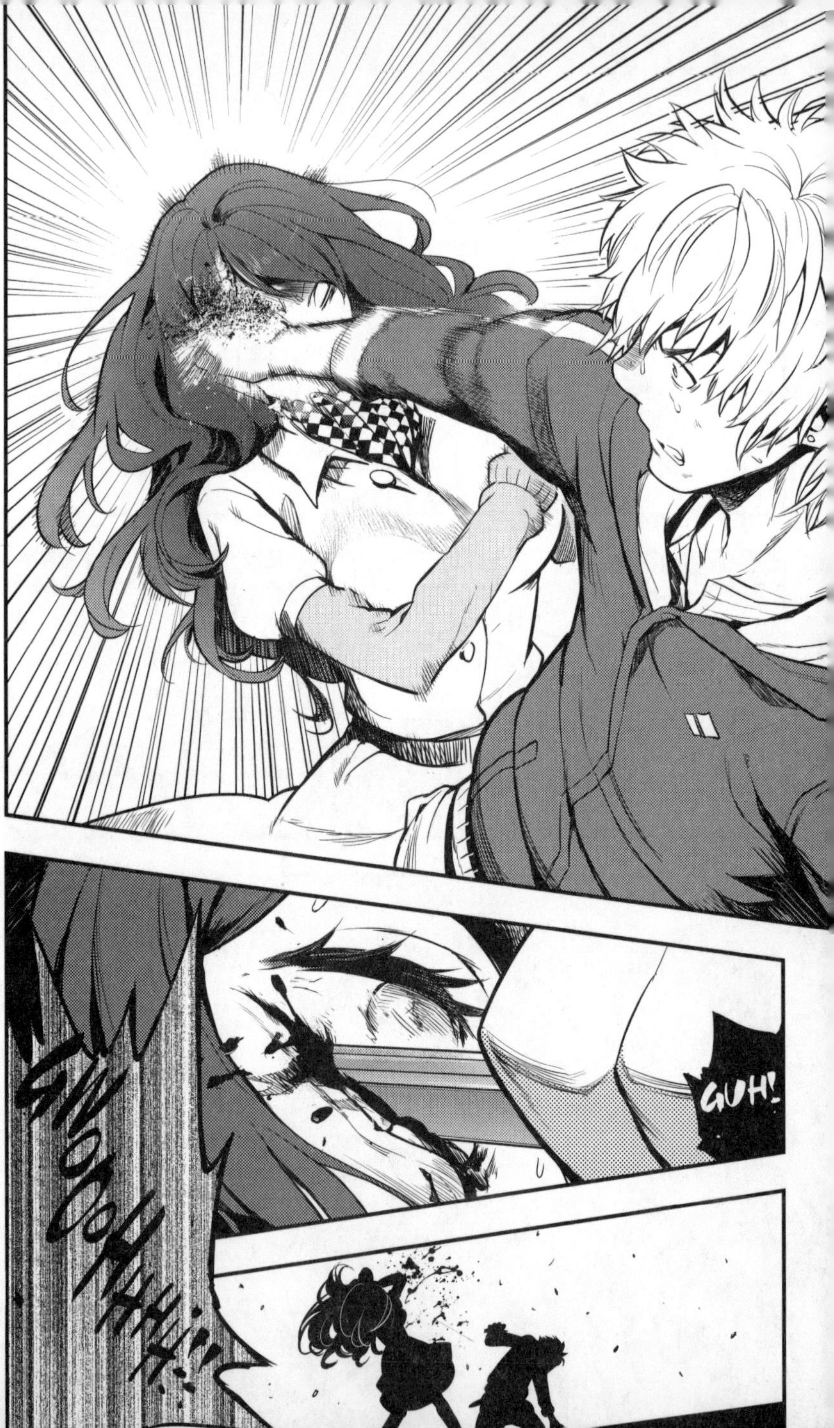
GUH!
SWOOHHH!!

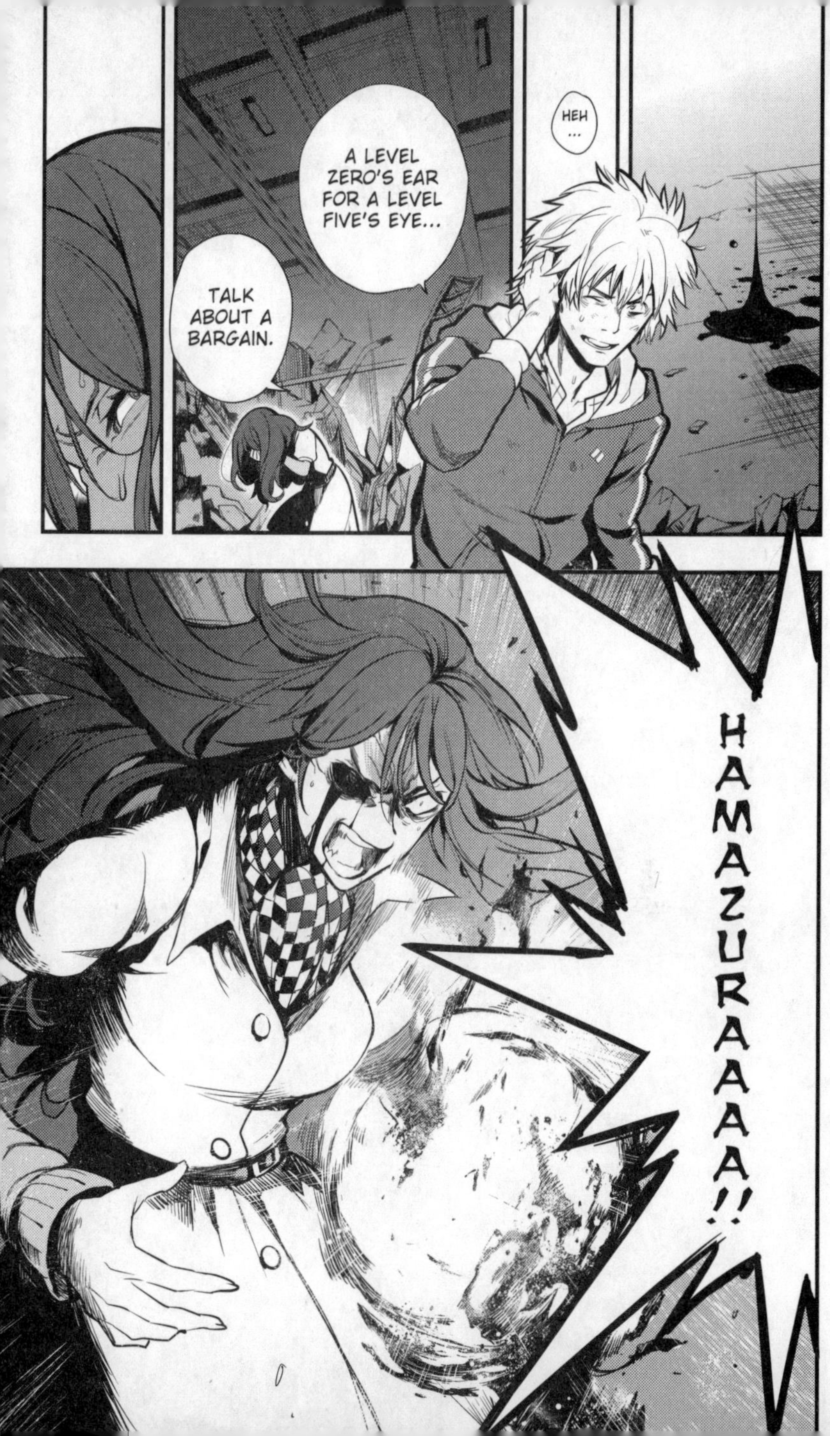
HEH...
A LEVEL ZERO'S EAR FOR A LEVEL FIVE'S EYE...
TALK ABOUT A BARGAIN.
HAMAZURAAAAA!!

A Certain Magical Index

#146 DISTRICT 3 REFINERY ②

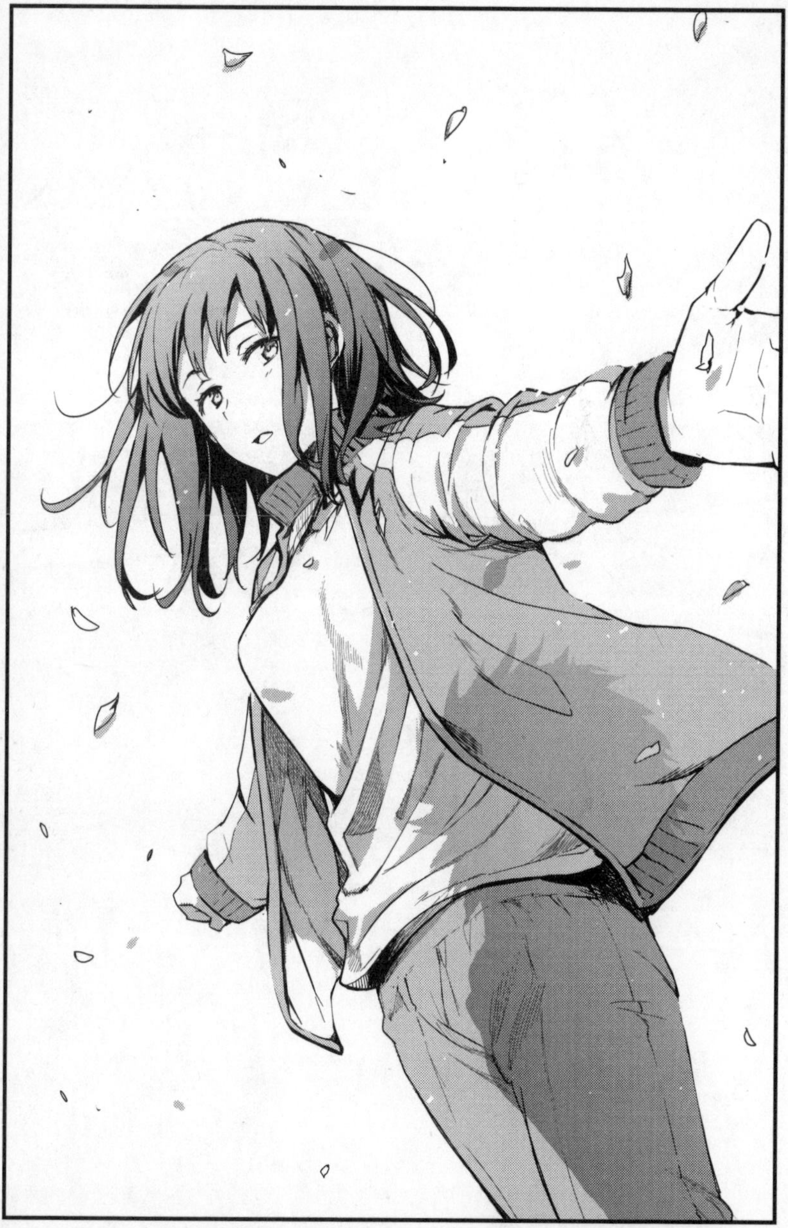

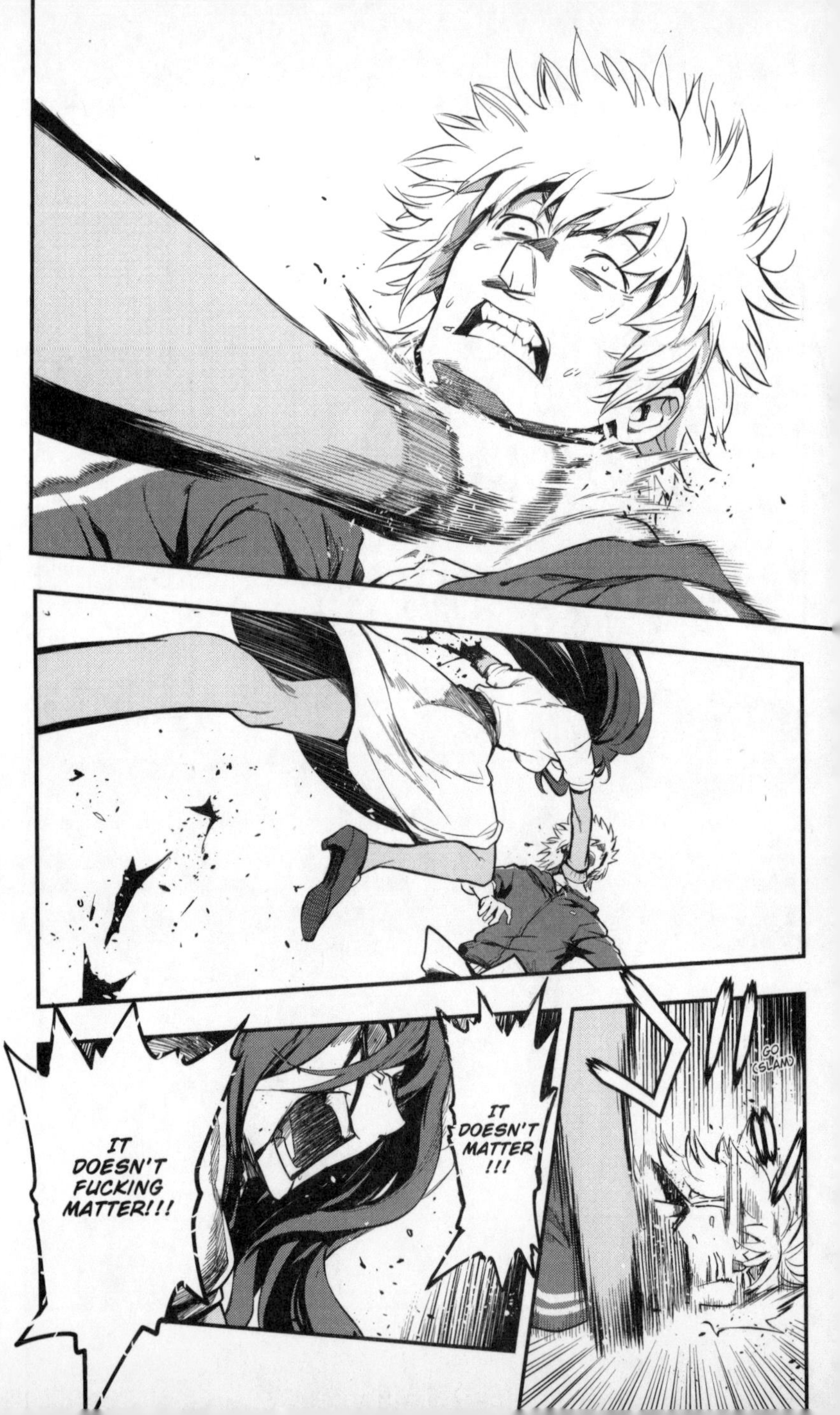
GO (SLAM)
IT DOESN'T MATTER!!!
IT DOESN'T FUCKING MATTER!!!

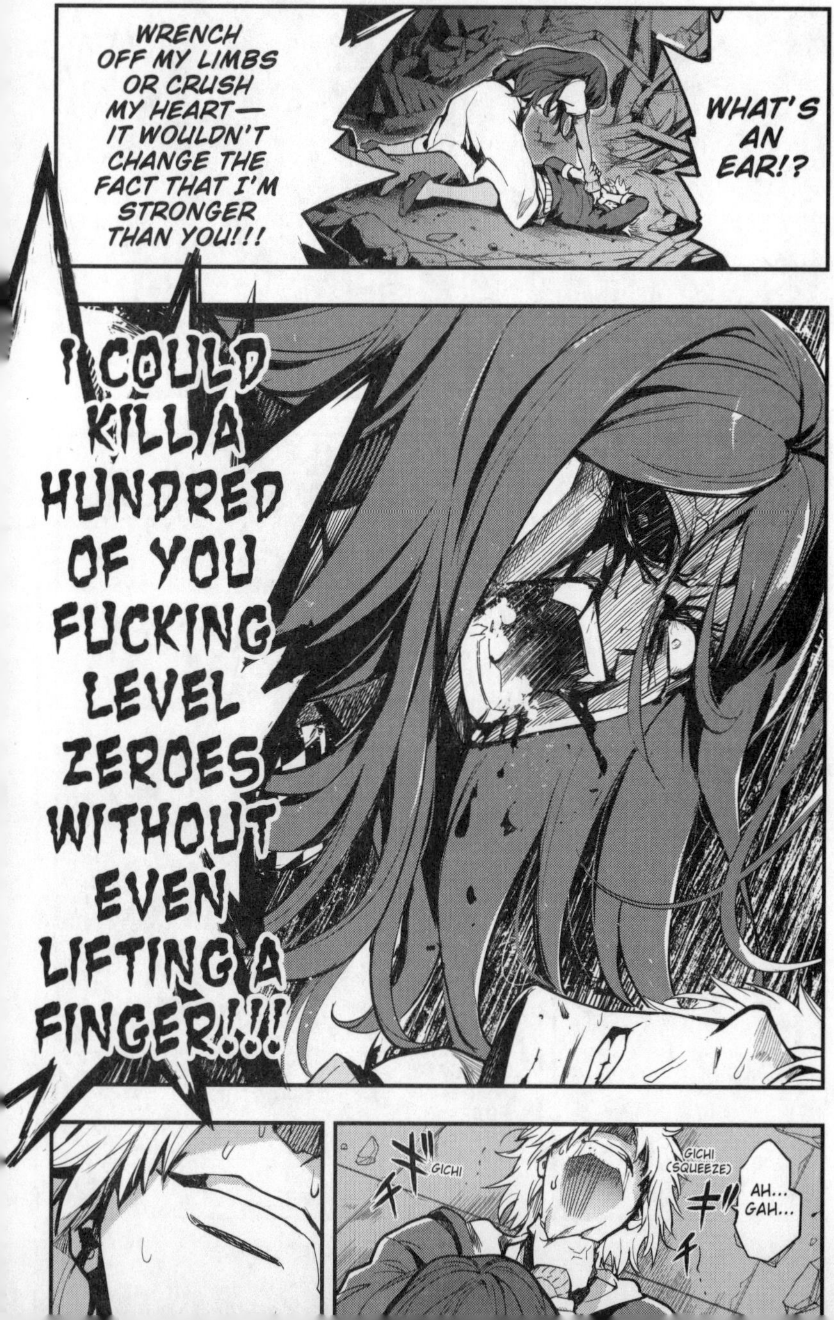
WHAT'S AN EAR!?
WRENCH OFF MY LIMBS OR CRUSH MY HEART— IT WOULDN'T CHANGE THE FACT THAT I'M STRONGER THAN YOU!!!
I COULD KILL A HUNDRED OF YOU FUCKING LEVEL ZEROES WITHOUT EVEN LIFTING A FINGER!!!
AH... GAH...
GICHI (SQUEEZE)
GICHI

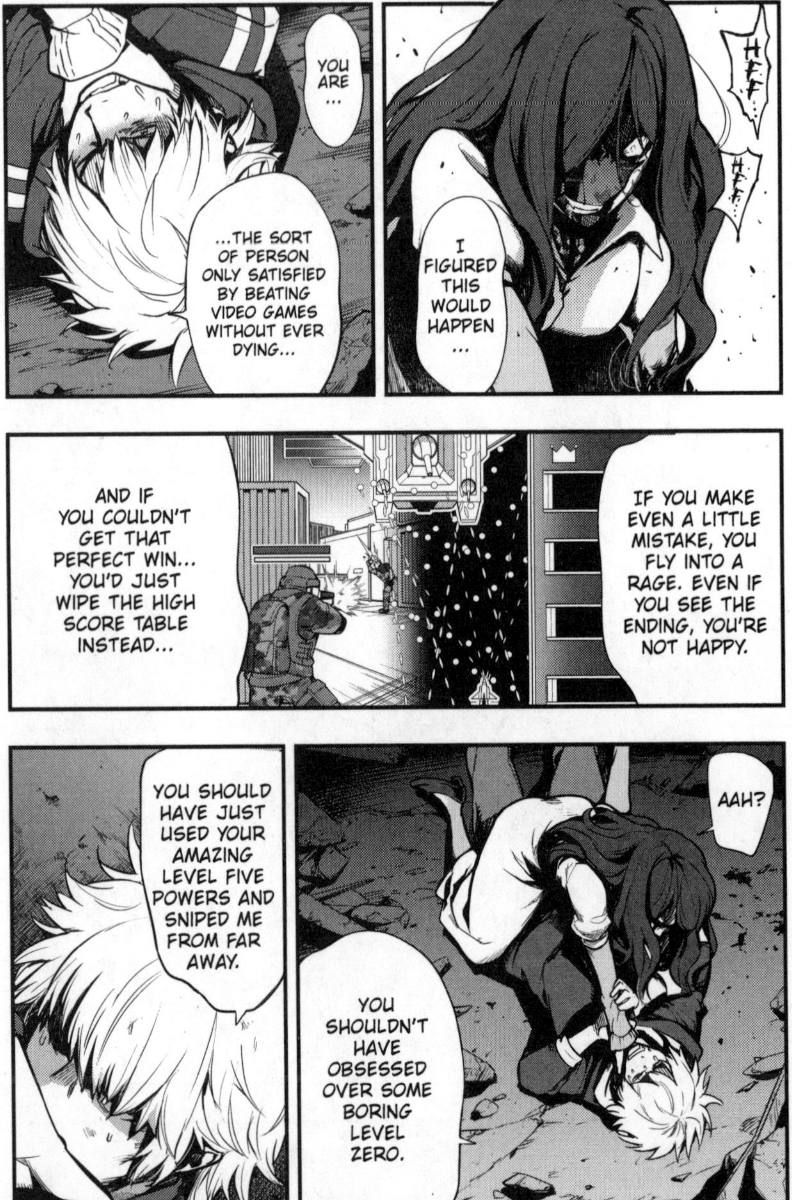
HFF...
HFF...
I FIGURED THIS WOULD HAPPEN...
YOU ARE...
...THE SORT OF PERSON ONLY SATISFIED BY BEATING VIDEO GAMES WITHOUT EVER DYING...
IF YOU MAKE EVEN A LITTLE MISTAKE, YOU FLY INTO A RAGE. EVEN IF YOU SEE THE ENDING, YOU'RE NOT HAPPY.
AND IF YOU COULDN'T GET THAT PERFECT WIN... YOU'D JUST WIPE THE HIGH SCORE TABLE INSTEAD...
AAH?
YOU SHOULDN'T HAVE OBSESSED OVER SOME BORING LEVEL ZERO.
YOU SHOULD HAVE JUST USED YOUR AMAZING LEVEL FIVE POWERS AND SNIPED ME FROM FAR AWAY.

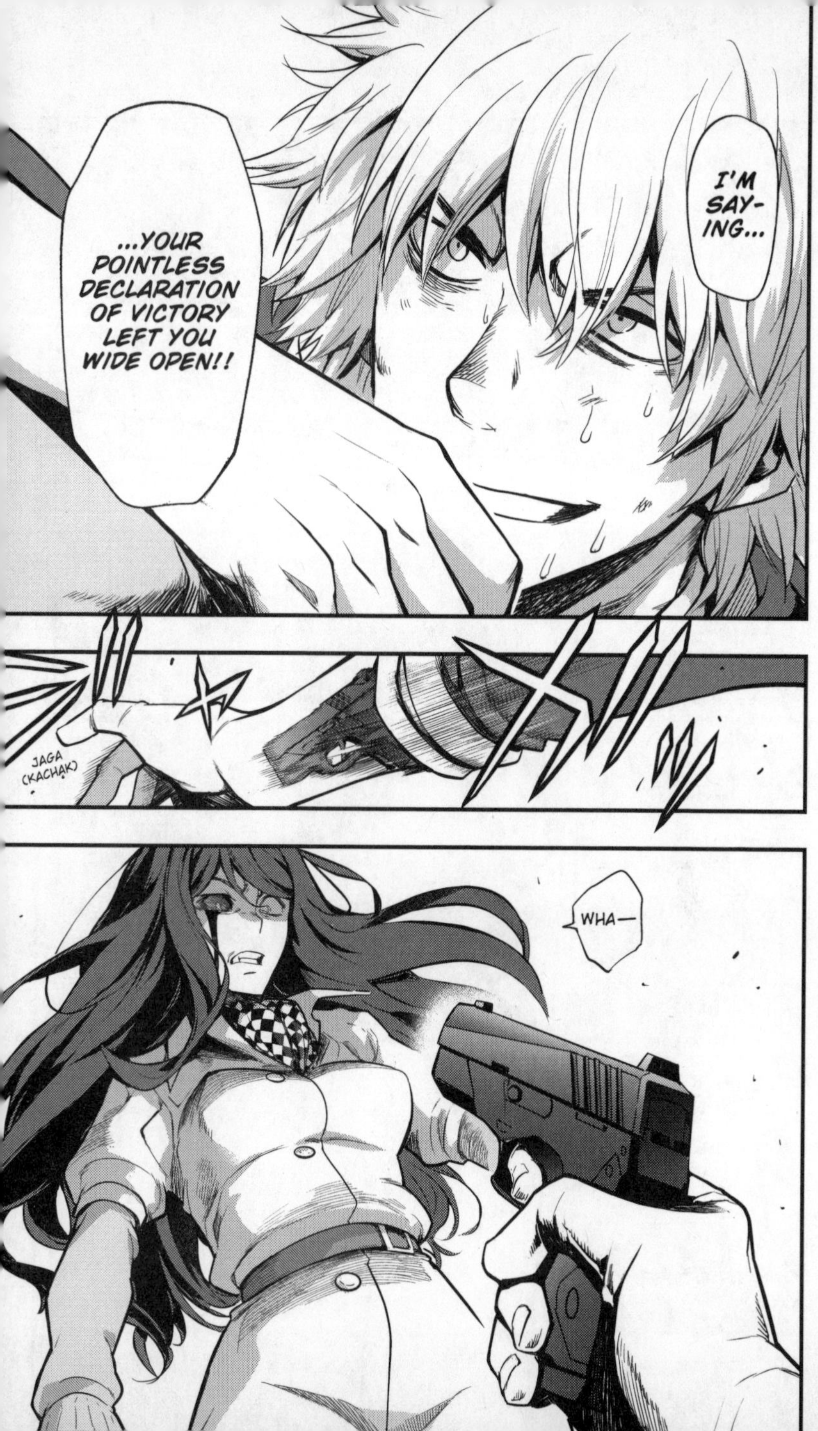
I'M SAY-ING...
...YOUR POINTLESS DECLARATION OF VICTORY LEFT YOU WIDE OPEN!!
JAGA (KACHAK)
WHA—

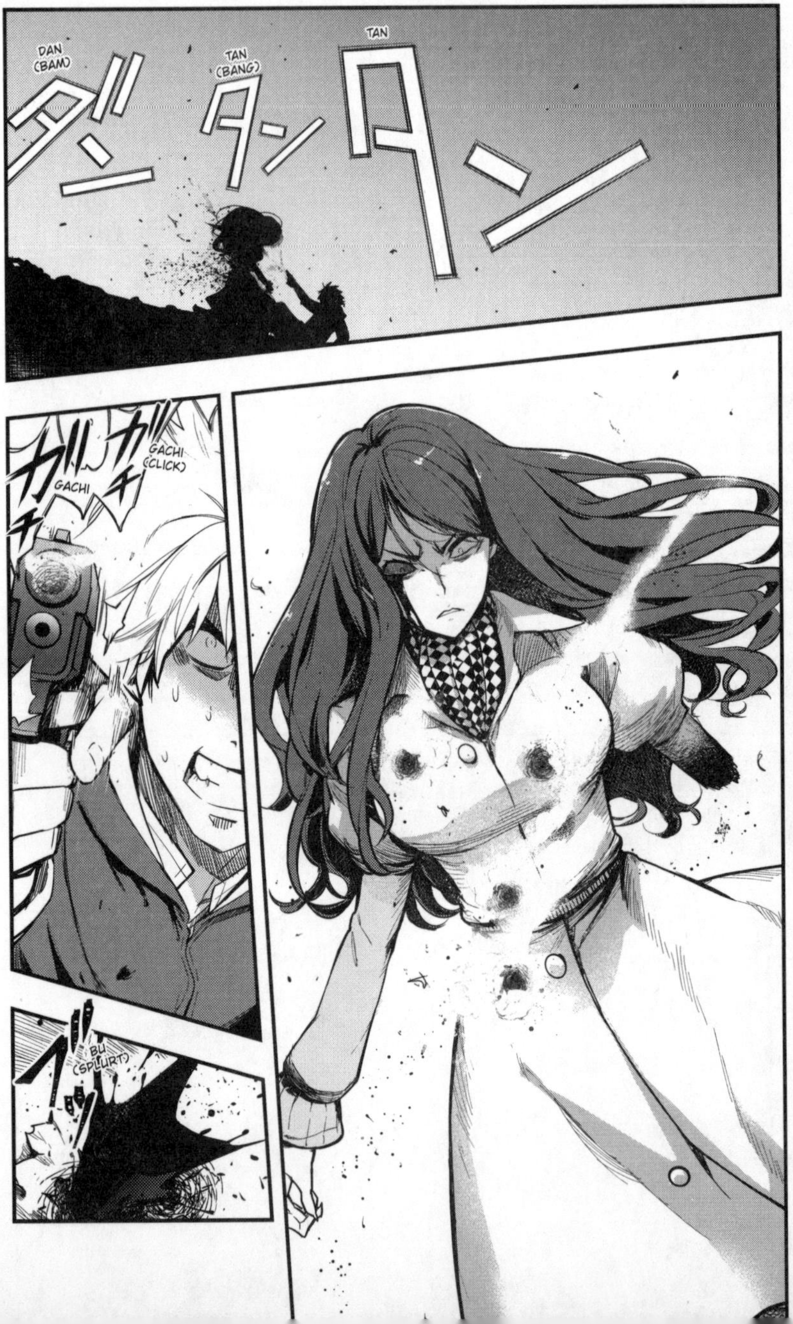
TAN
TAN (BANG)
DAN (BAM)
GACHI (CLICK)
GACHI
BU (SPLURT)

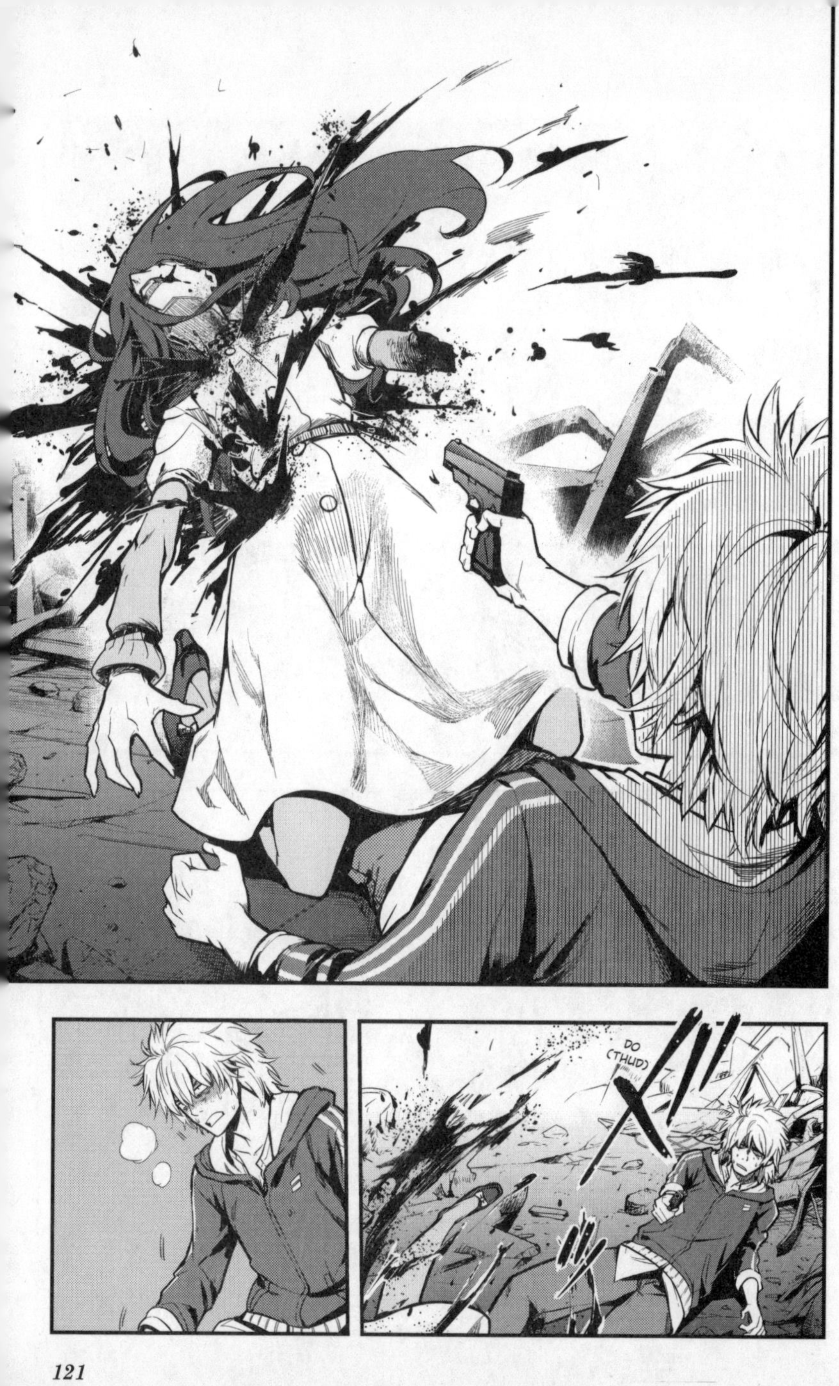
DO
(THUD)

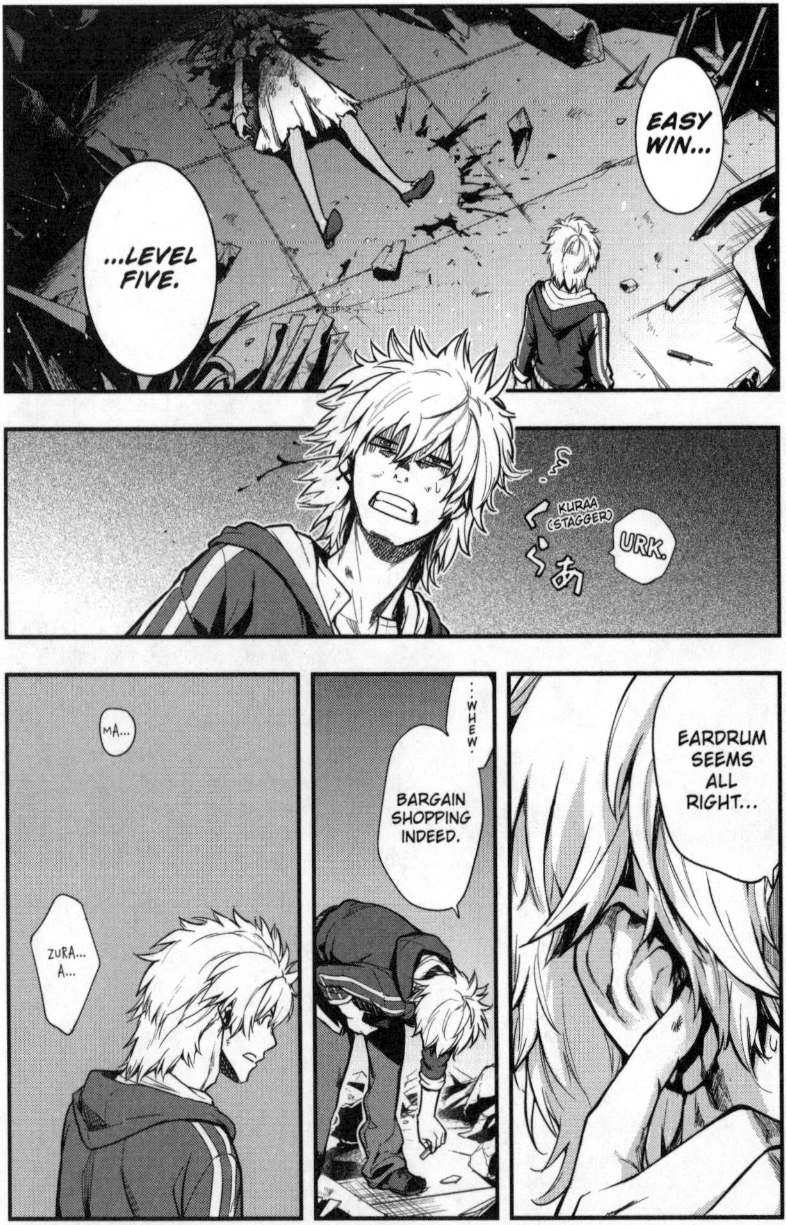
EASY WIN...
...LEVEL FIVE.
くらあ
KURAA (STAGGER)
URK.
EARDRUM SEEMS ALL RIGHT...
...WHEW.
BARGAIN SHOPPING INDEED.
MA...
ZURA... A...

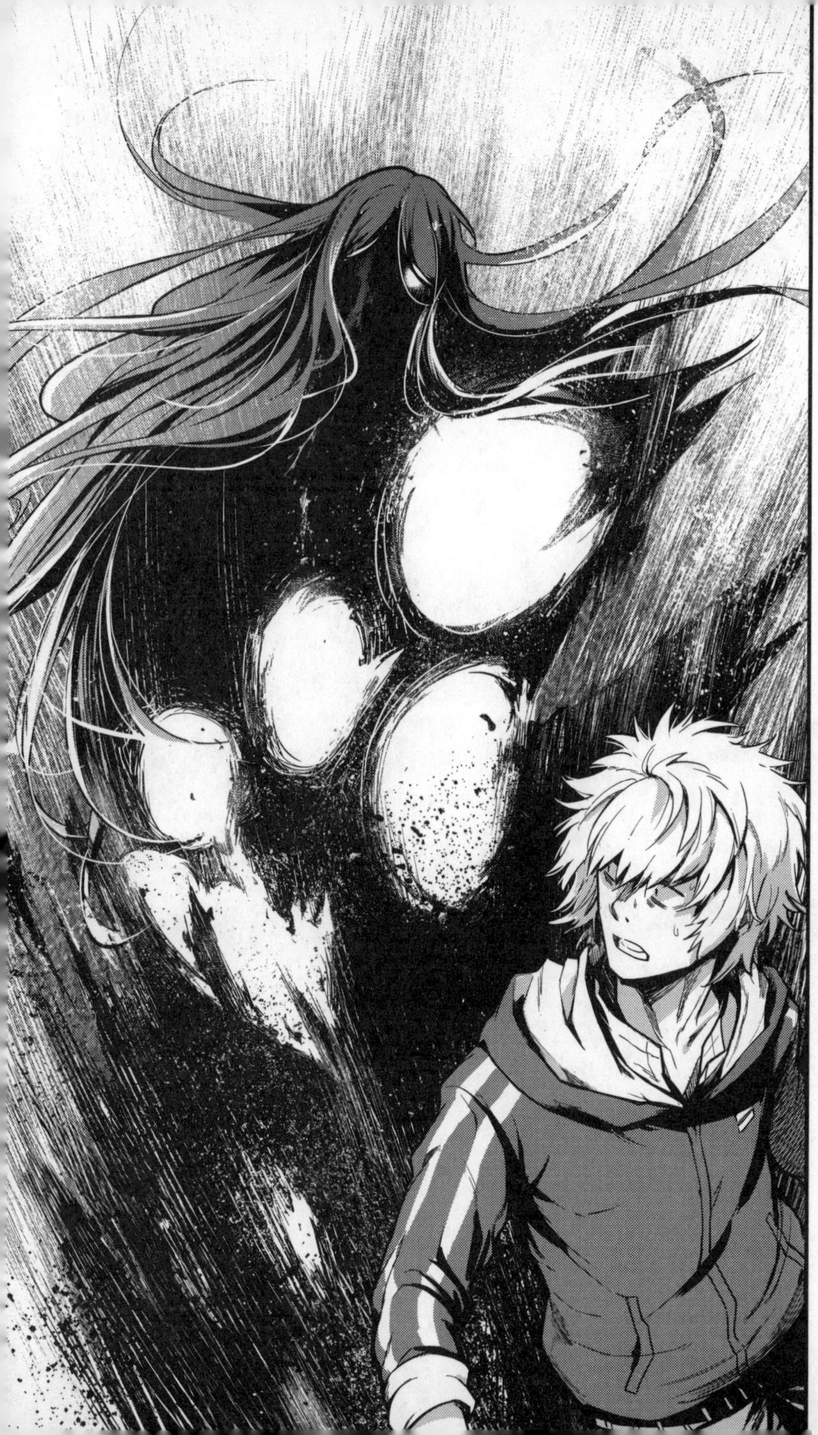

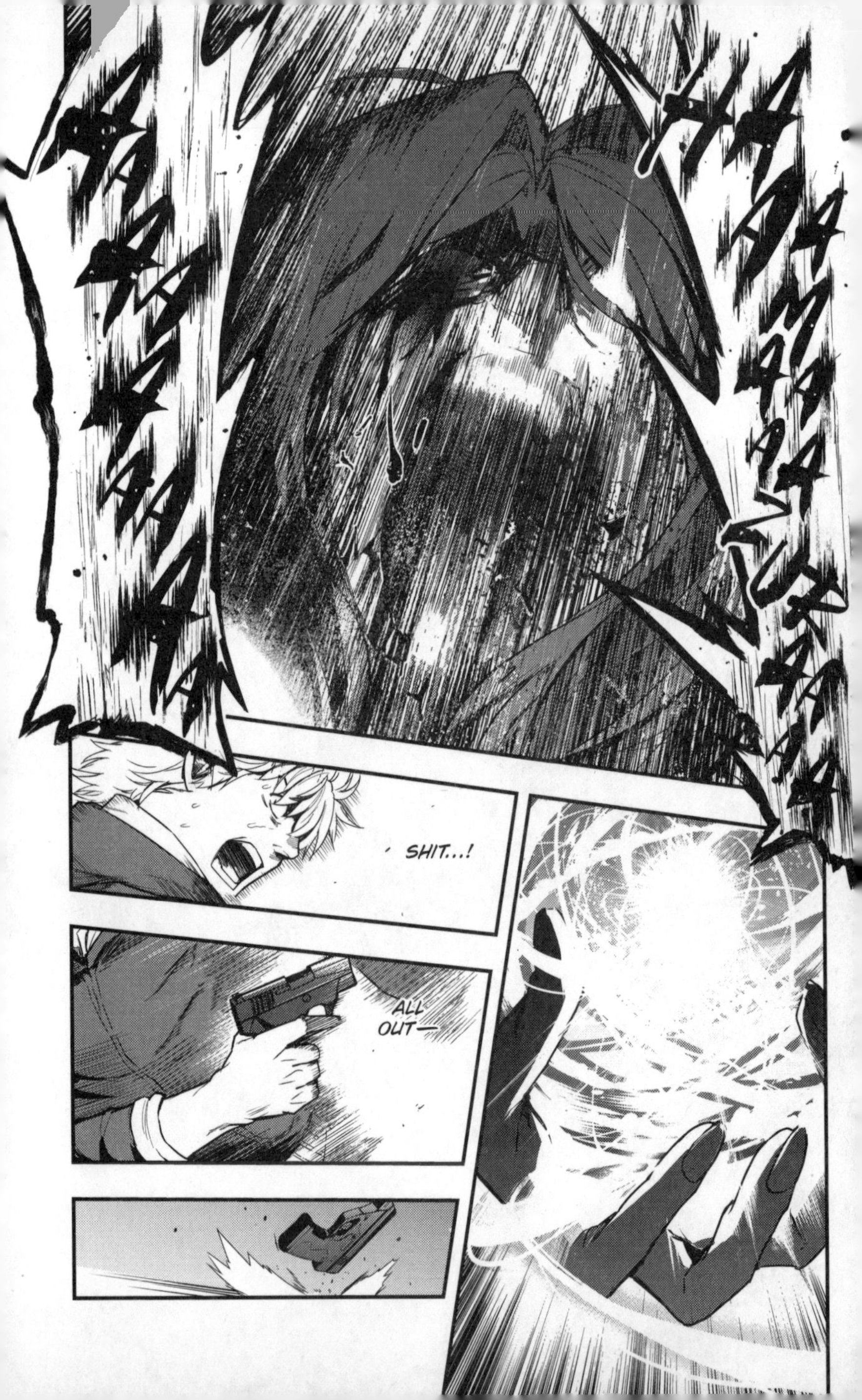
SHIT...!
ALL OUT—

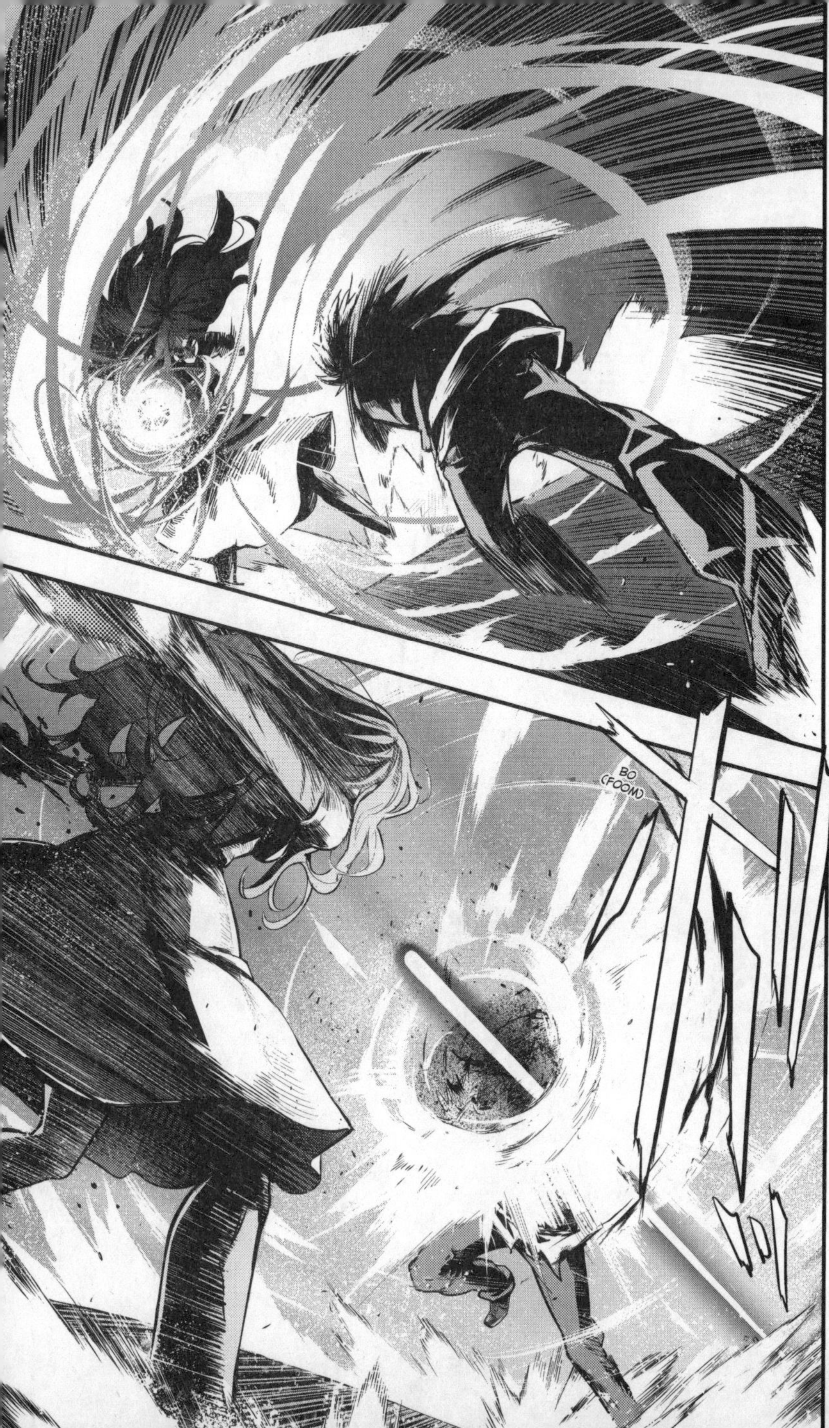
BO
(FOOM)

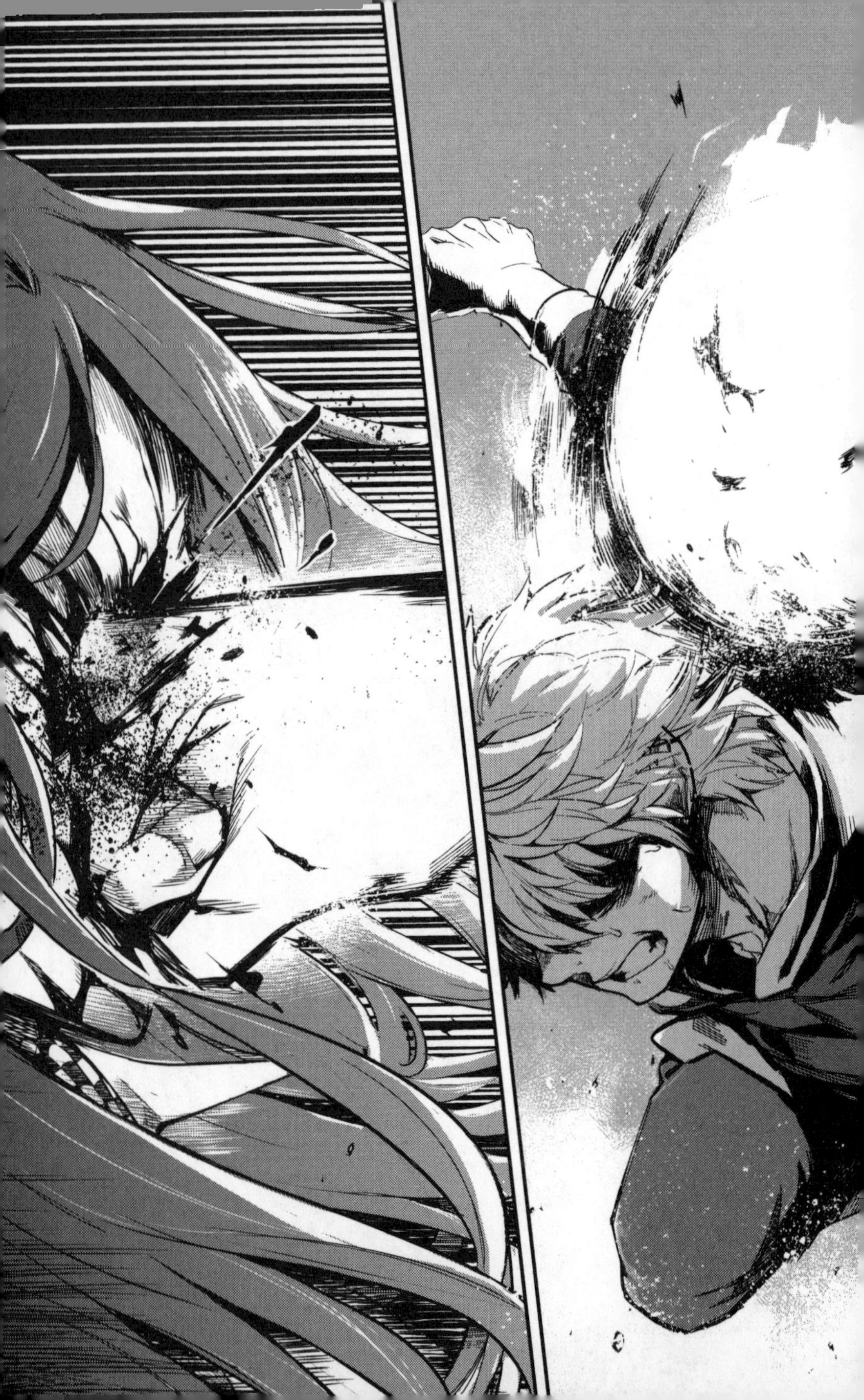

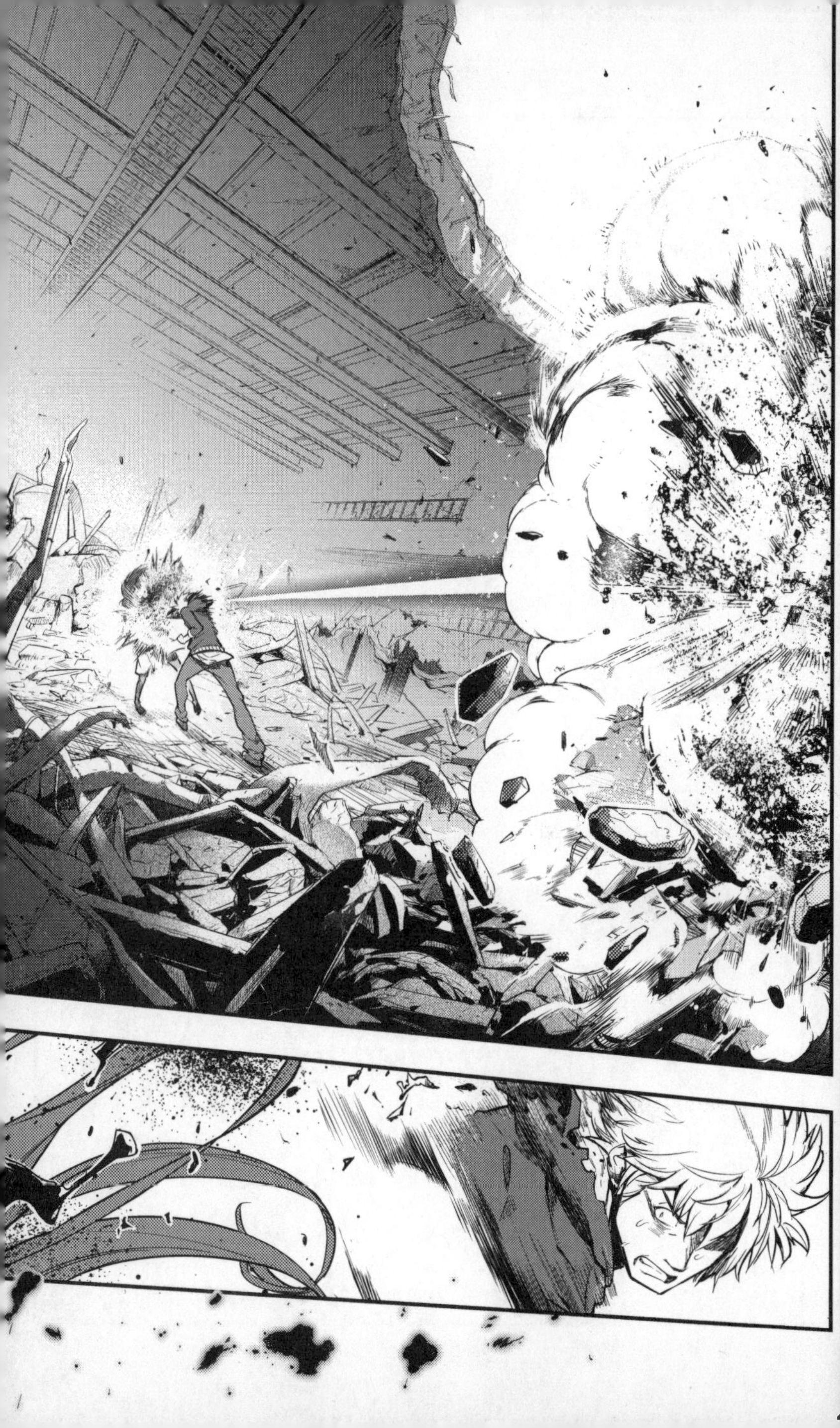

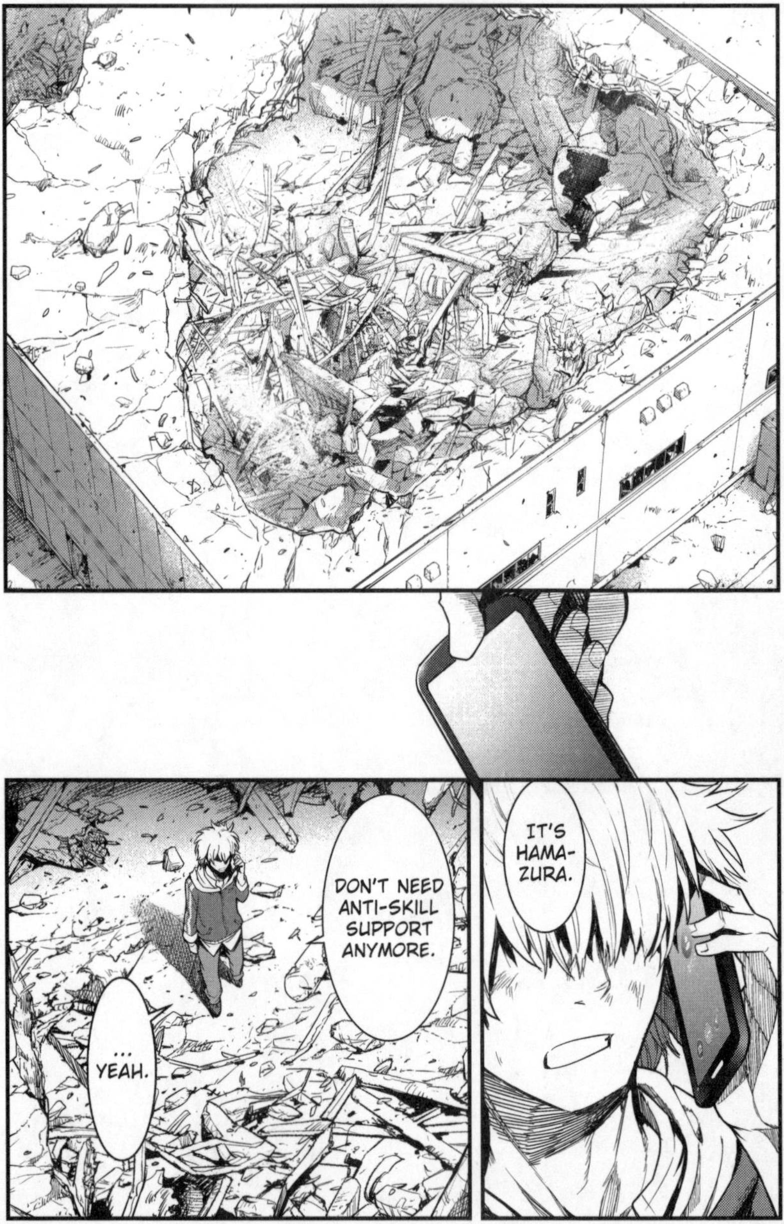
IT'S HAMA-ZURA.
DON'T NEED ANTI-SKILL SUPPORT ANYMORE.
... YEAH.

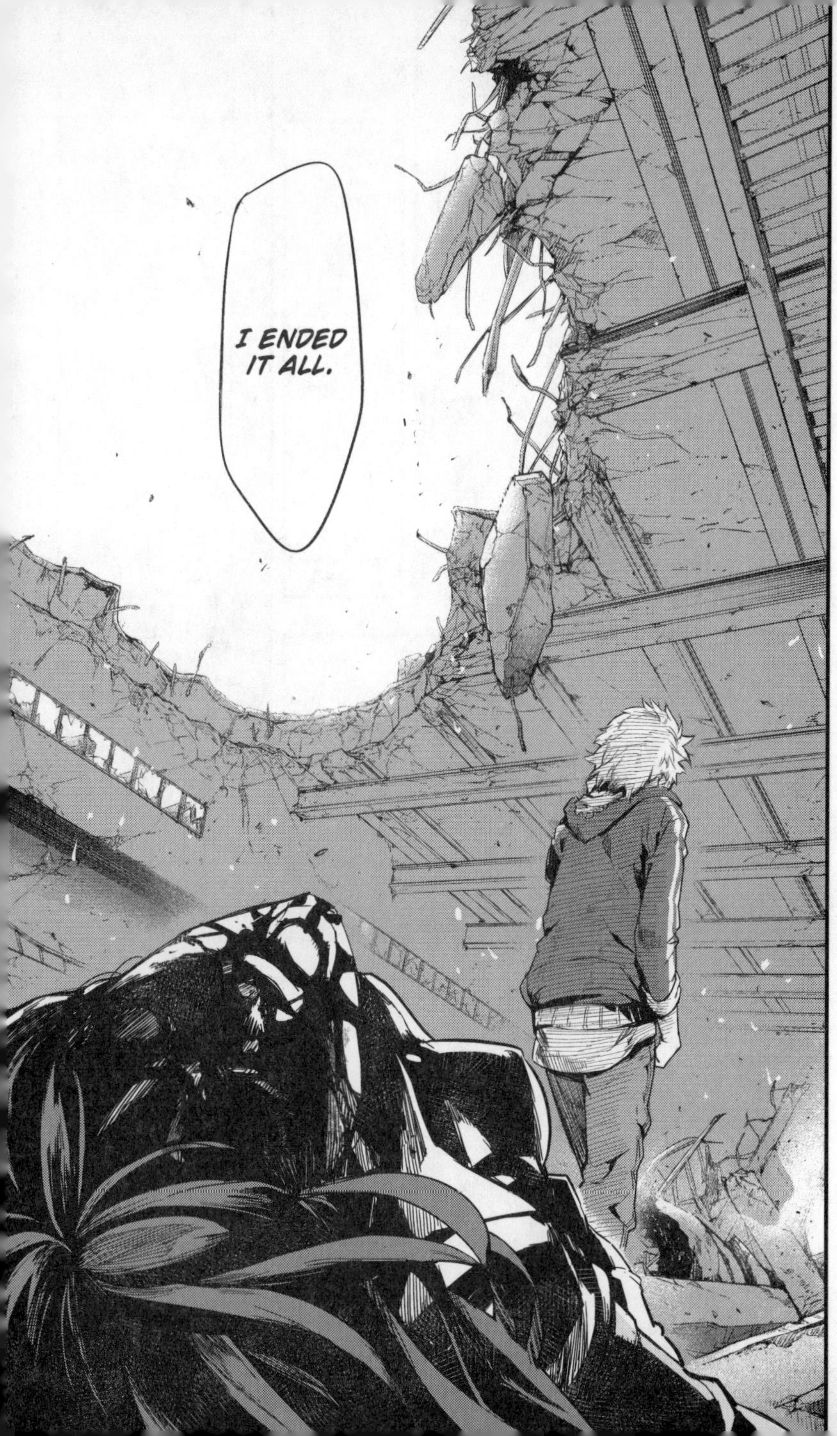
I ENDED IT ALL.

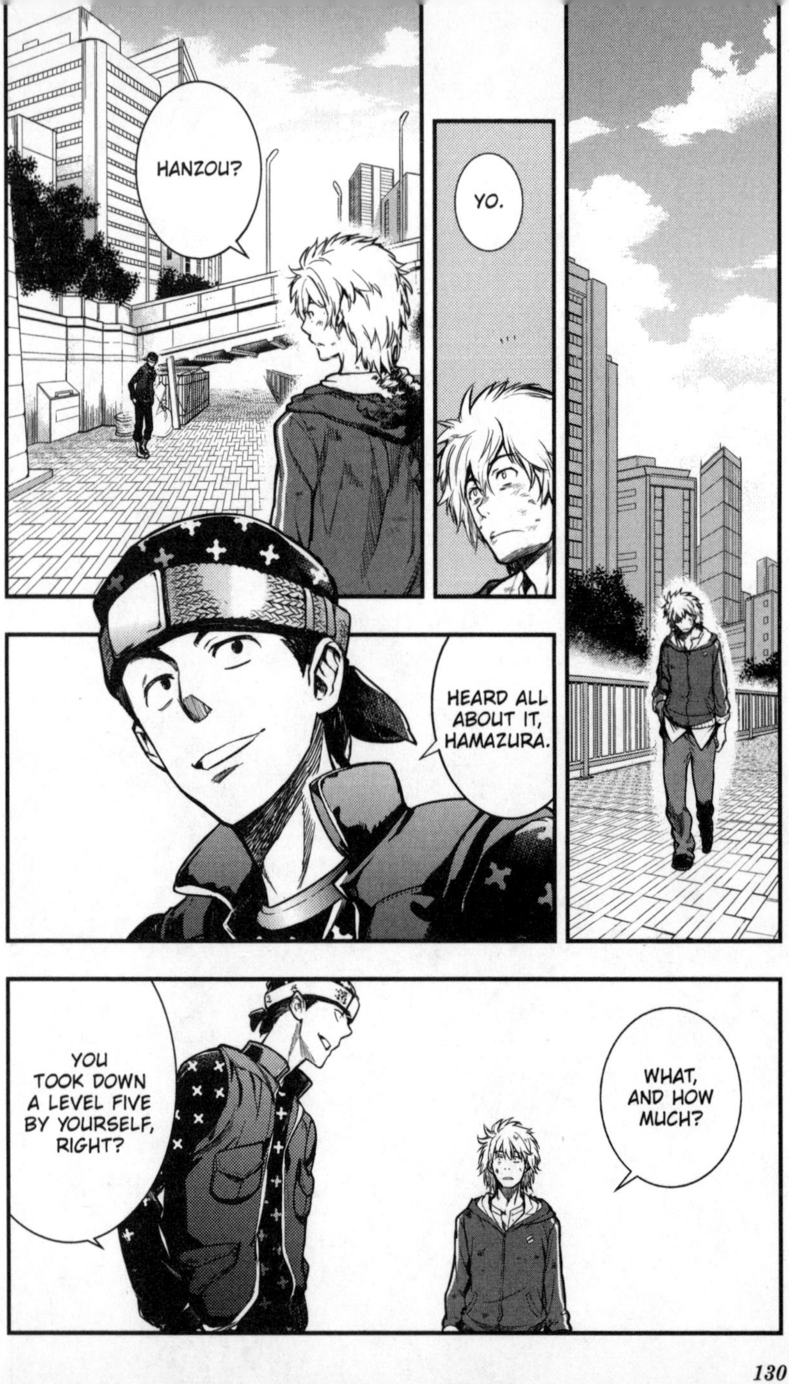
YO.
HANZOU?
HEARD ALL ABOUT IT, HAMAZURA.
WHAT, AND HOW MUCH?
YOU TOOK DOWN A LEVEL FIVE BY YOURSELF, RIGHT?

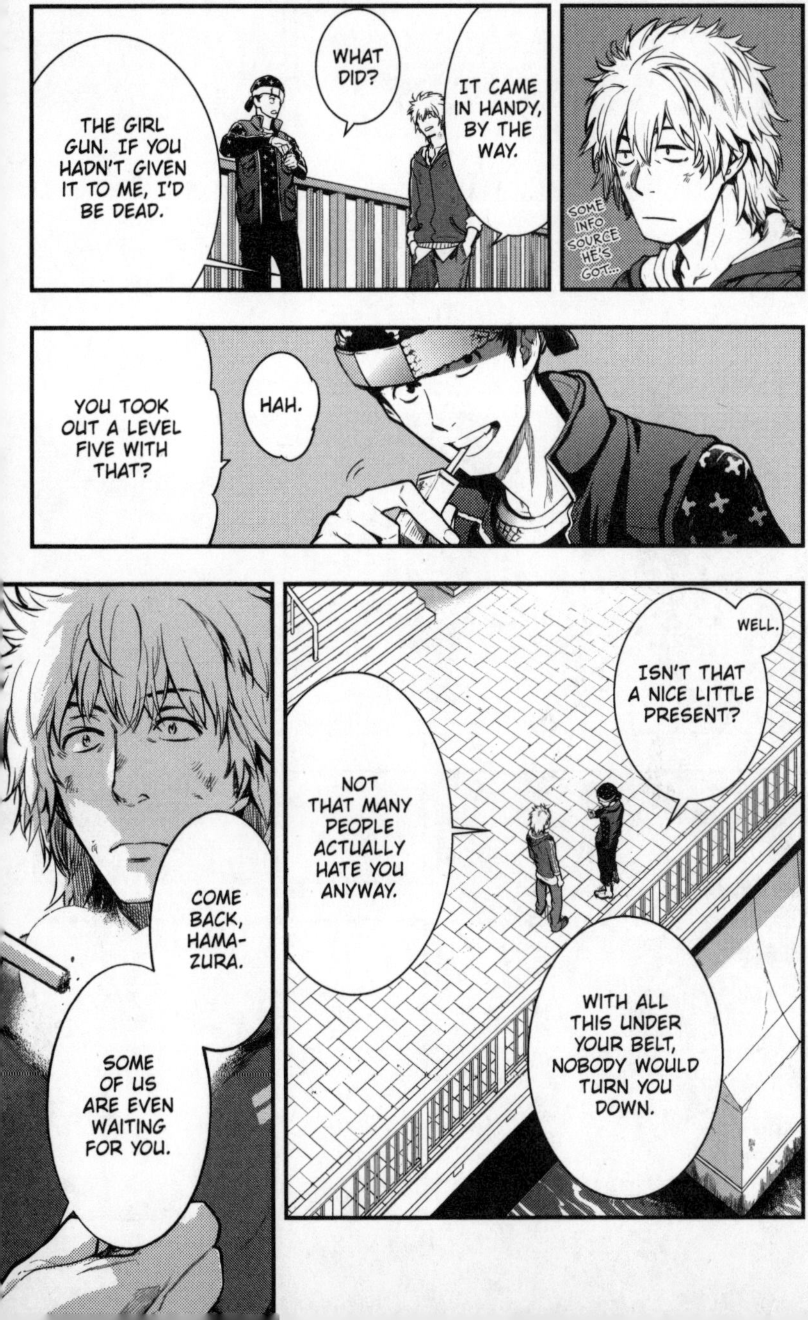
SOME INFO SOURCE HE'S GOT...
IT CAME IN HANDY, BY THE WAY.
WHAT DID?
THE GIRL GUN. IF YOU HADN'T GIVEN IT TO ME, I'D BE DEAD.
HAH.
YOU TOOK OUT A LEVEL FIVE WITH THAT?
WELL.
ISN'T THAT A NICE LITTLE PRESENT?
NOT THAT MANY PEOPLE ACTUALLY HATE YOU ANYWAY.
WITH ALL THIS UNDER YOUR BELT, NOBODY WOULD TURN YOU DOWN.
COME BACK, HAMA-ZURA.
SOME OF US ARE EVEN WAITING FOR YOU.

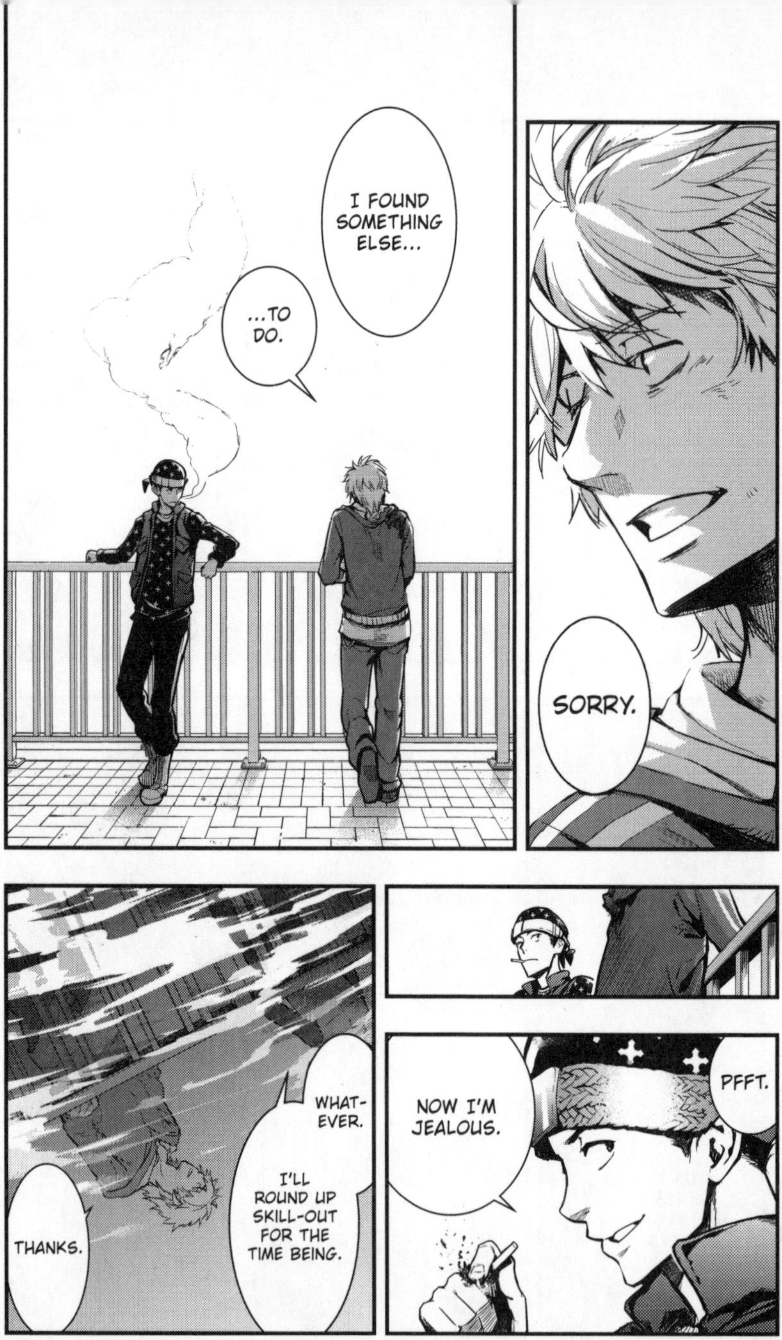
SORRY.
I FOUND SOMETHING ELSE...
...TO DO.
PFFT.
NOW I'M JEALOUS.
WHAT-EVER.
I'LL ROUND UP SKILL-OUT FOR THE TIME BEING.
THANKS.

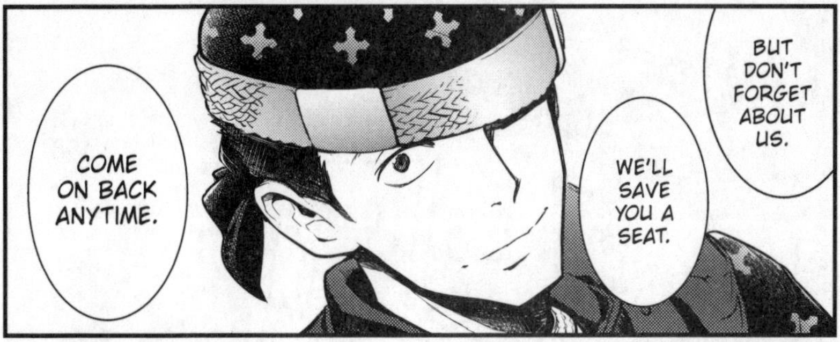
BUT DON'T FORGET ABOUT US.
WE'LL SAVE YOU A SEAT.
COME ON BACK ANYTIME.

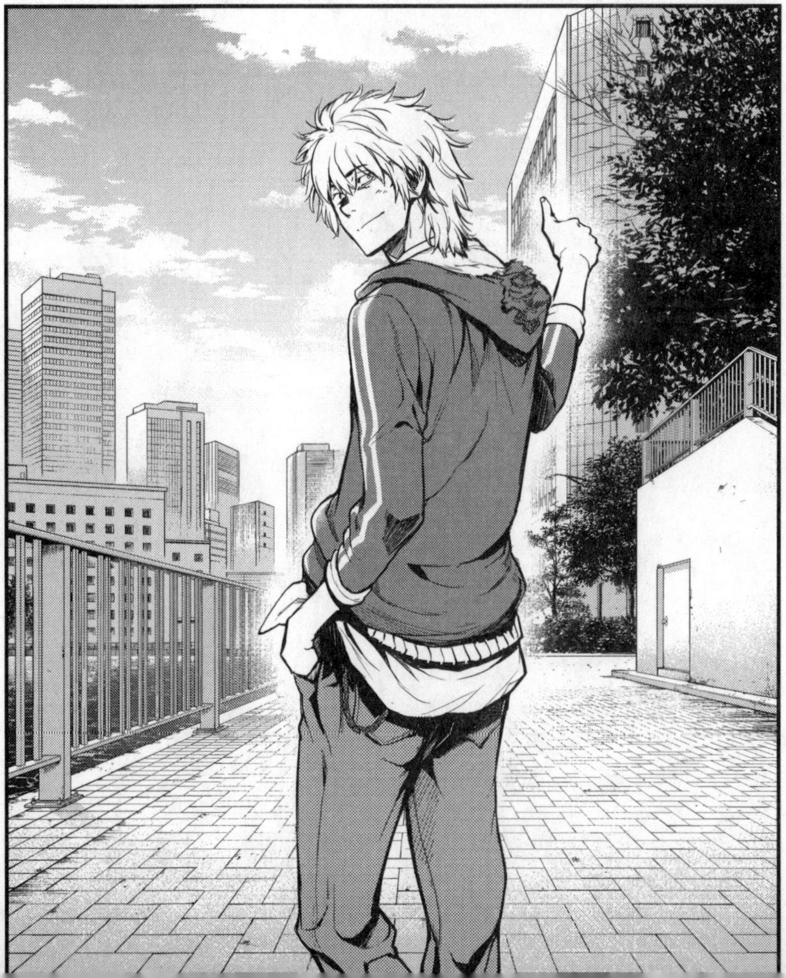

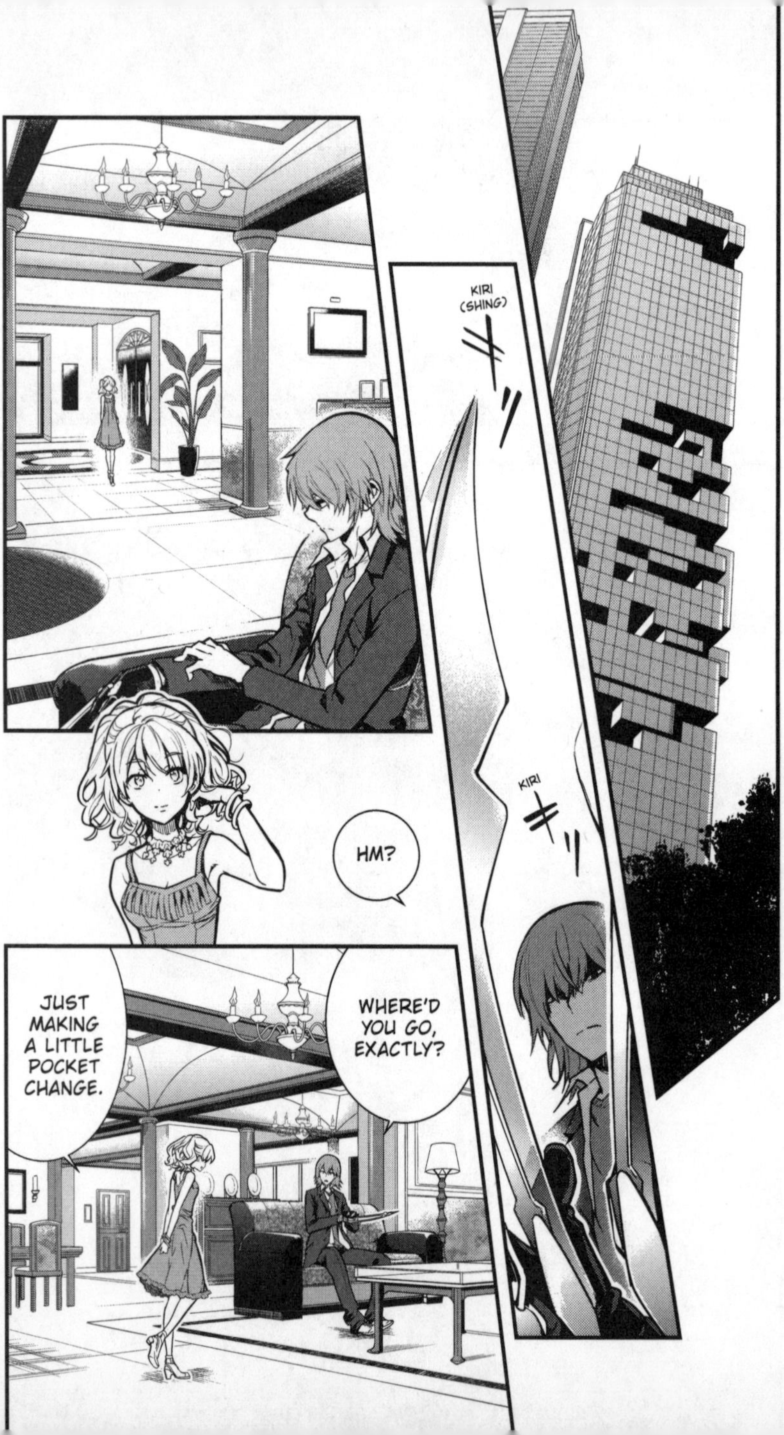
KIRI (SHING)
KIRI
HM?
WHERE'D YOU GO, EXACTLY?
JUST MAKING A LITTLE POCKET CHANGE.

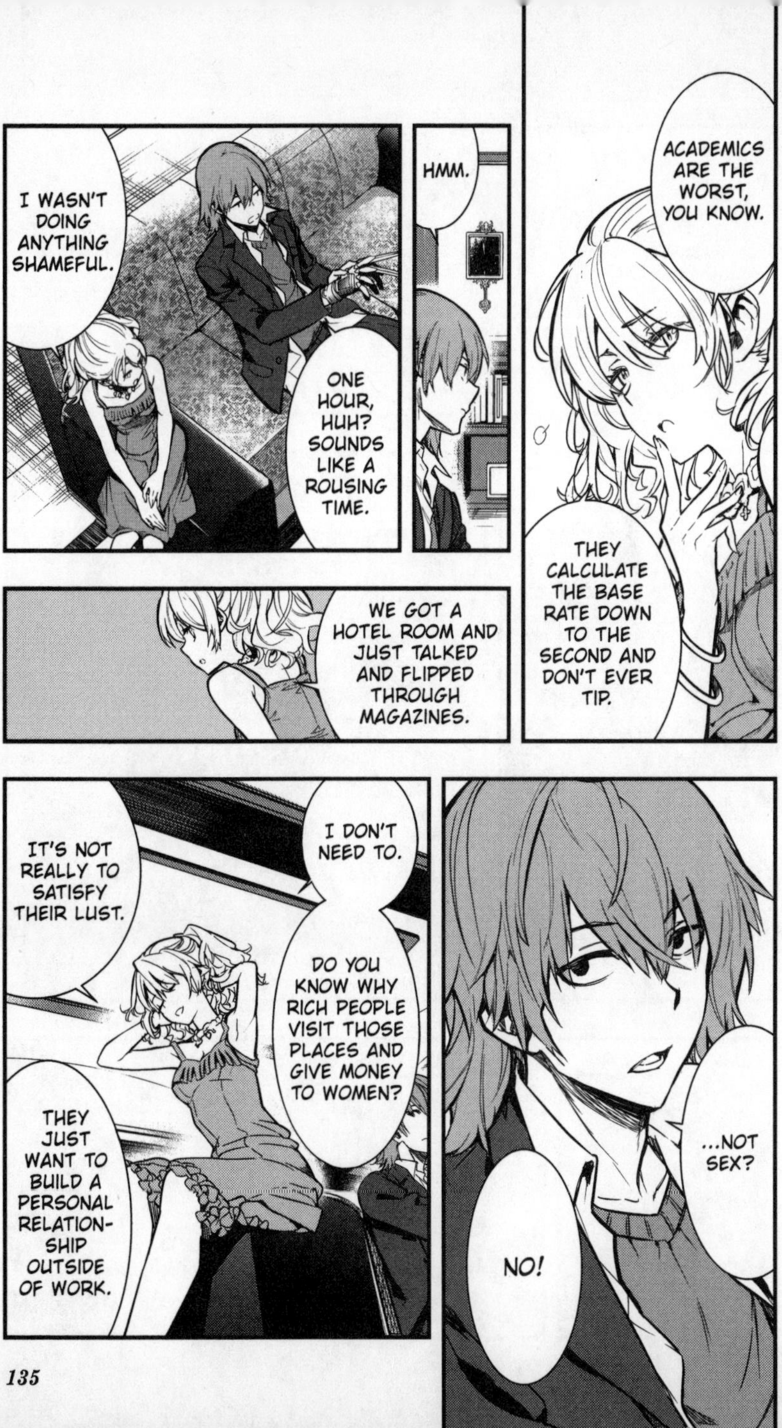
ACADEMICS ARE THE WORST, YOU KNOW.
THEY CALCULATE THE BASE RATE DOWN TO THE SECOND AND DON'T EVER TIP.
HMM.
ONE HOUR, HUH? SOUNDS LIKE A ROUSING TIME.
I WASN'T DOING ANYTHING SHAMEFUL.
WE GOT A HOTEL ROOM AND JUST TALKED AND FLIPPED THROUGH MAGAZINES.
...NOT SEX?
NO!
I DON'T NEED TO.
DO YOU KNOW WHY RICH PEOPLE VISIT THOSE PLACES AND GIVE MONEY TO WOMEN?
IT'S NOT REALLY TO SATISFY THEIR LUST.
THEY JUST WANT TO BUILD A PERSONAL RELATIONSHIP OUTSIDE OF WORK.

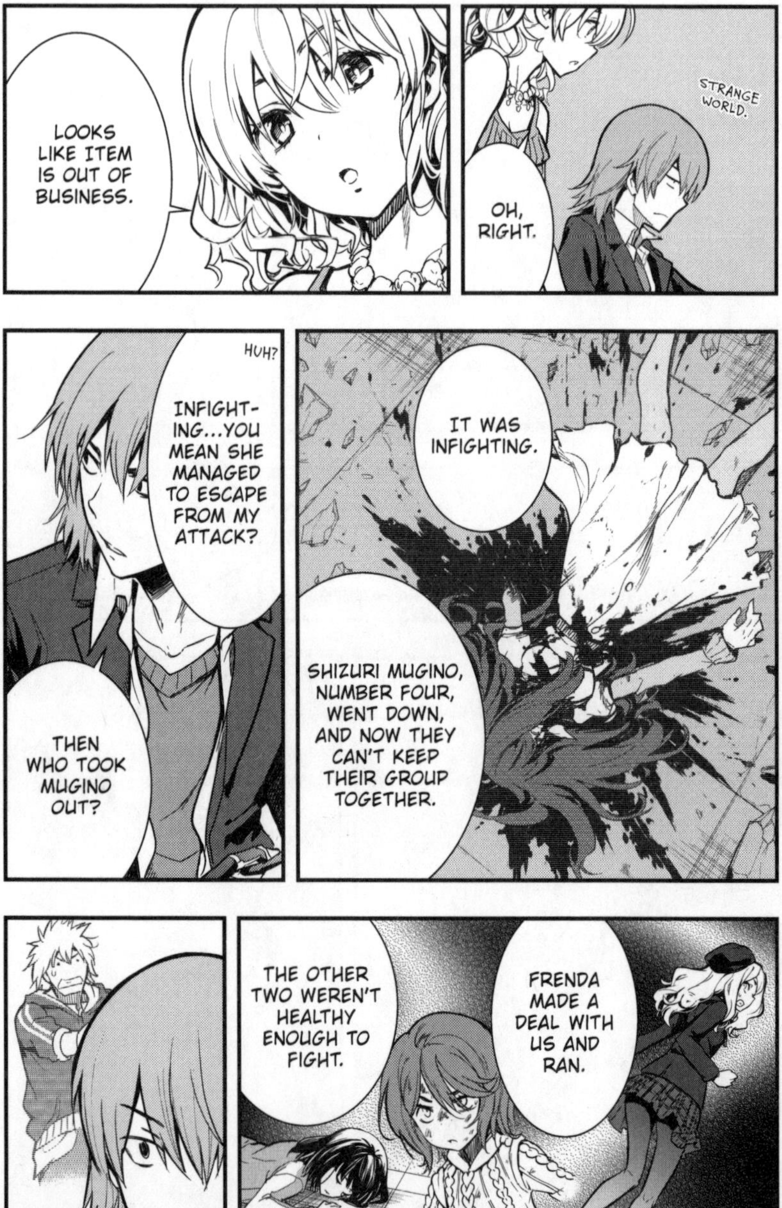
STRANGE WORLD.
OH, RIGHT.
LOOKS LIKE ITEM IS OUT OF BUSINESS.
IT WAS INFIGHTING.
SHIZURI MUGINO, NUMBER FOUR, WENT DOWN, AND NOW THEY CAN'T KEEP THEIR GROUP TOGETHER.
HUH?
INFIGHTING...YOU MEAN SHE MANAGED TO ESCAPE FROM MY ATTACK?
THEN WHO TOOK MUGINO OUT?
FRENDA MADE A DEAL WITH US AND RAN.
THE OTHER TWO WEREN'T HEALTHY ENOUGH TO FIGHT.

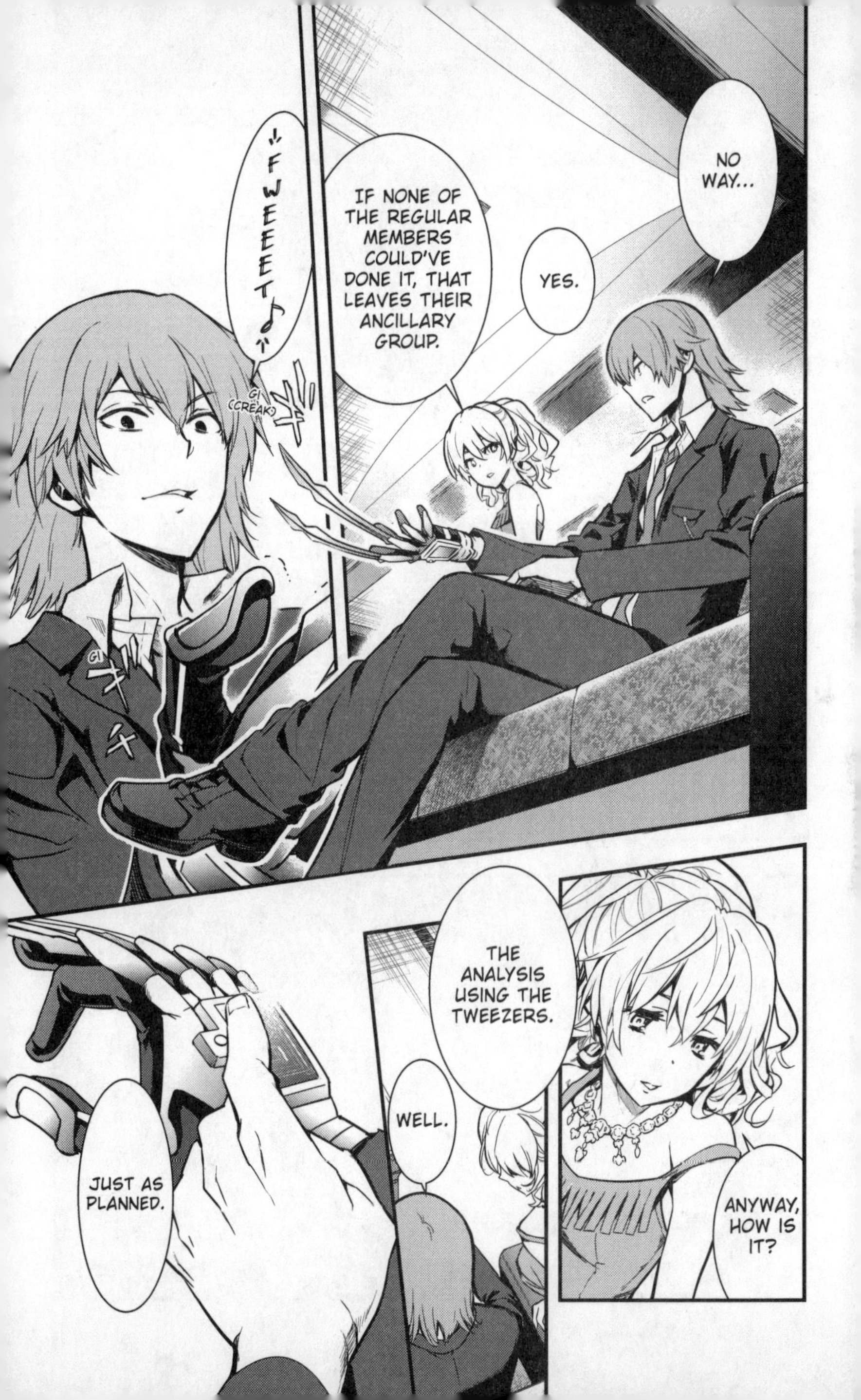
NO WAY...
YES.
IF NONE OF THE REGULAR MEMBERS COULD'VE DONE IT, THAT LEAVES THEIR ANCILLARY GROUP.
FWEEET♪
GI (CREAK)
GI
ANYWAY, HOW IS IT?
THE ANALYSIS USING THE TWEEZERS.
WELL.
JUST AS PLANNED.

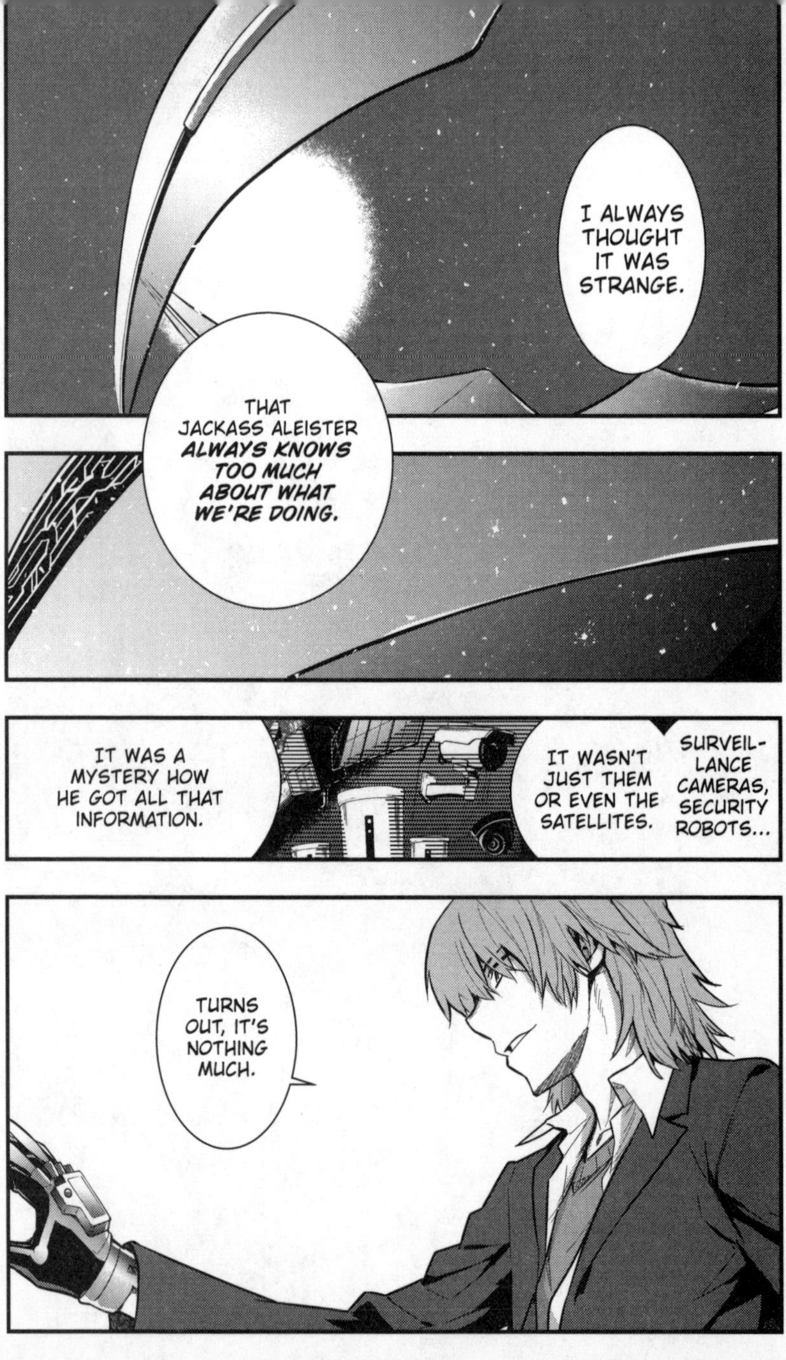
I ALWAYS THOUGHT IT WAS STRANGE.
THAT JACKASS ALEISTER ***ALWAYS KNOWS TOO MUCH ABOUT WHAT WE'RE DOING.***
SURVEIL-LANCE CAMERAS, SECURITY ROBOTS...
IT WASN'T JUST THEM OR EVEN THE SATELLITES.
IT WAS A MYSTERY HOW HE GOT ALL THAT INFORMATION.
TURNS OUT, IT'S NOTHING MUCH.

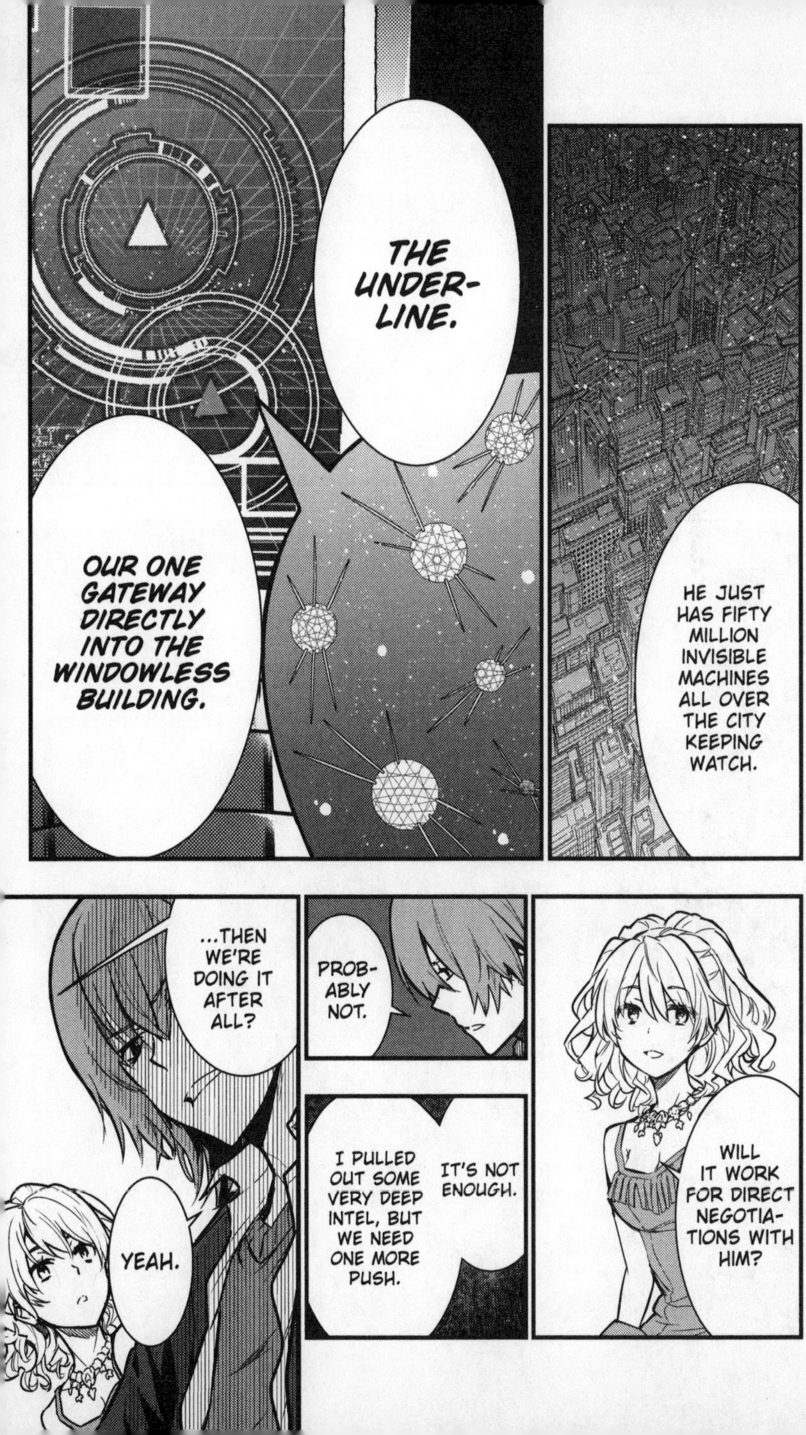
HE JUST HAS FIFTY MILLION INVISIBLE MACHINES ALL OVER THE CITY KEEPING WATCH.
THE UNDER-LINE.
OUR ONE GATEWAY DIRECTLY INTO THE WINDOWLESS BUILDING.
WILL IT WORK FOR DIRECT NEGOTIA-TIONS WITH HIM?
PROB-ABLY NOT.
IT'S NOT ENOUGH.
I PULLED OUT SOME VERY DEEP INTEL, BUT WE NEED ONE MORE PUSH.
...THEN WE'RE DOING IT AFTER ALL?
YEAH.

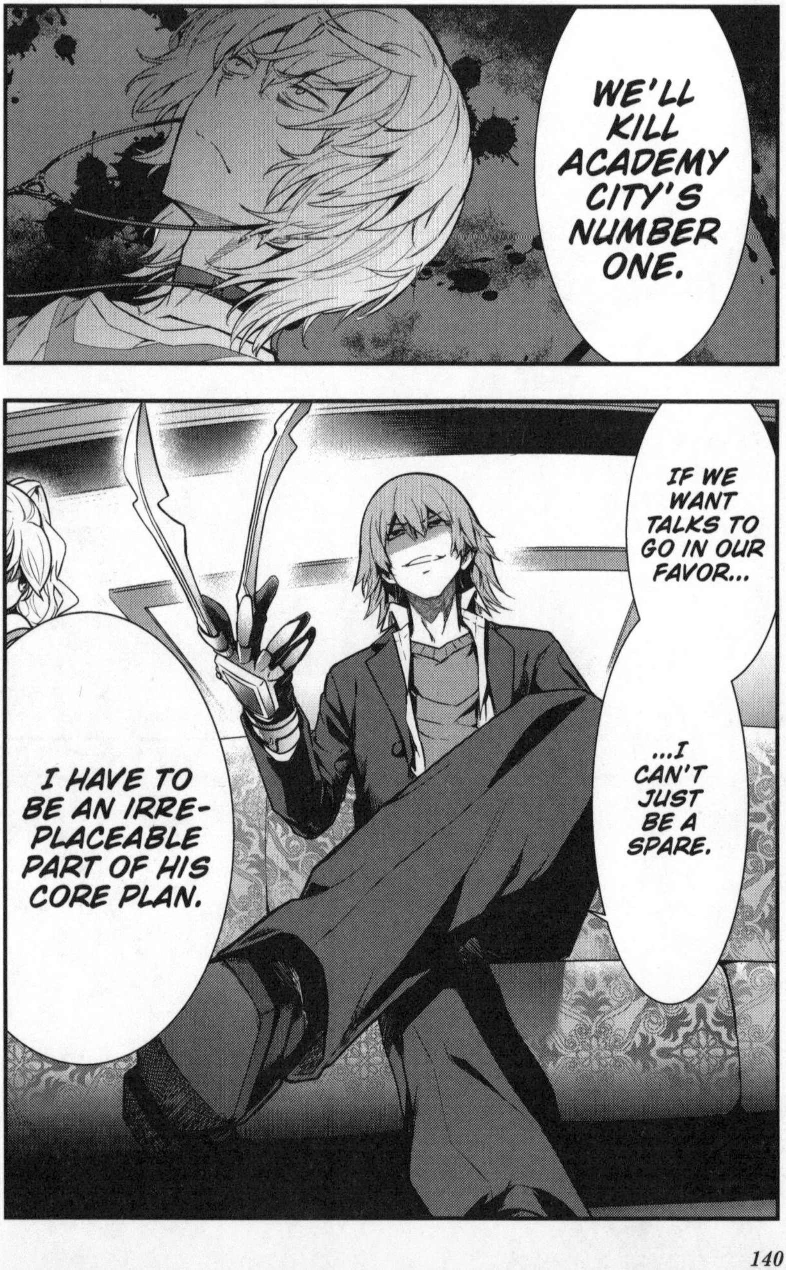
WE'LL KILL ACADEMY CITY'S NUMBER ONE.
IF WE WANT TALKS TO GO IN OUR FAVOR...
...I CAN'T JUST BE A SPARE.
I HAVE TO BE AN IRRE-PLACEABLE PART OF HIS CORE PLAN.

Transmission data from "UNDER_LINE"

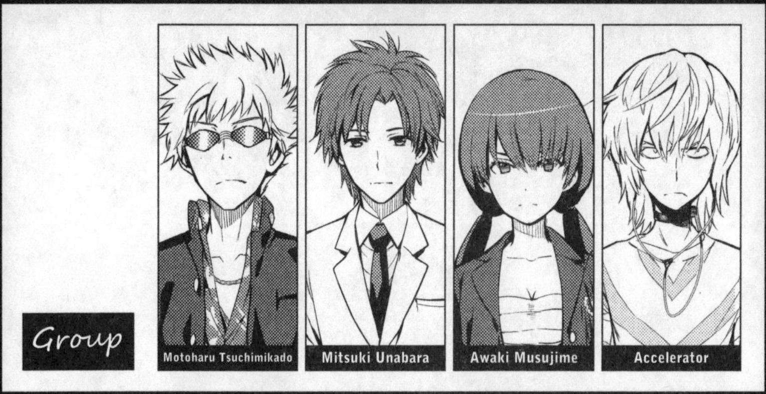
Group
Motoharu Tsuchimikado
Mitsuki Unabara
Awaki Musujime
Accelerator

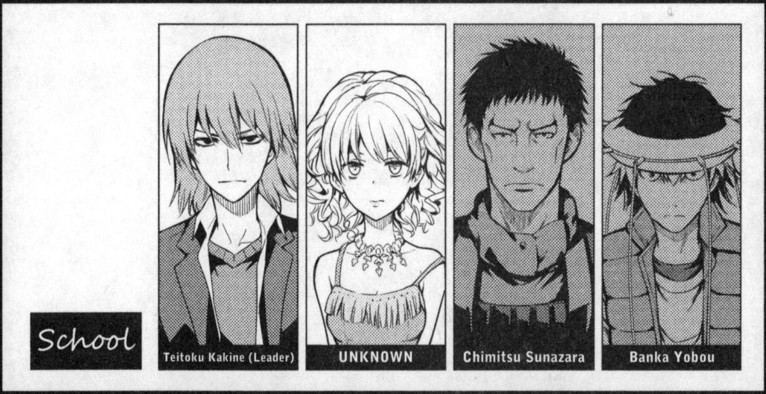
School
Teitoku Kakine (Leader)
UNKNOWN
Chimitsu Sunazara
Banka Yobou

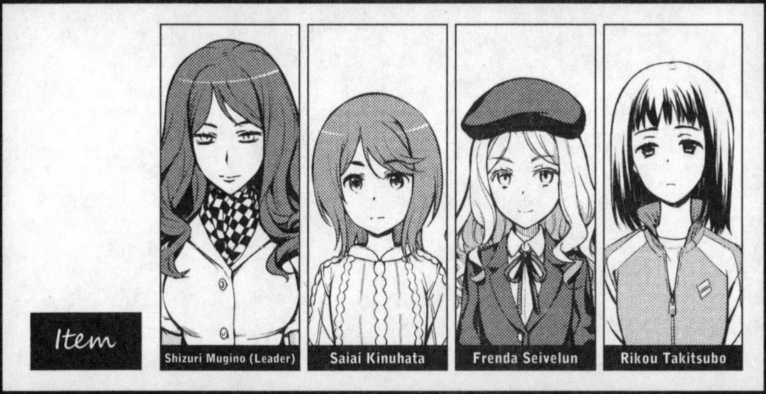
Item
Shizuri Mugino (Leader)
Saiai Kinuhata
Frenda Seivelun
Rikou Takitsubo

A Certain Magical Index

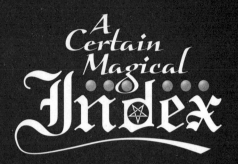

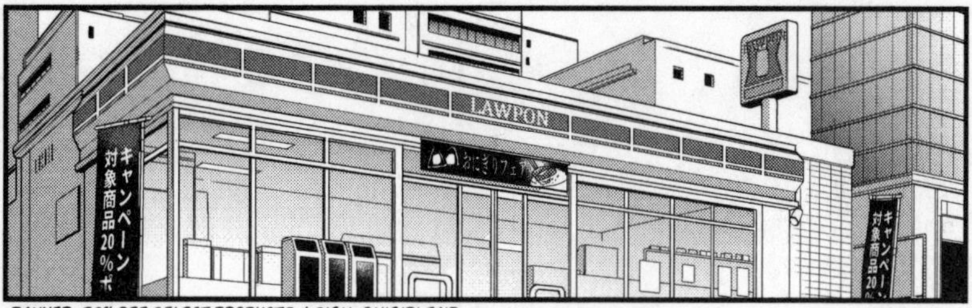
LAWPON
キャンペーン
対象商品20%
おにぎりフェア

BANNER: 20% OFF SELECT PRODUCTS / SIGN: ONIGIRI FAIR

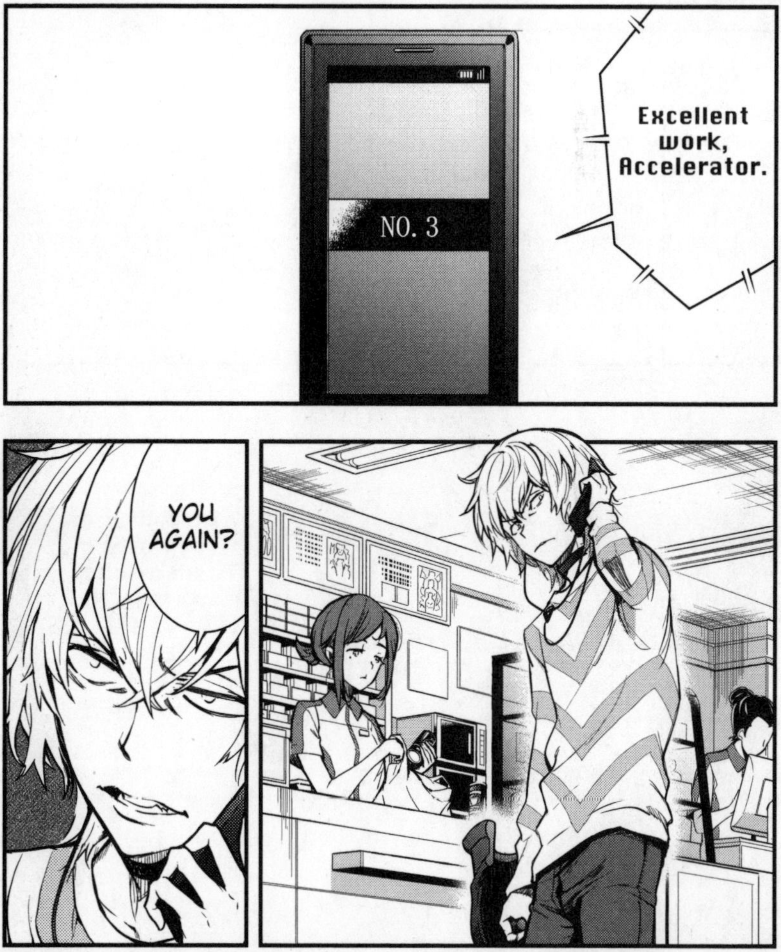
Excellent work, Accelerator.
NO. 3
YOU AGAIN?

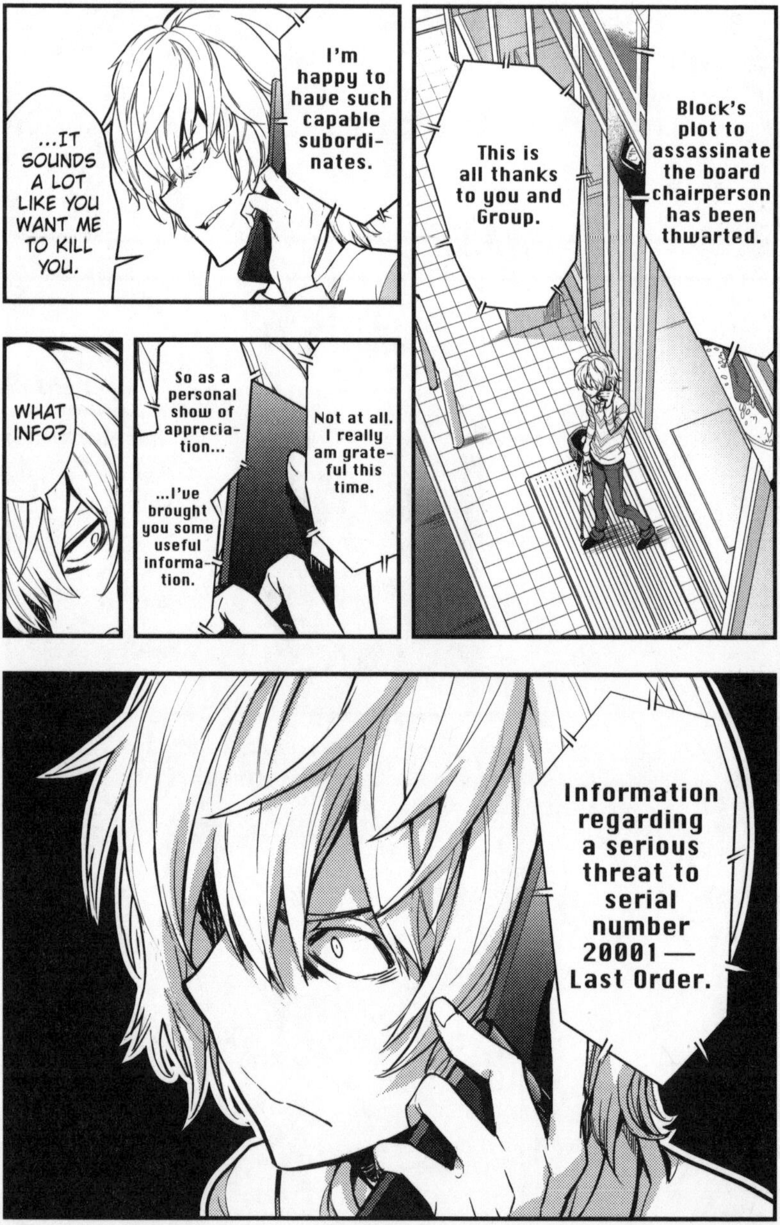
Block's plot to assassinate the board chairperson has been thwarted.
This is all thanks to you and Group.
I'm happy to have such capable subordi-nates.
...IT SOUNDS A LOT LIKE YOU WANT ME TO KILL YOU.
Not at all. I really am grate-ful this time.
So as a personal show of apprecia-tion...
...I've brought you some useful informa-tion.
WHAT INFO?
Information regarding a serious threat to serial number 20001 — Last Order.

#147 DISTRICT 7 OPEN CAFÉ

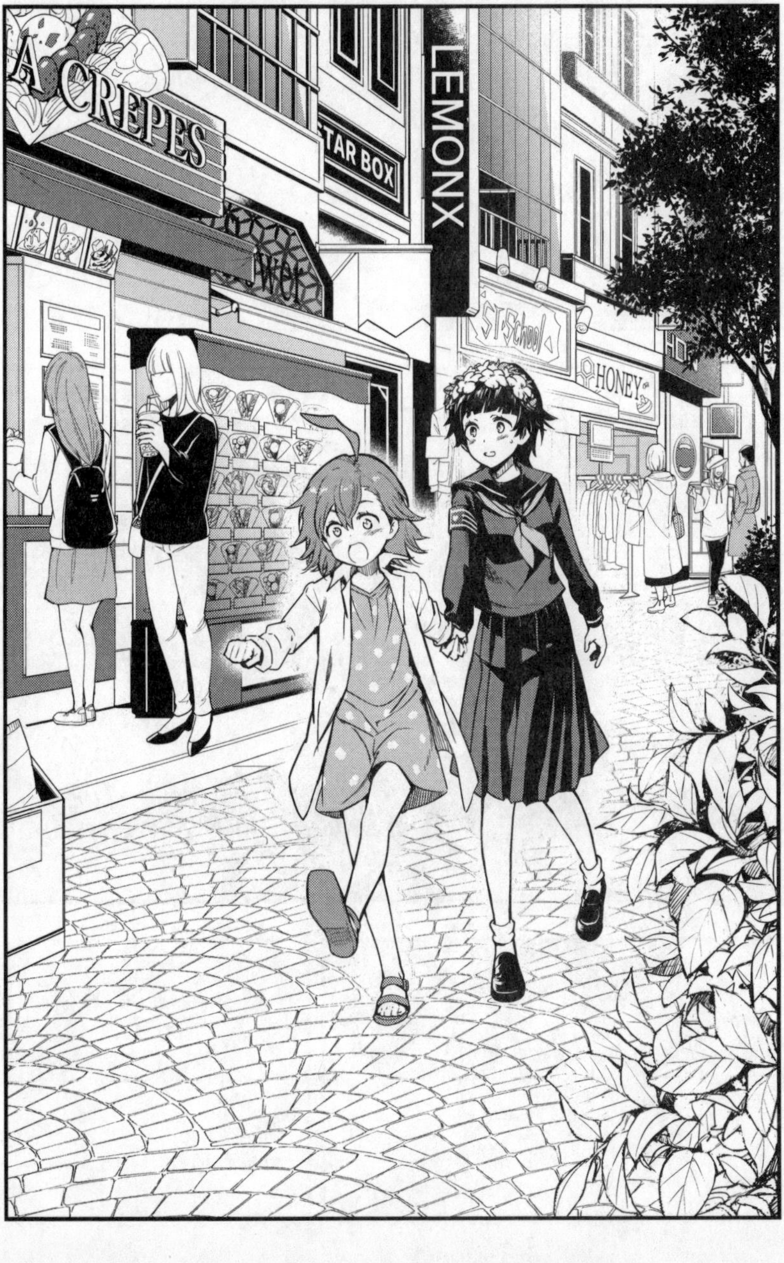
CREPES
STAR BOX
LEMONX
ST School
HONEY

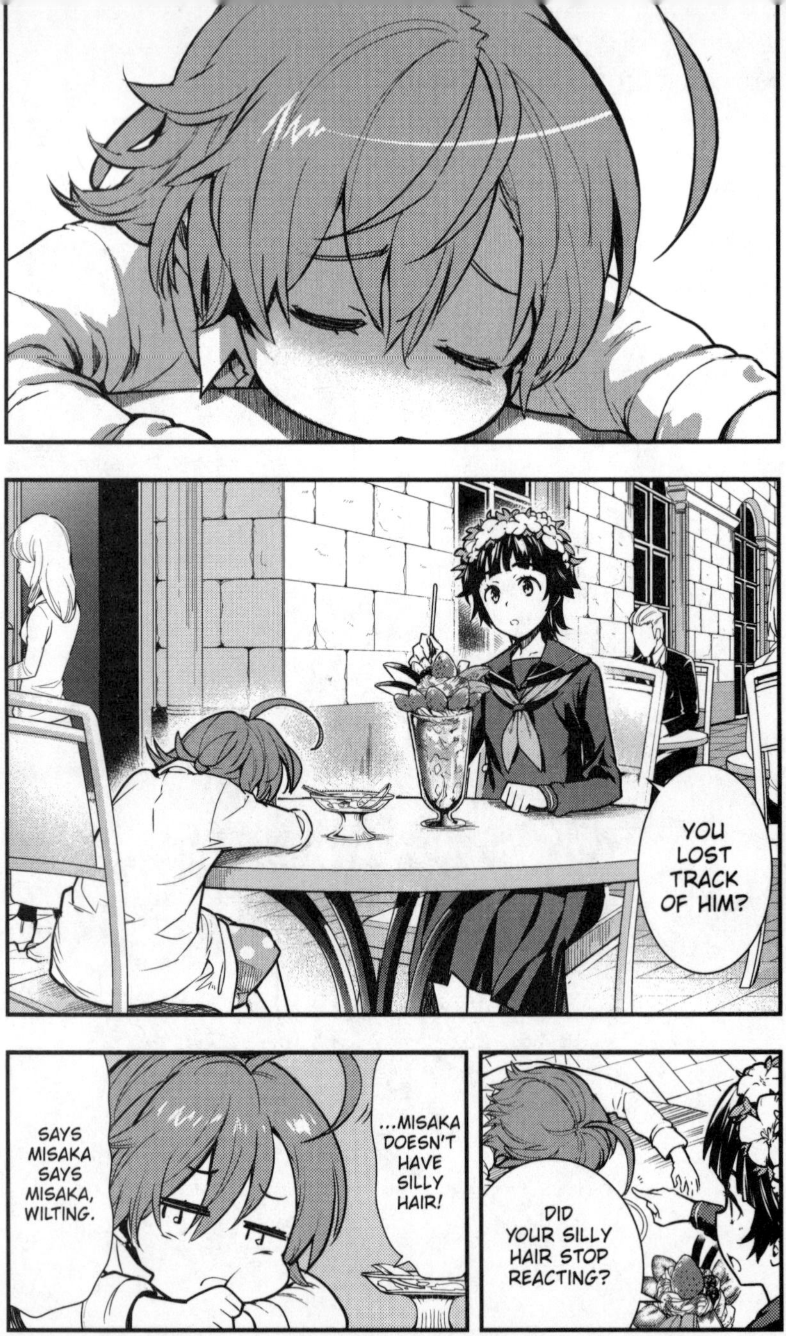
YOU LOST TRACK OF HIM?
DID YOUR SILLY HAIR STOP REACTING?
...MISAKA DOESN'T HAVE SILLY HAIR!
SAYS MISAKA SAYS MISAKA, WILTING.

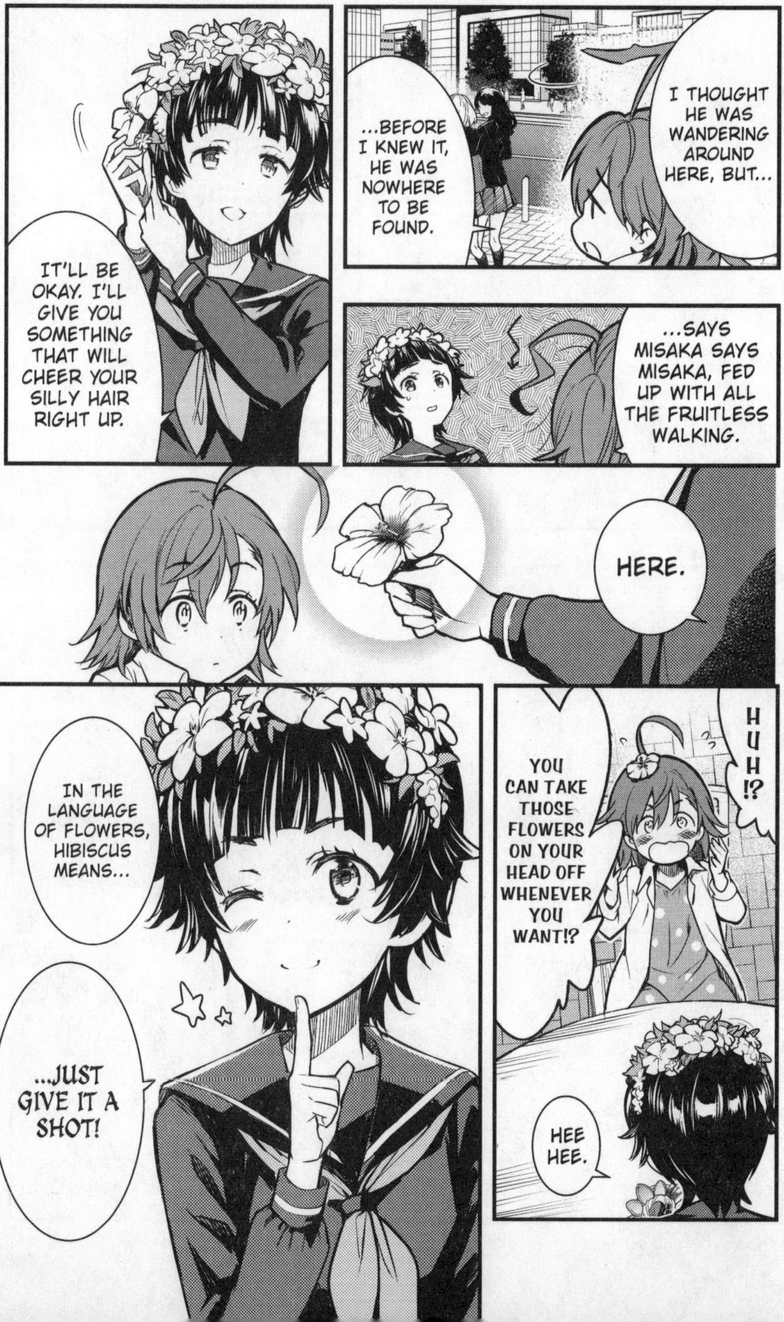
I THOUGHT HE WAS WANDERING AROUND HERE, BUT...
...BEFORE I KNEW IT, HE WAS NOWHERE TO BE FOUND.
...SAYS MISAKA SAYS MISAKA, FED UP WITH ALL THE FRUITLESS WALKING.
IT'LL BE OKAY. I'LL GIVE YOU SOMETHING THAT WILL CHEER YOUR SILLY HAIR RIGHT UP.
HERE.
HUH!?
YOU CAN TAKE THOSE FLOWERS ON YOUR HEAD OFF WHENEVER YOU WANT!?
HEE HEE.
IN THE LANGUAGE OF FLOWERS, HIBISCUS MEANS...
...JUST GIVE IT A SHOT!

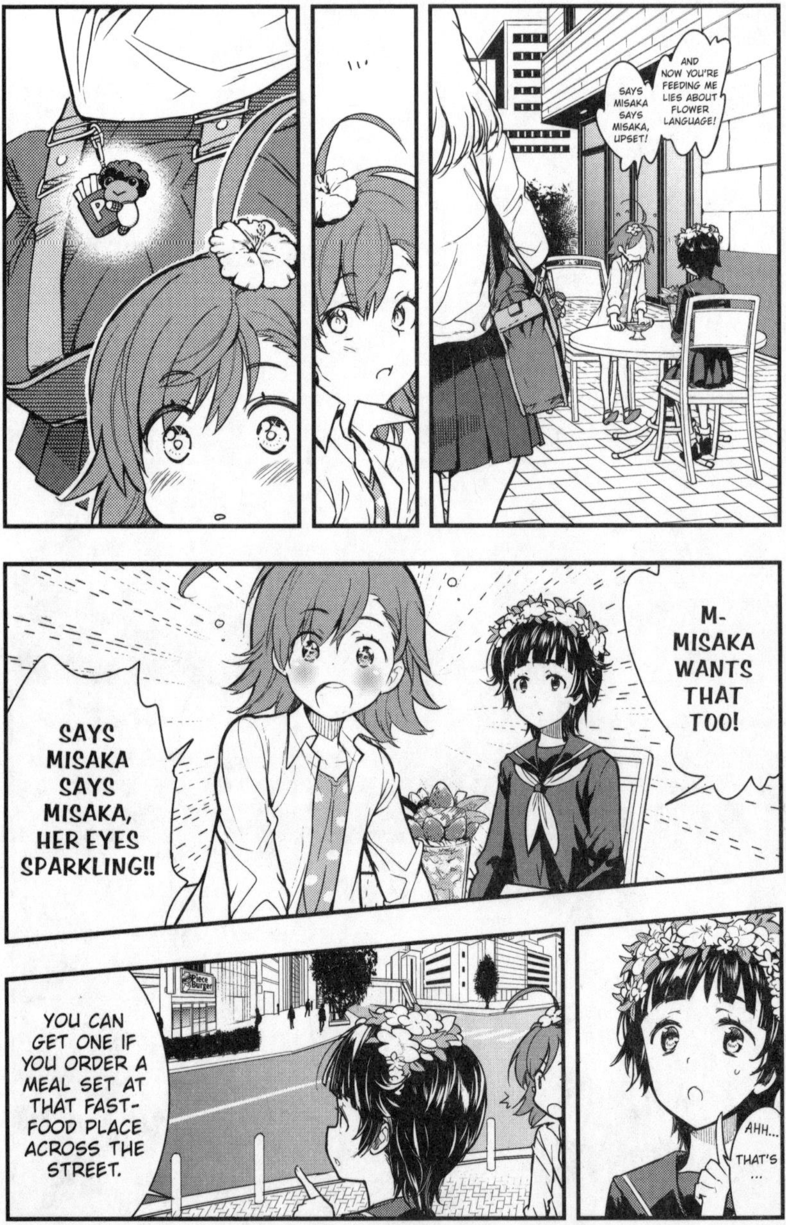
AND NOW YOU'RE FEEDING ME LIES ABOUT FLOWER LANGUAGE!
SAYS MISAKA SAYS MISAKA, UPSET!
M-MISAKA WANTS THAT TOO!
SAYS MISAKA SAYS MISAKA, HER EYES SPARKLING!!
AHH... THAT'S ...
Piece Burger
YOU CAN GET ONE IF YOU ORDER A MEAL SET AT THAT FAST-FOOD PLACE ACROSS THE STREET.

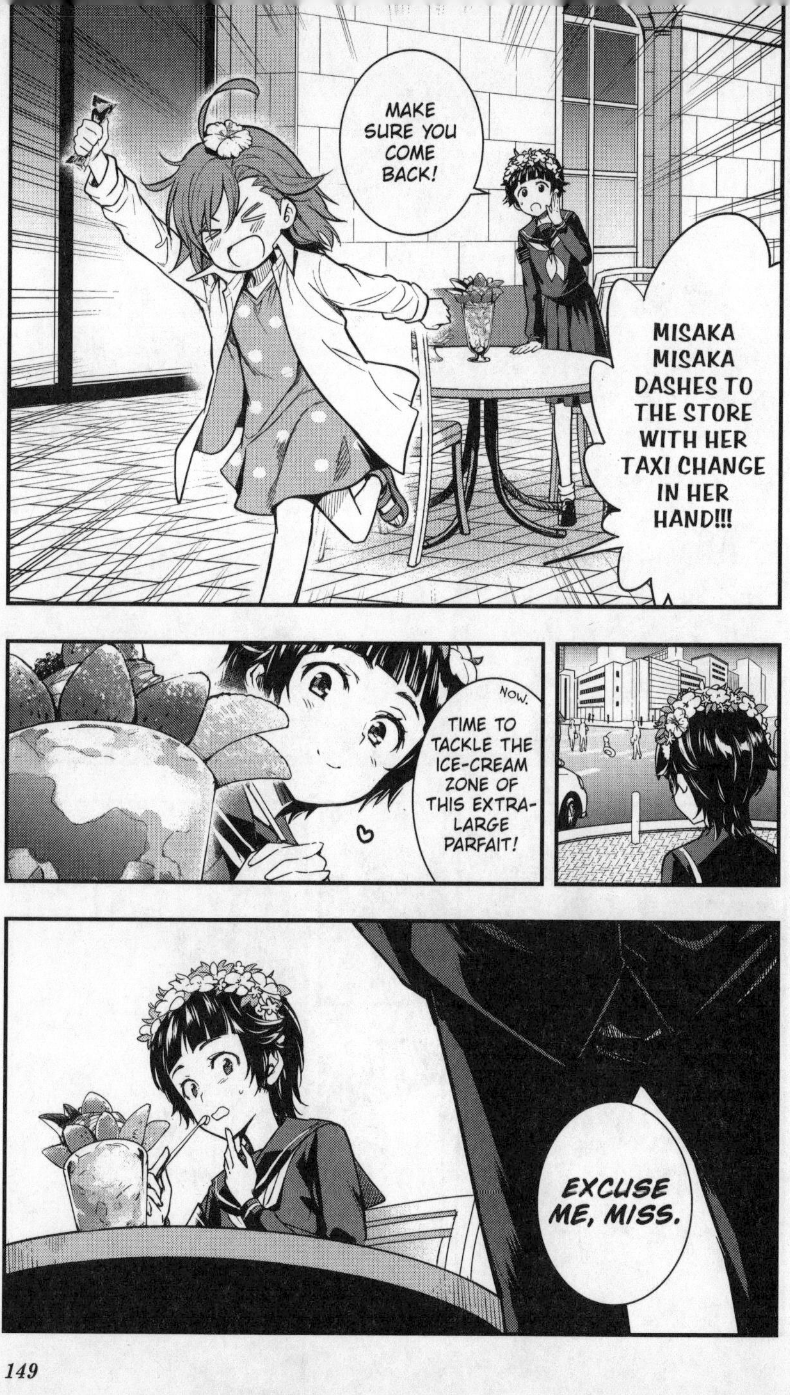
MISAKA MISAKA DASHES TO THE STORE WITH HER TAXI CHANGE IN HER HAND!!!
MAKE SURE YOU COME BACK!
NOW.
TIME TO TACKLE THE ICE-CREAM ZONE OF THIS EXTRA-LARGE PARFAIT!
EXCUSE ME, MISS.

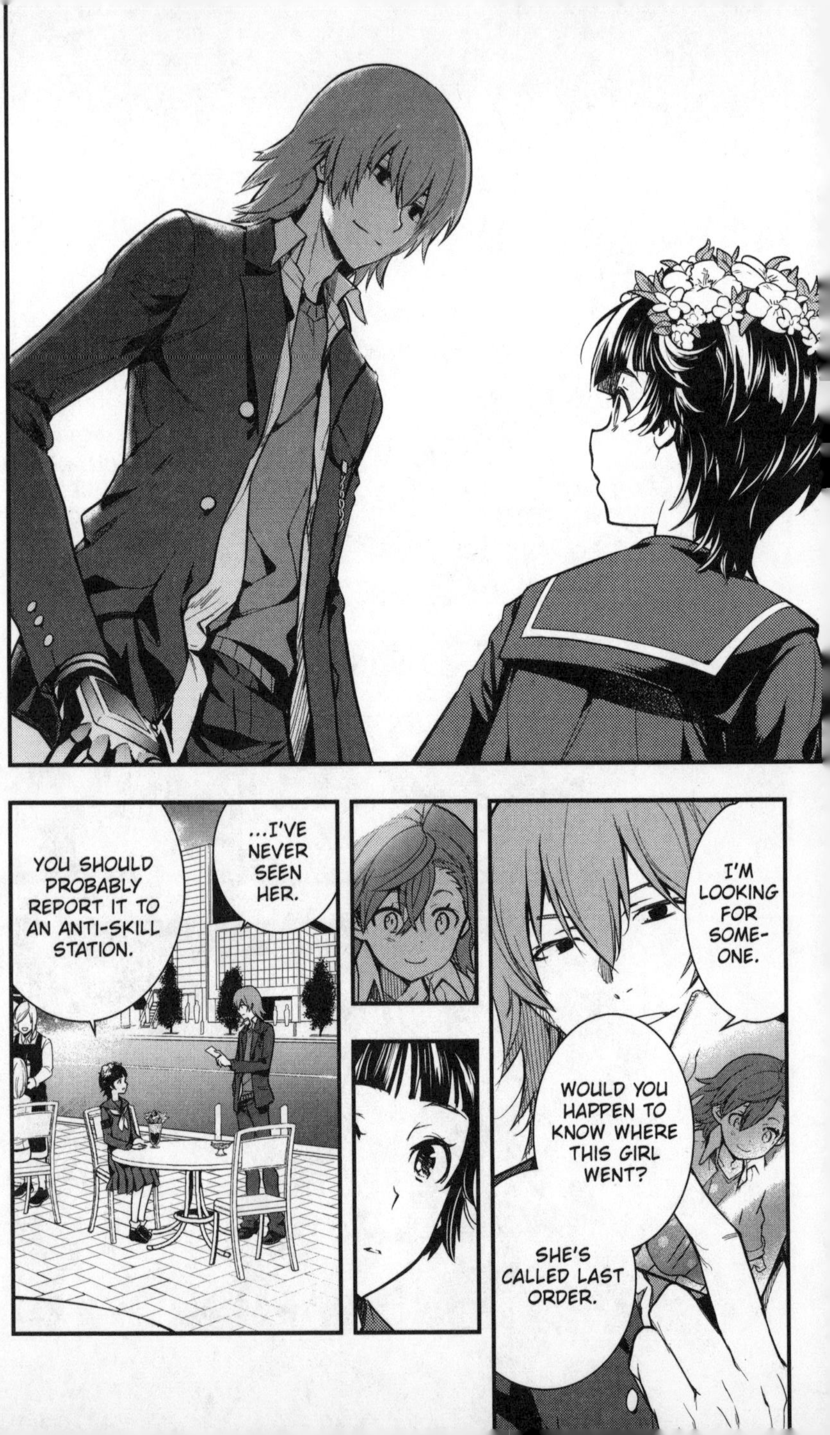
I'M LOOKING FOR SOME-ONE.
WOULD YOU HAPPEN TO KNOW WHERE THIS GIRL WENT?
SHE'S CALLED LAST ORDER.
...I'VE NEVER SEEN HER.
YOU SHOULD PROBABLY REPORT IT TO AN ANTI-SKILL STATION.

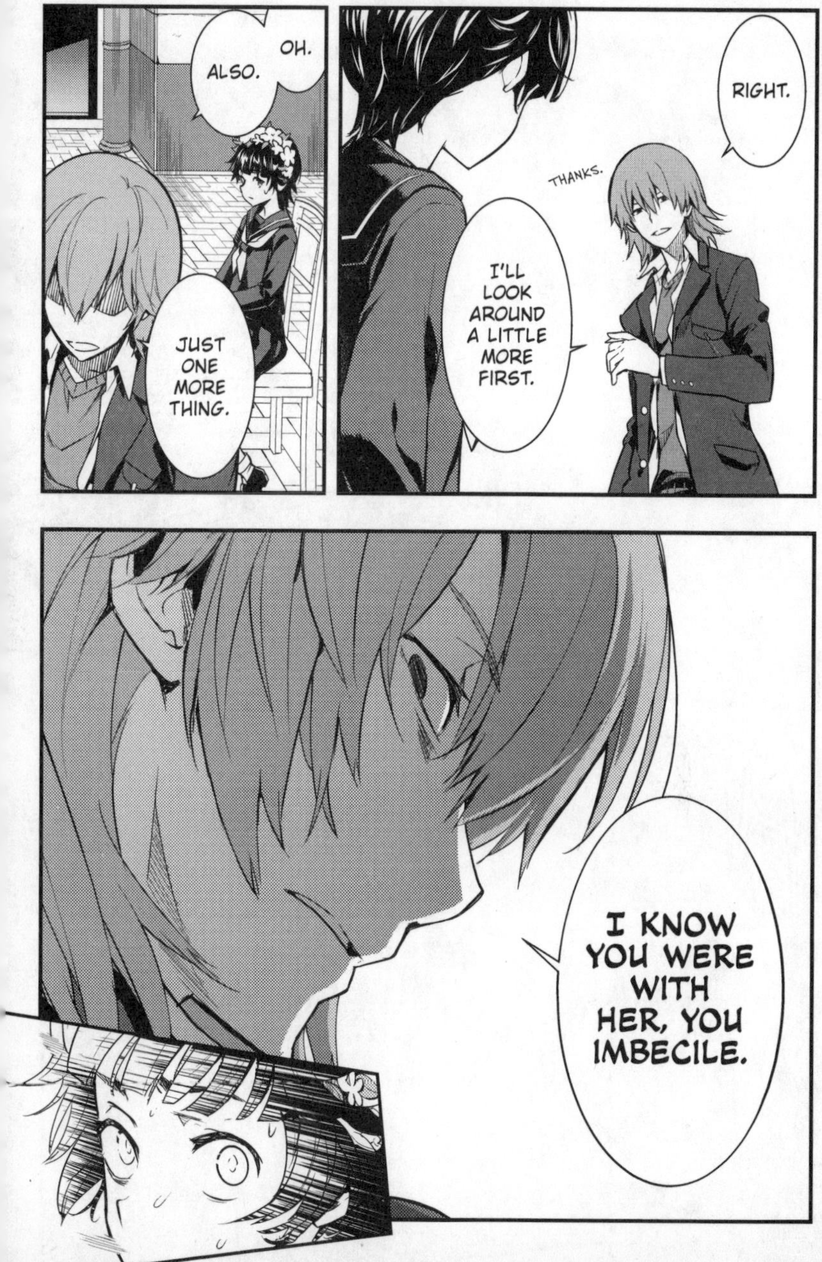
RIGHT.
THANKS.
I'LL LOOK AROUND A LITTLE MORE FIRST.
OH. ALSO.
JUST ONE MORE THING.
I KNOW YOU WERE WITH HER, YOU IMBECILE.

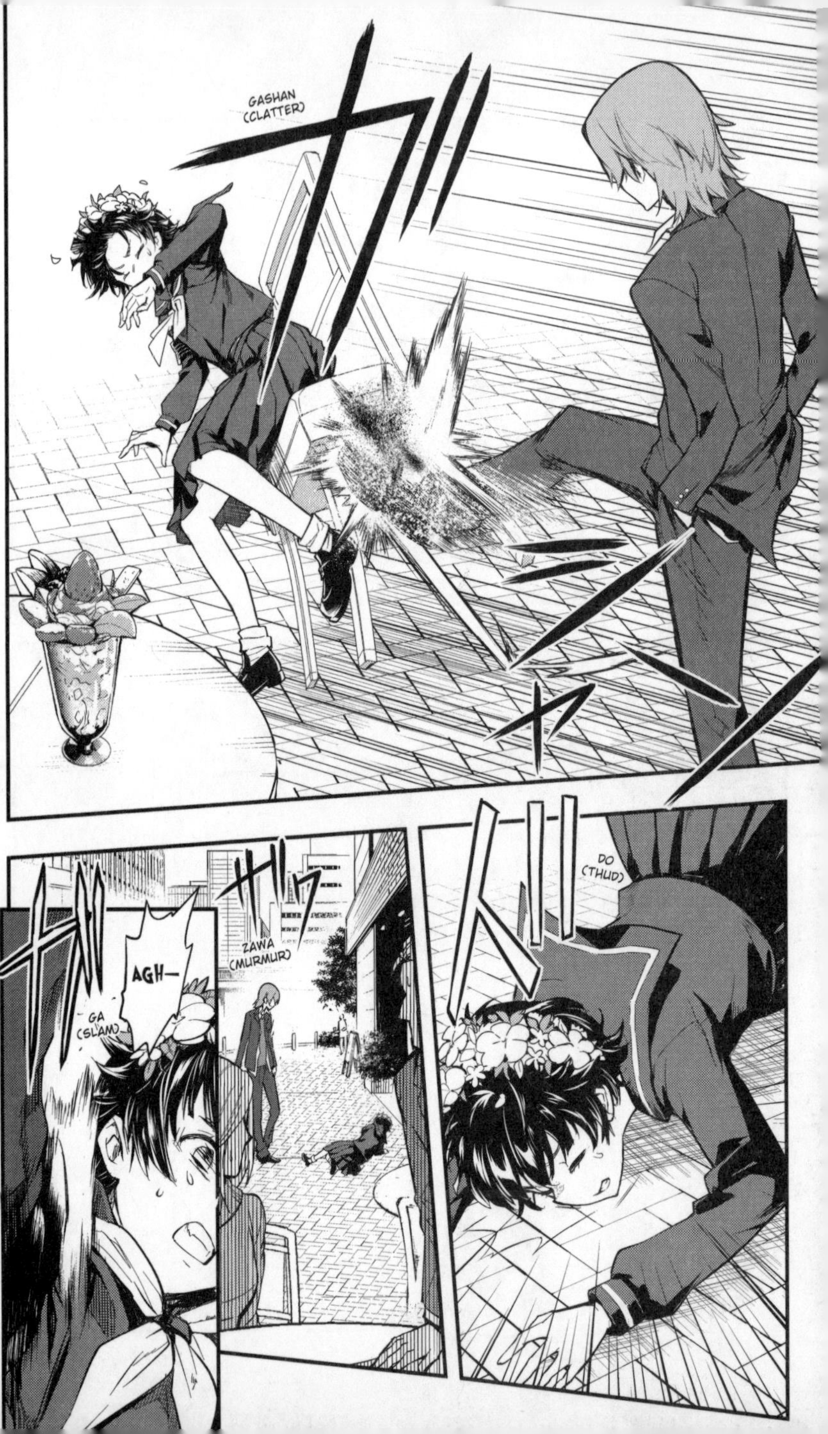
GASHAN (CLATTER)
DO (THUD)
ZAWA (MURMUR)
AGH—
GA (SLAM)

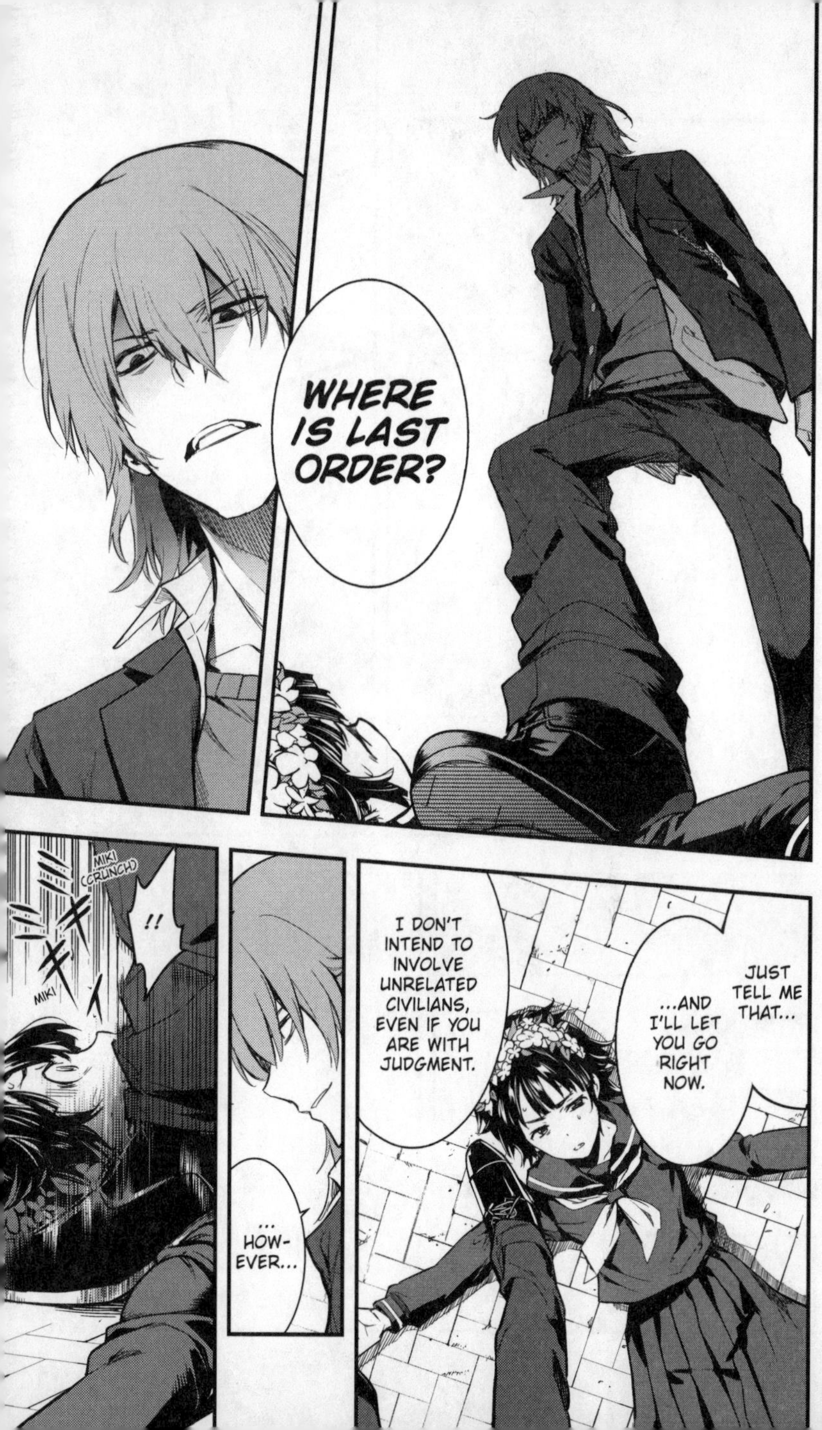

WHERE IS LAST ORDER?
JUST TELL ME THAT...
...AND I'LL LET YOU GO RIGHT NOW.
I DON'T INTEND TO INVOLVE UNRELATED CIVILIANS, EVEN IF YOU ARE WITH JUDGMENT.
... HOW-EVER...
MIKI (CRUNCH)
!!
MIKI

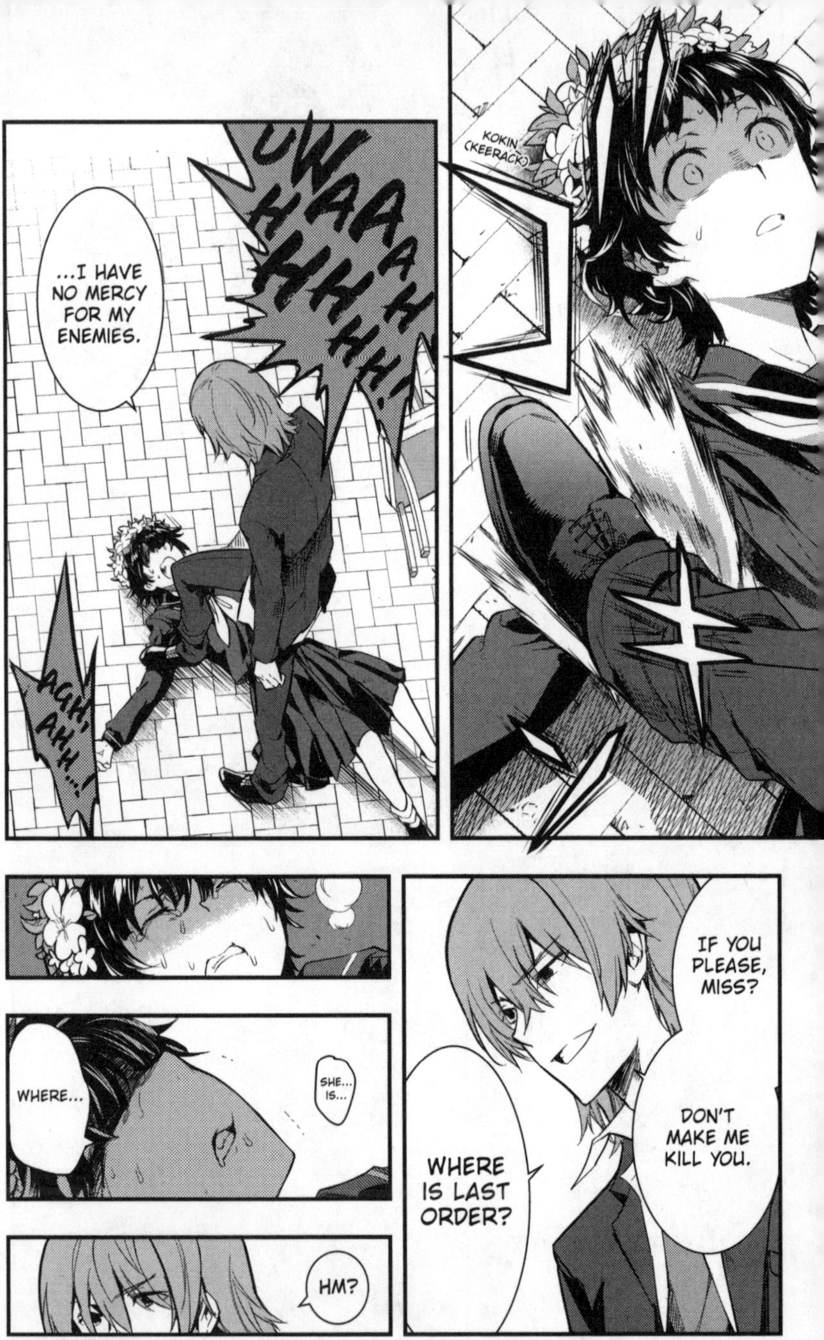
KOKIN (KEERACK)
UWAAAAHHHHHH!!
...I HAVE NO MERCY FOR MY ENEMIES.
AGH, AHH...!
IF YOU PLEASE, MISS?
DON'T MAKE ME KILL YOU.
WHERE IS LAST ORDER?
WHERE...
SHE... IS...
HM?

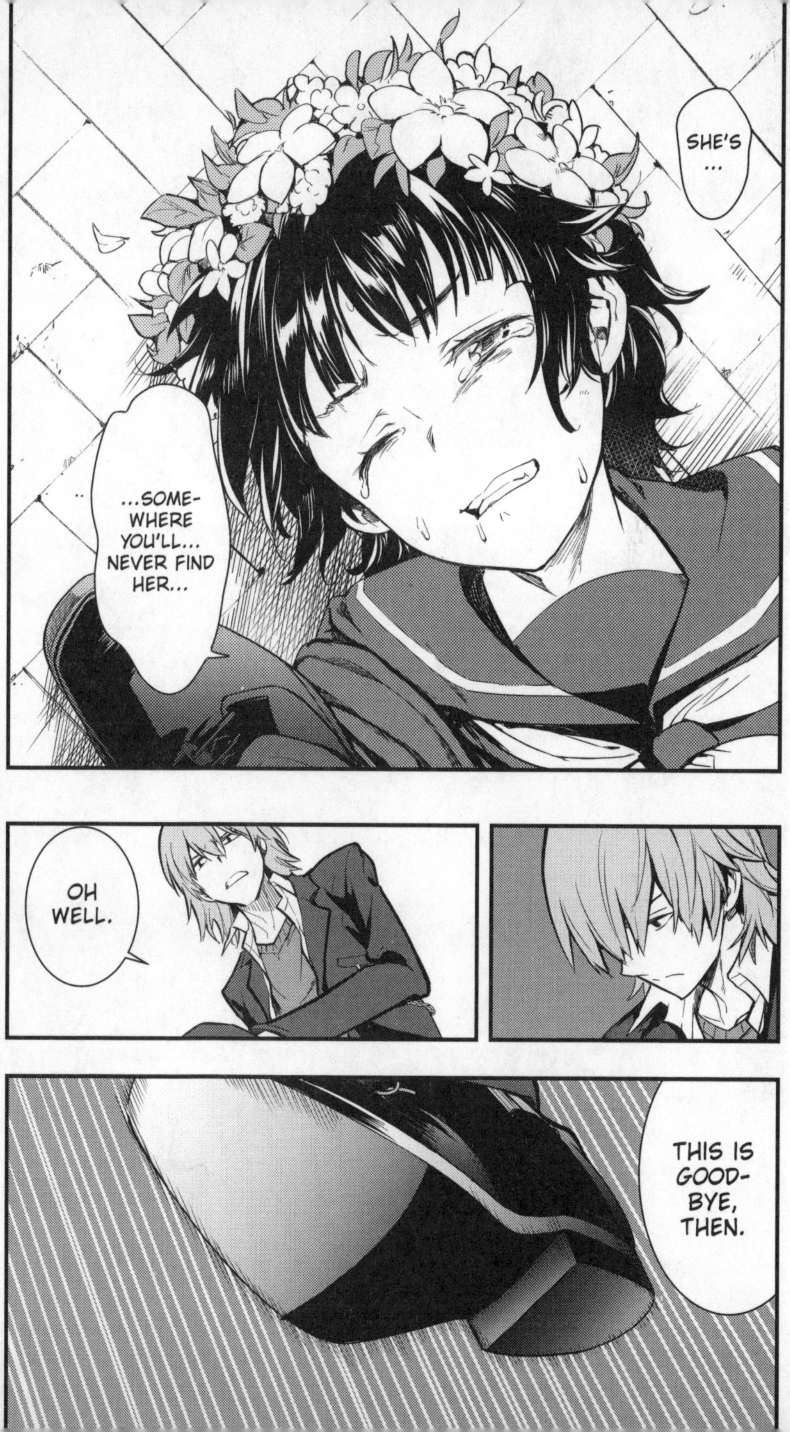
SHE'S ...
...SOME-WHERE YOU'LL... NEVER FIND HER...
OH WELL.
THIS IS GOOD-BYE, THEN.

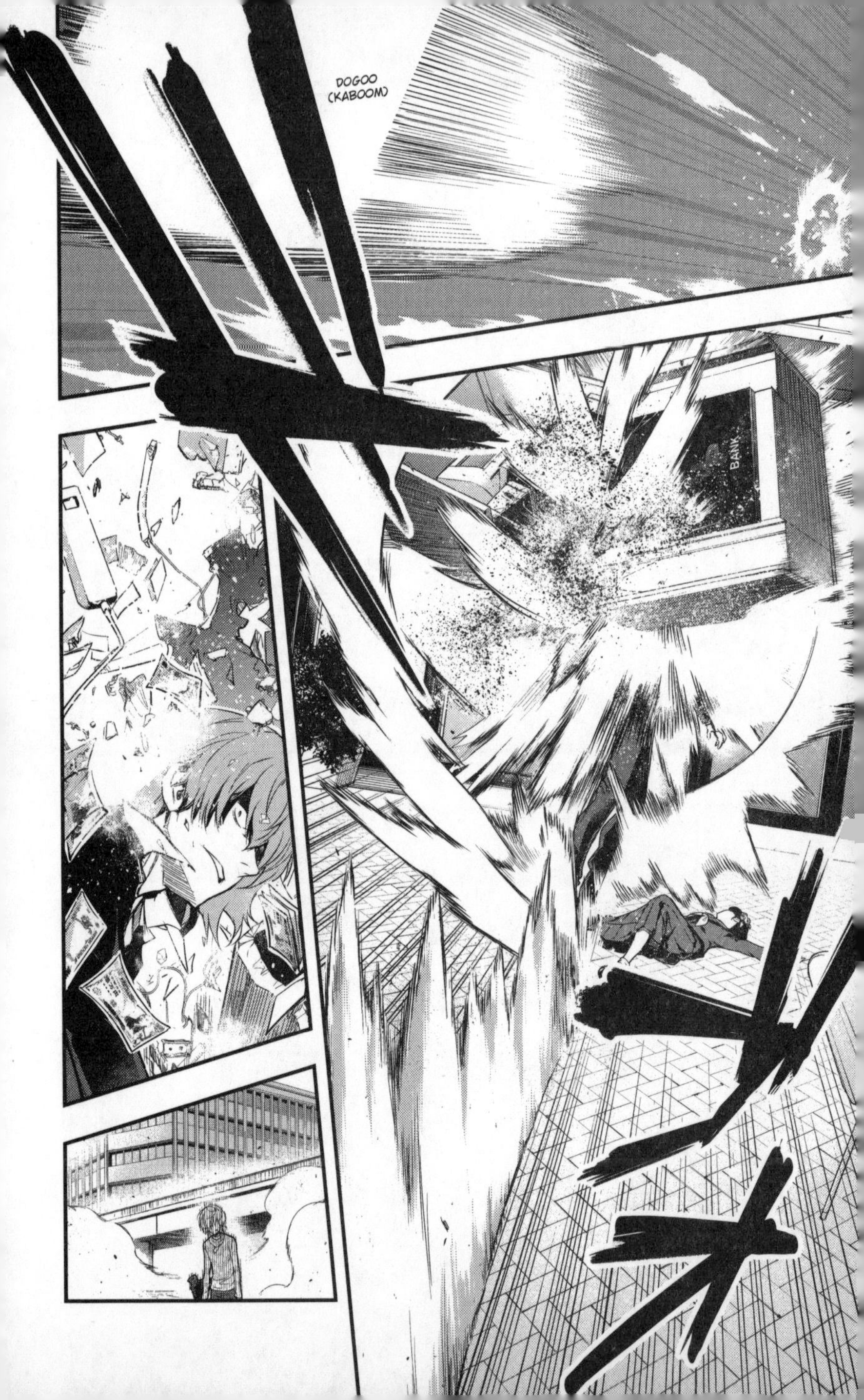
DOGOO
(KABOOM)
BANK

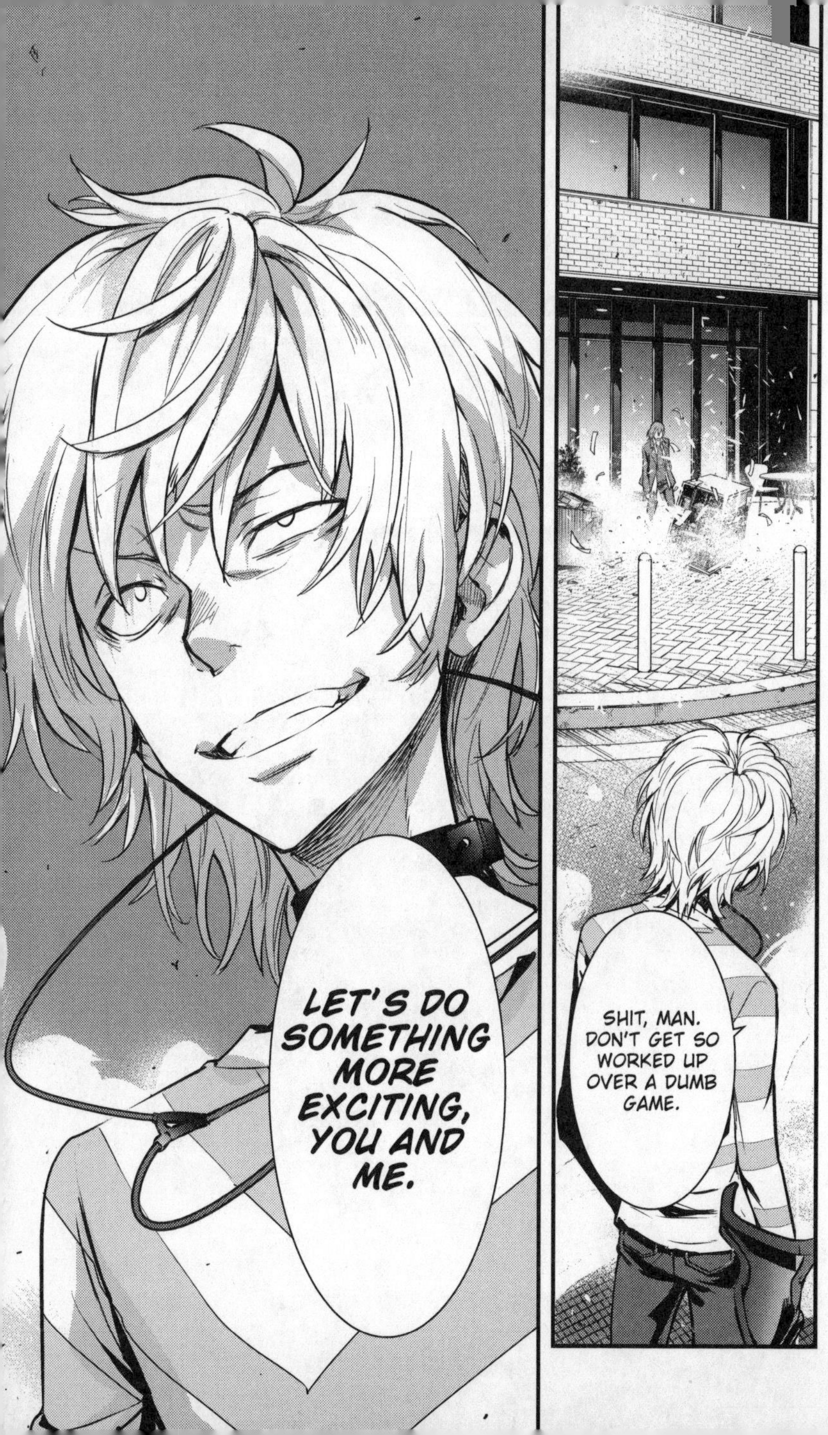
SHIT, MAN. DON'T GET SO WORKED UP OVER A DUMB GAME.
LET'S DO SOMETHING MORE EXCITING, YOU AND ME.

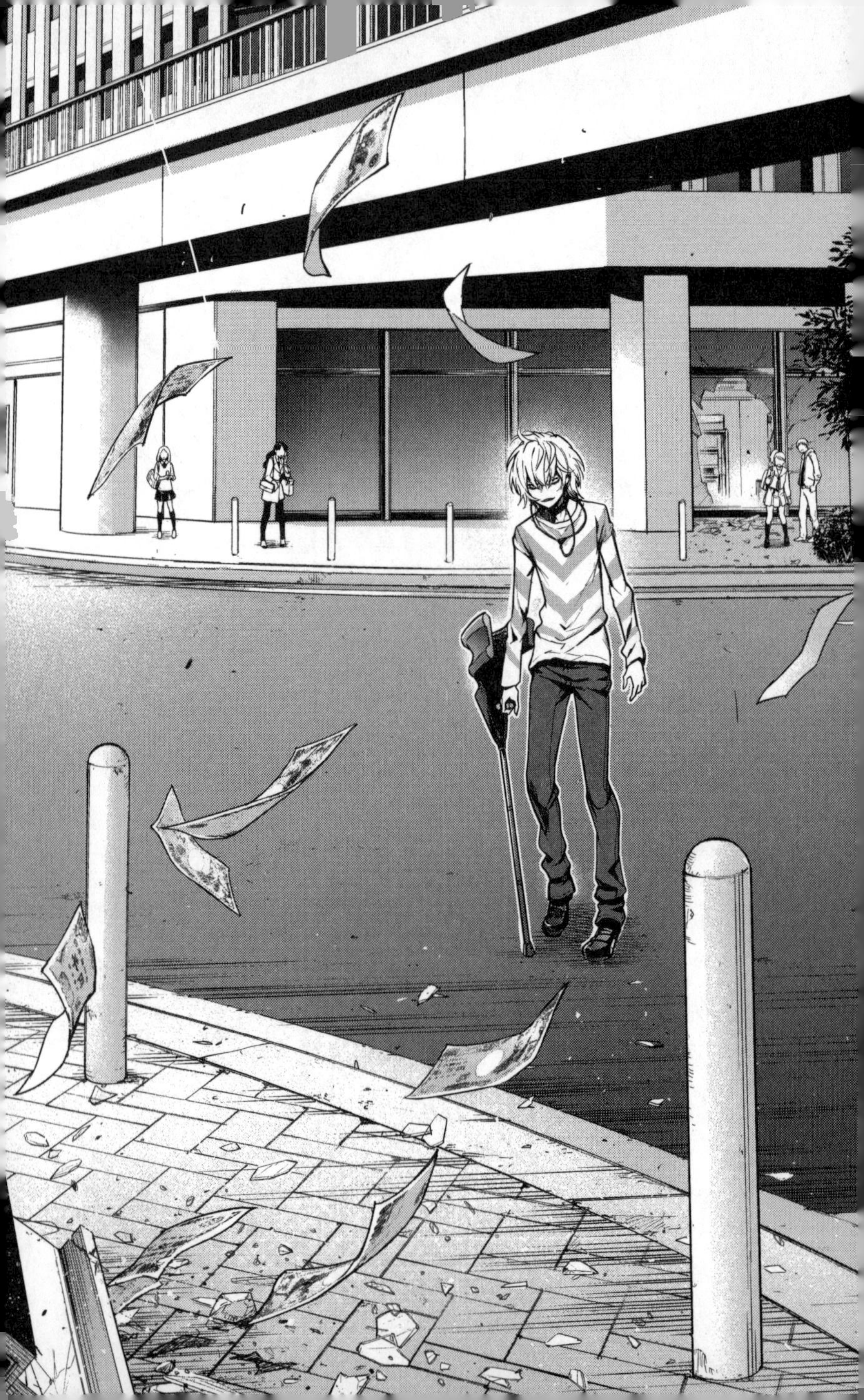

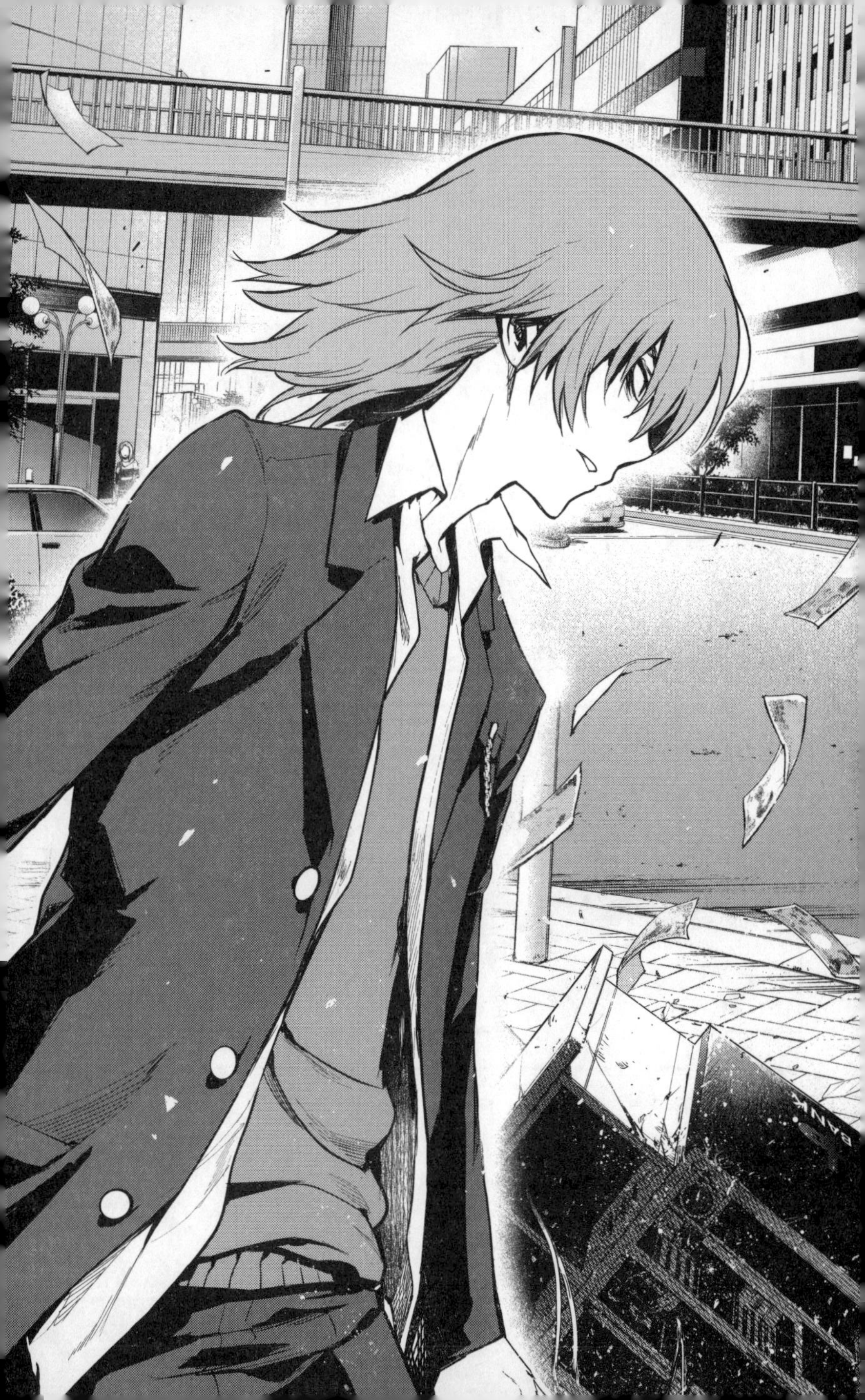
BANK

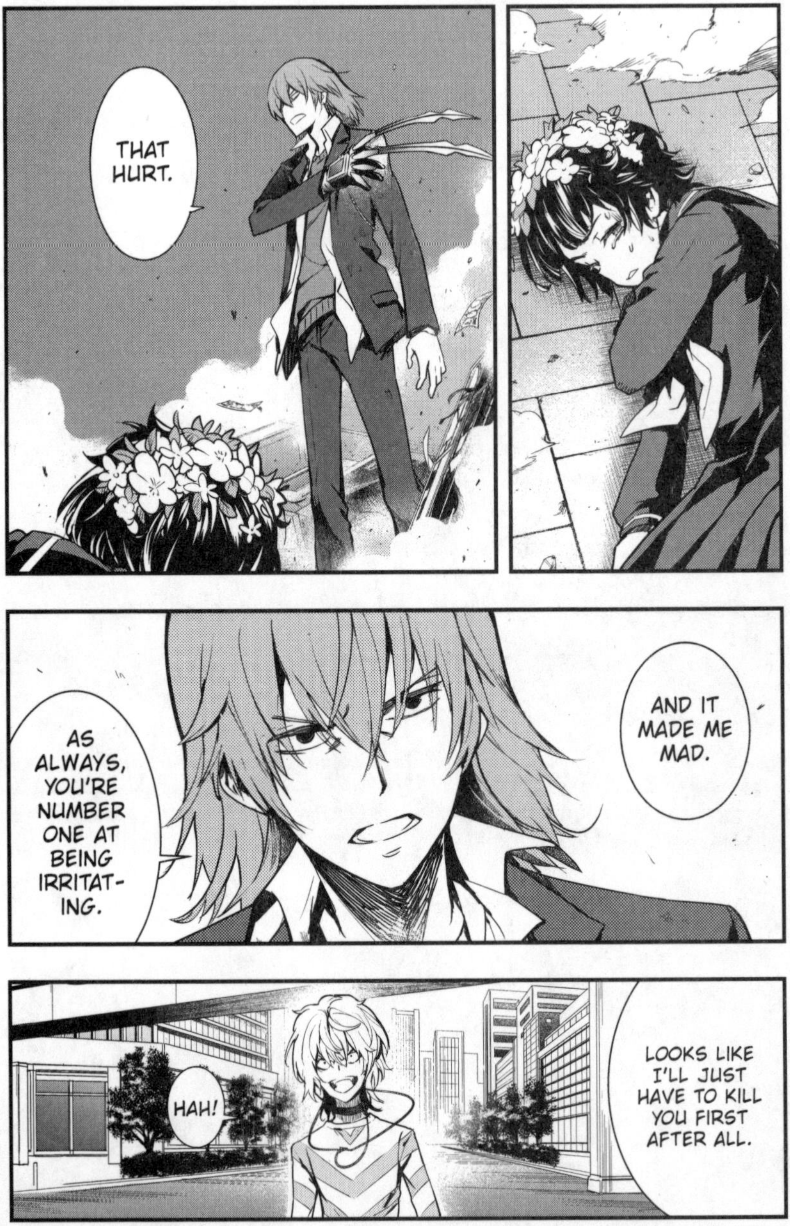
THAT HURT.
AND IT MADE ME MAD.
AS ALWAYS, YOU'RE NUMBER ONE AT BEING IRRITAT-ING.
LOOKS LIKE I'LL JUST HAVE TO KILL YOU FIRST AFTER ALL.
HAH!

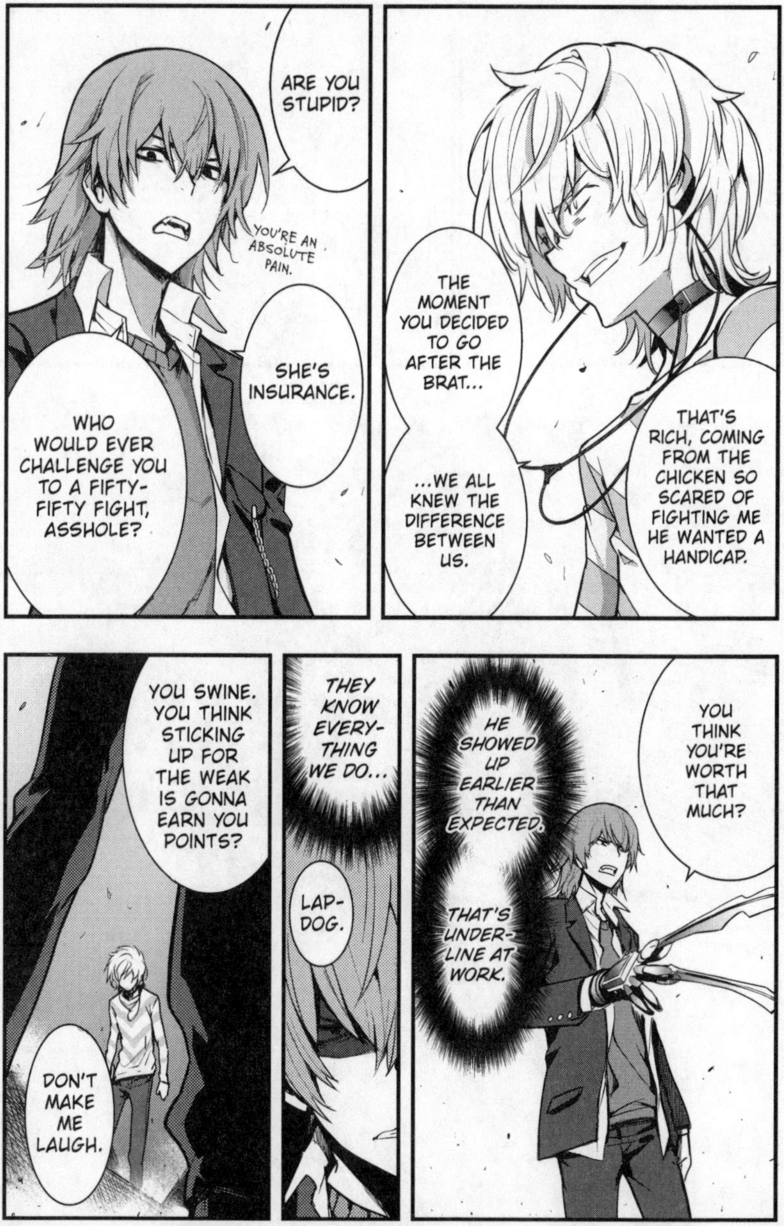
THAT'S RICH, COMING FROM THE CHICKEN SO SCARED OF FIGHTING ME HE WANTED A HANDICAP.
THE MOMENT YOU DECIDED TO GO AFTER THE BRAT...
...WE ALL KNEW THE DIFFERENCE BETWEEN US.
ARE YOU STUPID?
YOU'RE AN ABSOLUTE PAIN.
SHE'S INSURANCE.
WHO WOULD EVER CHALLENGE YOU TO A FIFTY-FIFTY FIGHT, ASSHOLE?
YOU THINK YOU'RE WORTH THAT MUCH?
HE SHOWED UP EARLIER THAN EXPECTED.
THAT'S UNDER-LINE AT WORK.
THEY KNOW EVERY-THING WE DO...
LAP-DOG.
YOU SWINE. YOU THINK STICKING UP FOR THE WEAK IS GONNA EARN YOU POINTS?
DON'T MAKE ME LAUGH.

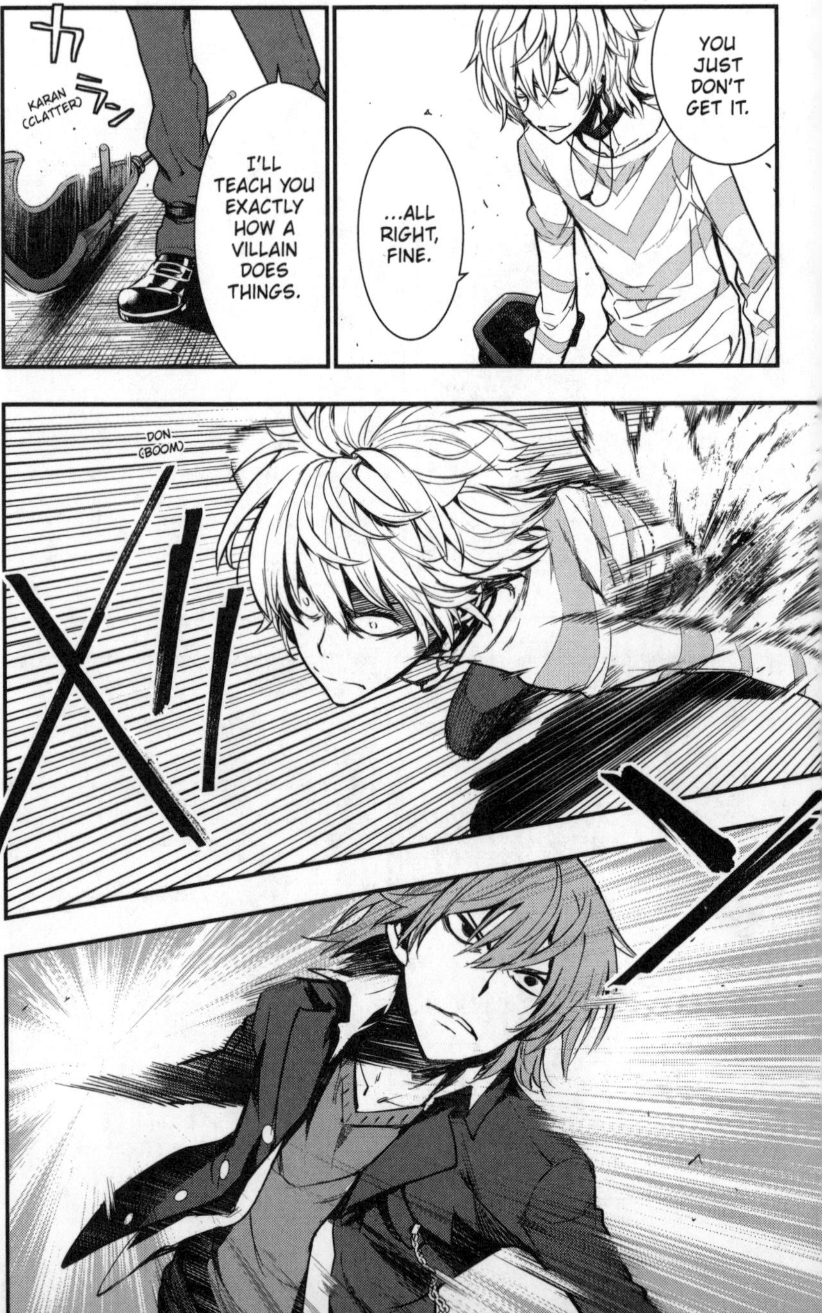
YOU JUST DON'T GET IT.
...ALL RIGHT, FINE.
I'LL TEACH YOU EXACTLY HOW A VILLAIN DOES THINGS.
KARAN (CLATTER)
DON (BOOM)

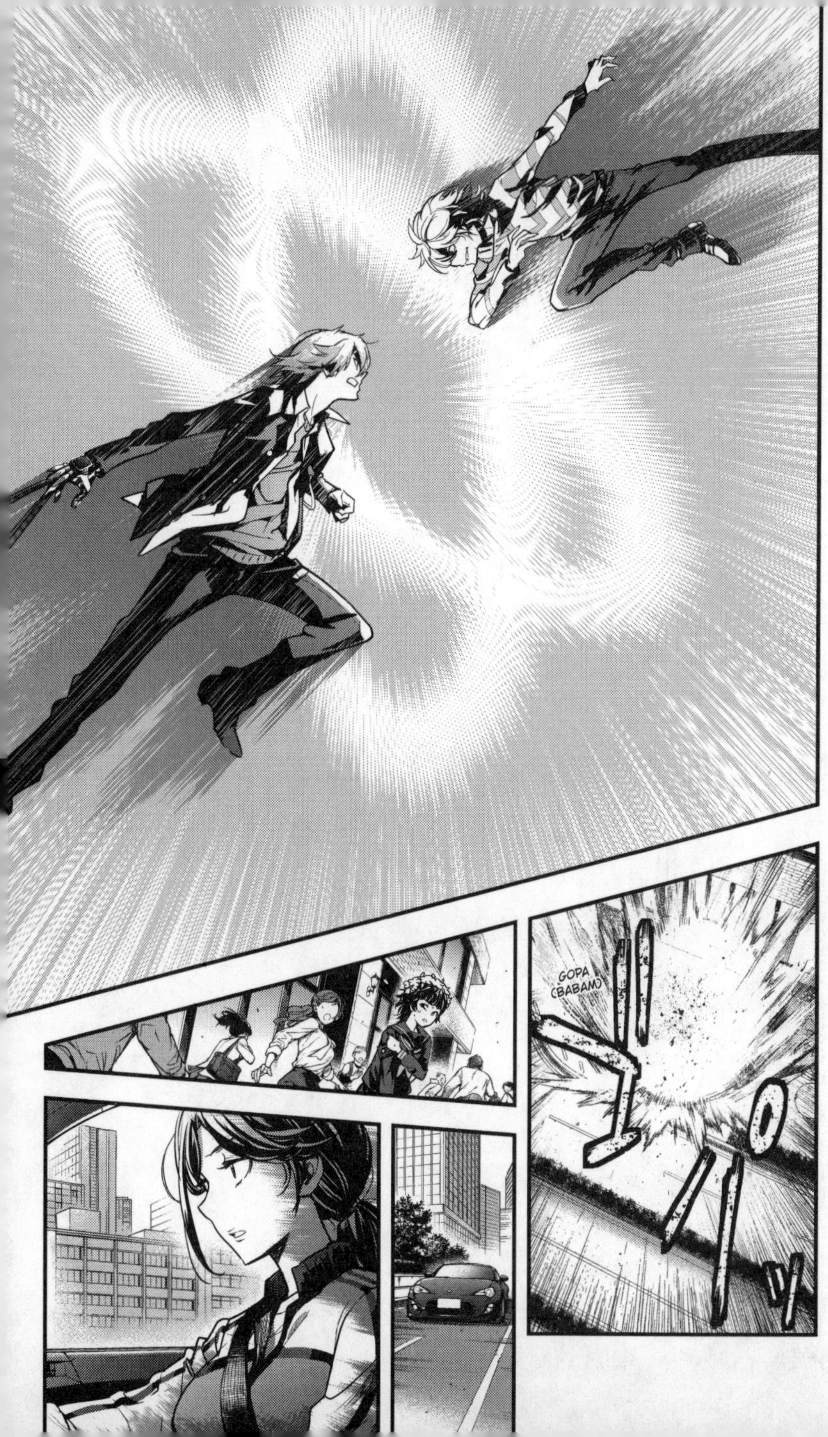
GOPA
(BABAM)

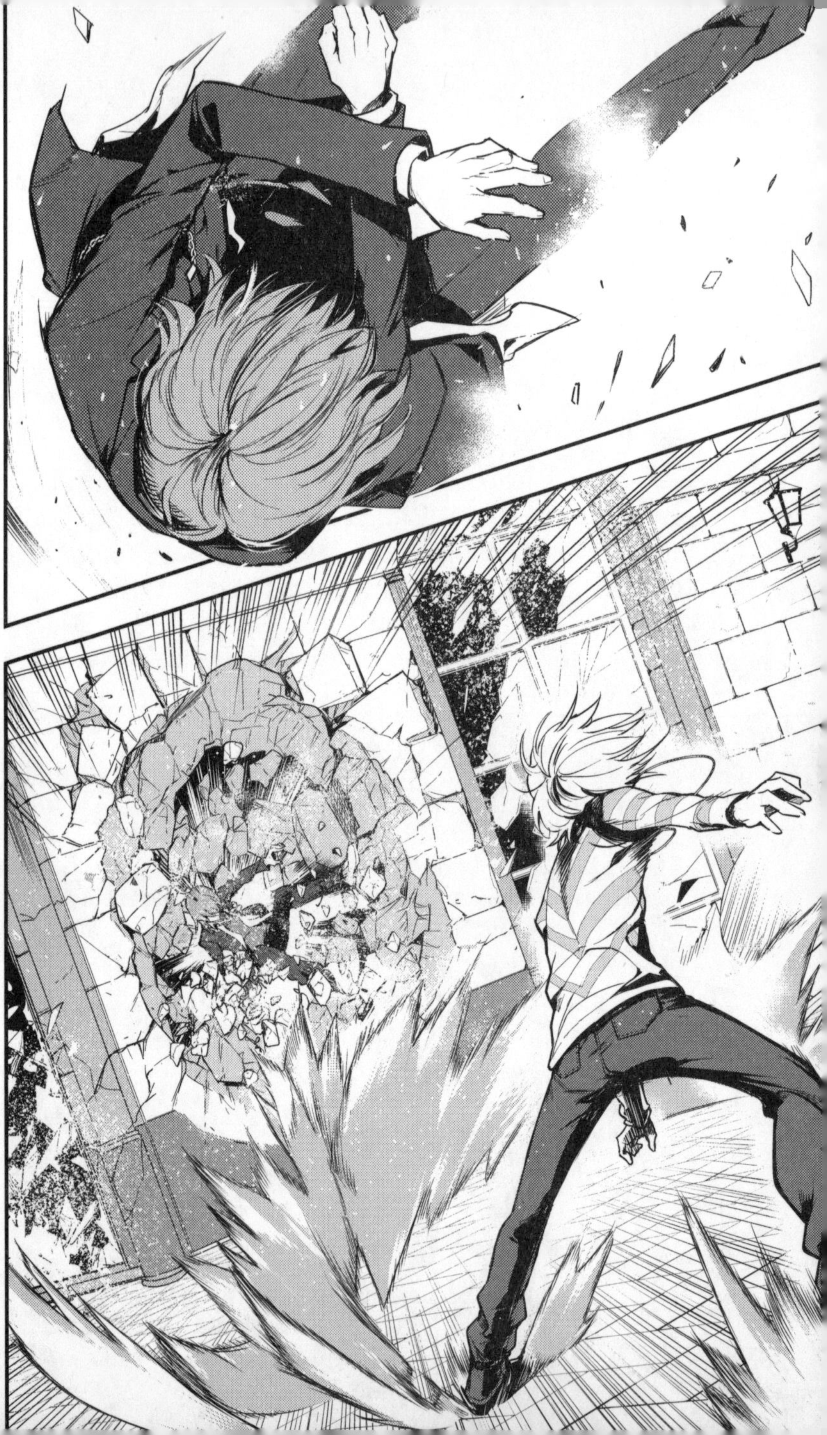

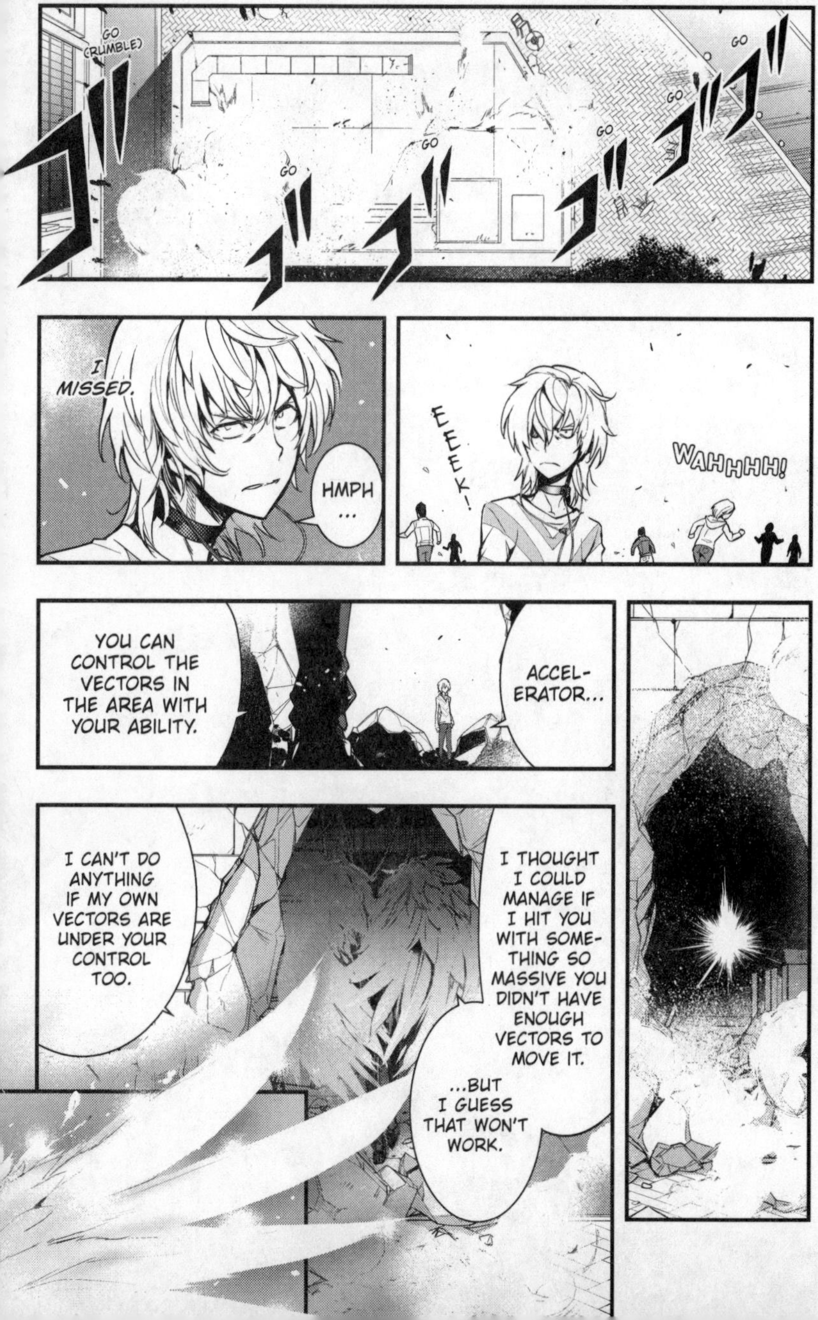
GO
GO
GO
GO
GO (RUMBLE)
WAHHHH!
EEEEK!
I MISSED.
HMPH...
ACCEL-ERATOR...
YOU CAN CONTROL THE VECTORS IN THE AREA WITH YOUR ABILITY.
I THOUGHT I COULD MANAGE IF I HIT YOU WITH SOME-THING SO MASSIVE YOU DIDN'T HAVE ENOUGH VECTORS TO MOVE IT.
...BUT I GUESS THAT WON'T WORK.
I CAN'T DO ANYTHING IF MY OWN VECTORS ARE UNDER YOUR CONTROL TOO.

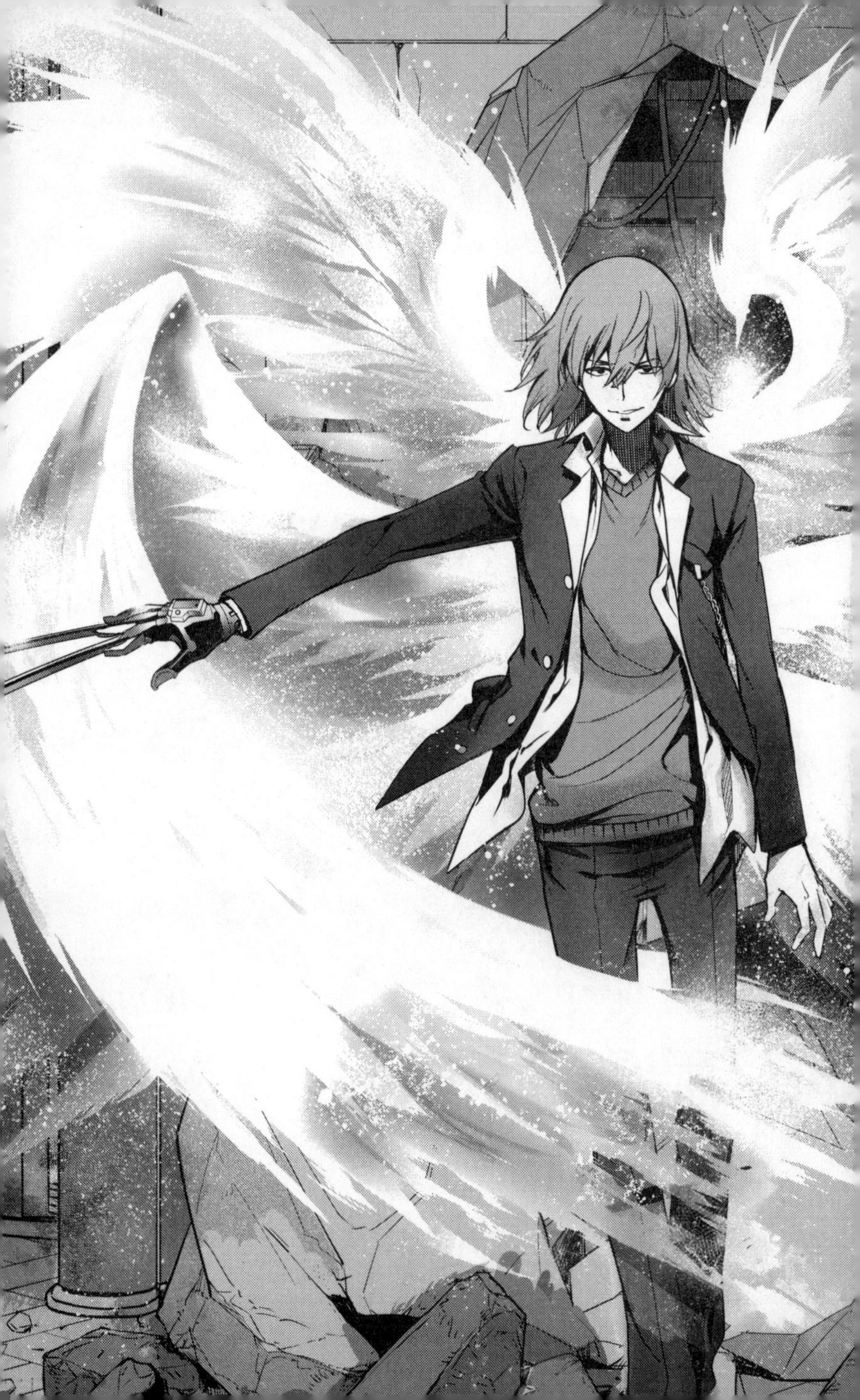

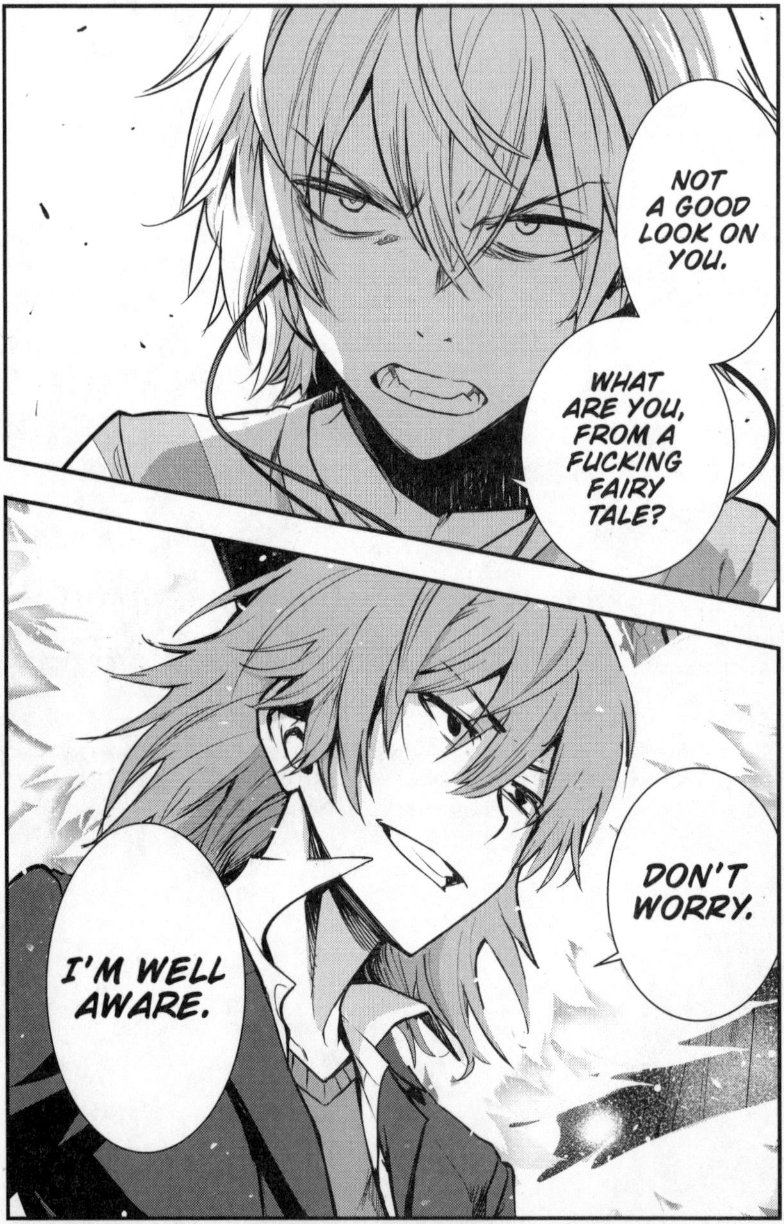
NOT A GOOD LOOK ON YOU.
WHAT ARE YOU, FROM A FUCKING FAIRY TALE?
DON'T WORRY.
I'M WELL AWARE.

A Certain Magical Index

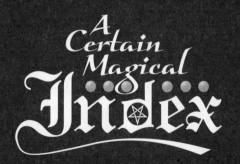

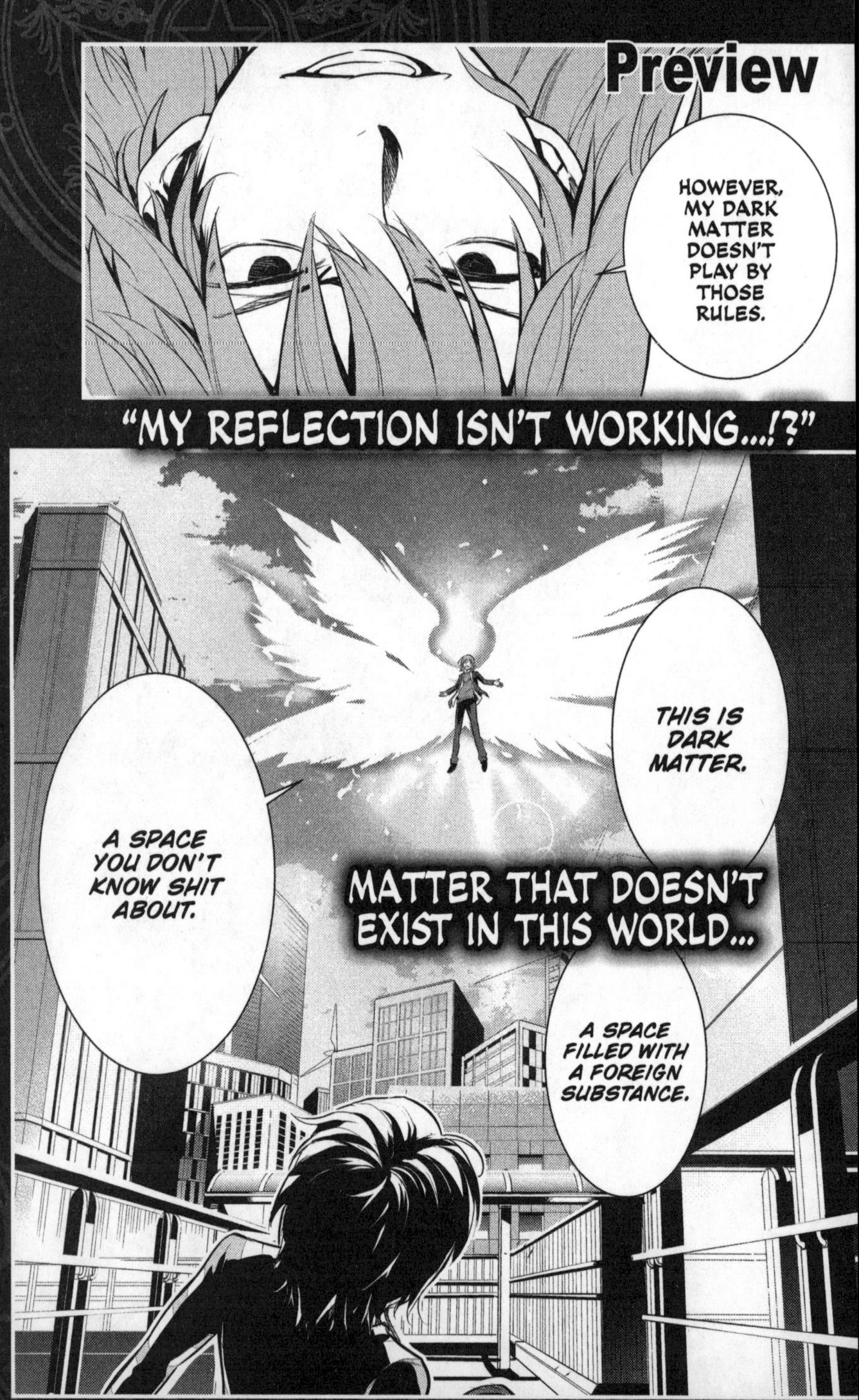
Preview
HOWEVER, MY DARK MATTER DOESN'T PLAY BY THOSE RULES.
"MY REFLECTION ISN'T WORKING...!?"
THIS IS DARK MATTER.
A SPACE FILLED WITH A FOREIGN SUBSTANCE.
A SPACE YOU DON'T KNOW SHIT ABOUT.
MATTER THAT DOESN'T EXIST IN THIS WORLD...

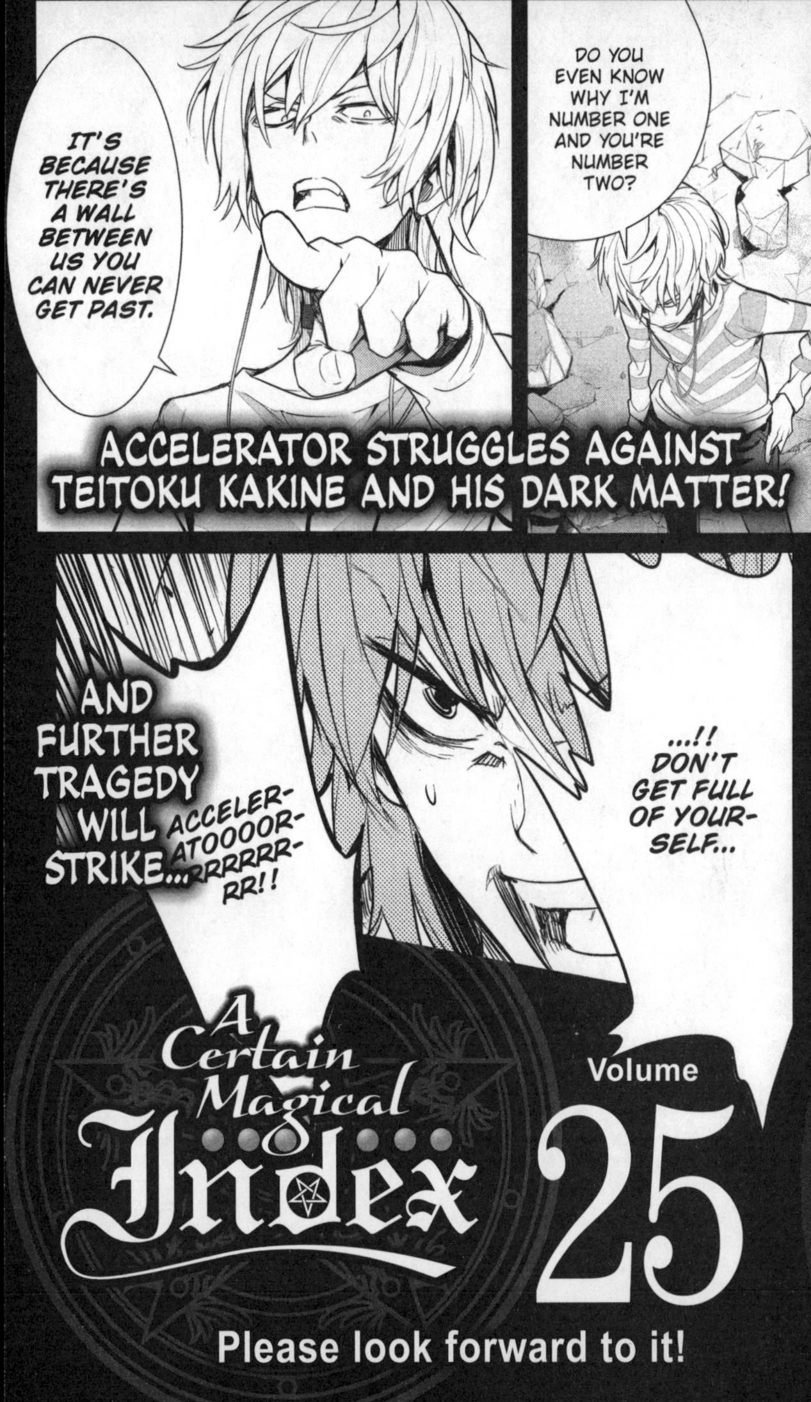
DO YOU EVEN KNOW WHY I'M NUMBER ONE AND YOU'RE NUMBER TWO?
IT'S BECAUSE THERE'S A WALL BETWEEN US YOU CAN NEVER GET PAST.
ACCELERATOR STRUGGLES AGAINST TEITOKU KAKINE AND HIS DARK MATTER!
...!! DON'T GET FULL OF YOURSELF...
ACCELERATOOOORRRRRRRR!!
AND FURTHER TRAGEDY WILL STRIKE...
A Certain Magical Index
Volume 25
Please look forward to it!

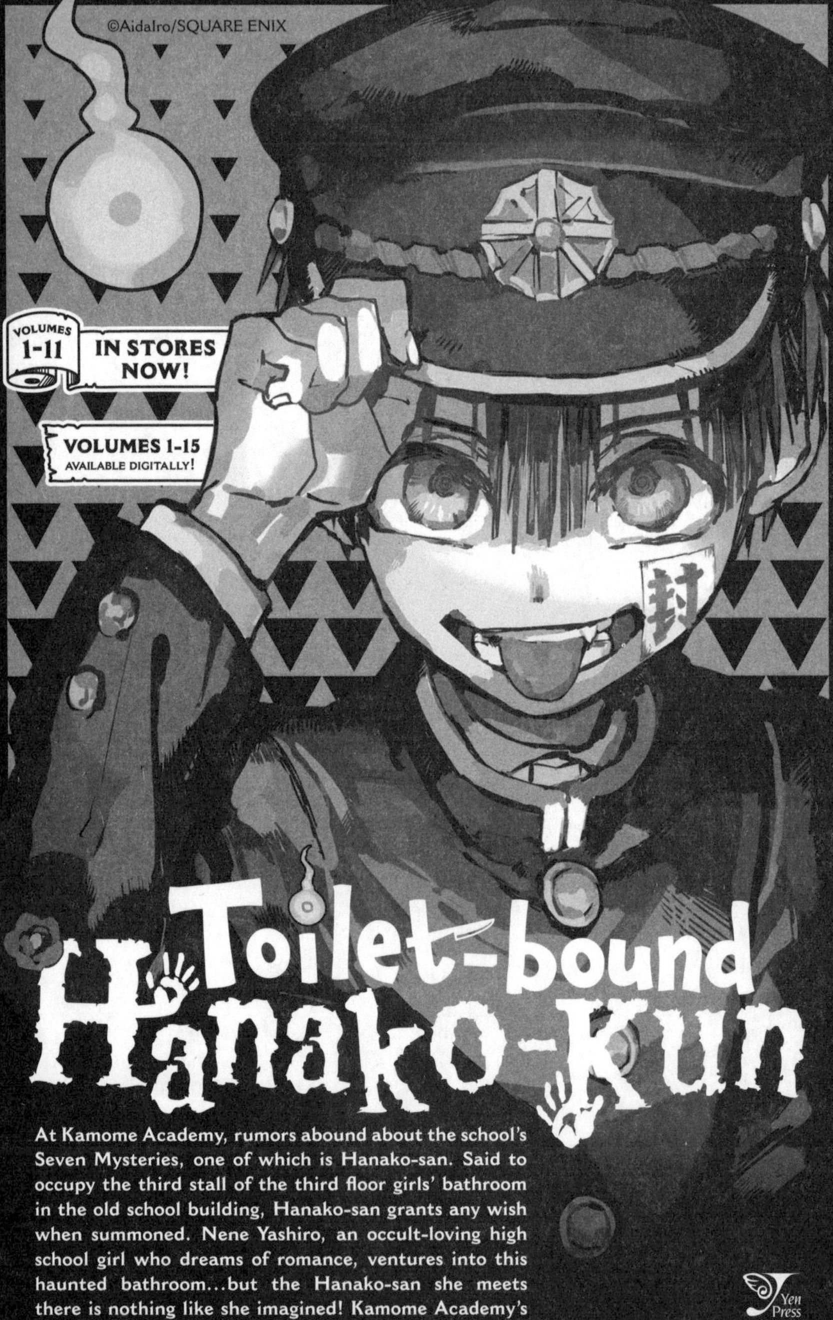
©AidaIro/SQUARE ENIX
VOLUMES 1-11 IN STORES NOW!
VOLUMES 1-15 AVAILABLE DIGITALLY!
Toilet-bound Hanako-Kun
At Kamome Academy, rumors abound about the school's Seven Mysteries, one of which is Hanako-san. Said to occupy the third stall of the third floor girls' bathroom in the old school building, Hanako-san grants any wish when summoned. Nene Yashiro, an occult-loving high school girl who dreams of romance, ventures into this haunted bathroom...but the Hanako-san she meets there is nothing like she imagined! Kamome Academy's Hanako-san...is a boy!

A fallen angel with falling grades!

Gɑbriel DROPOUT

Vol. 1–9 on sale now!

Gabriel Dropout ©UKAMI / KADOKAWA CORPORATION

Yen Press
www.yenpress.com

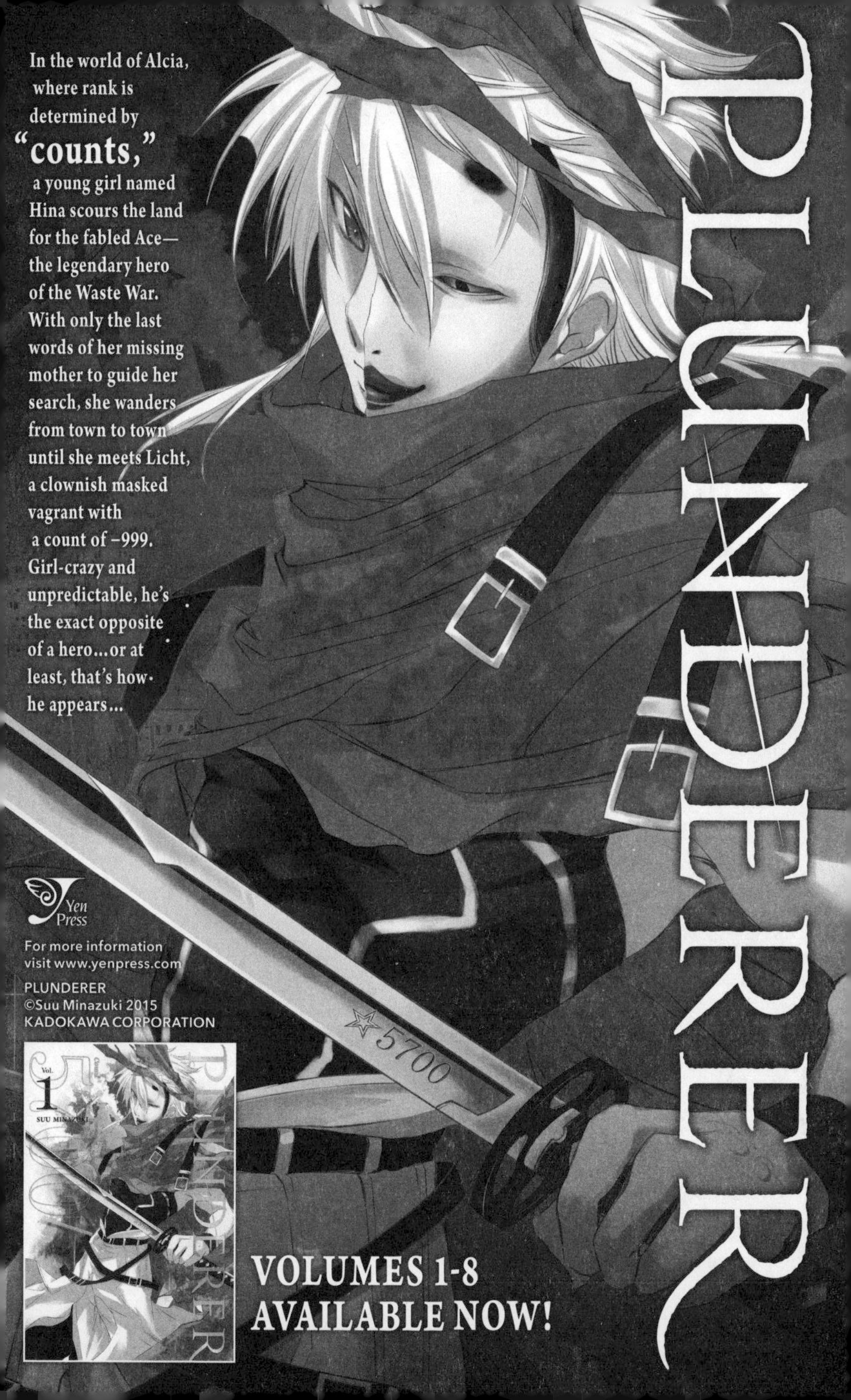
PLUNDERER
In the world of Alcia, where rank is determined by
"counts,"
a young girl named Hina scours the land for the fabled Ace—the legendary hero of the Waste War. With only the last words of her missing mother to guide her search, she wanders from town to town until she meets Licht, a clownish masked vagrant with a count of −999. Girl-crazy and unpredictable, he's the exact opposite of a hero...or at least, that's how he appears...
☆5700
Yen Press
For more information visit www.yenpress.com
PLUNDERER
©Suu Minazuki 2015
KADOKAWA CORPORATION
Vol. 1
SUU MINAZUKI
VOLUMES 1-8
AVAILABLE NOW!

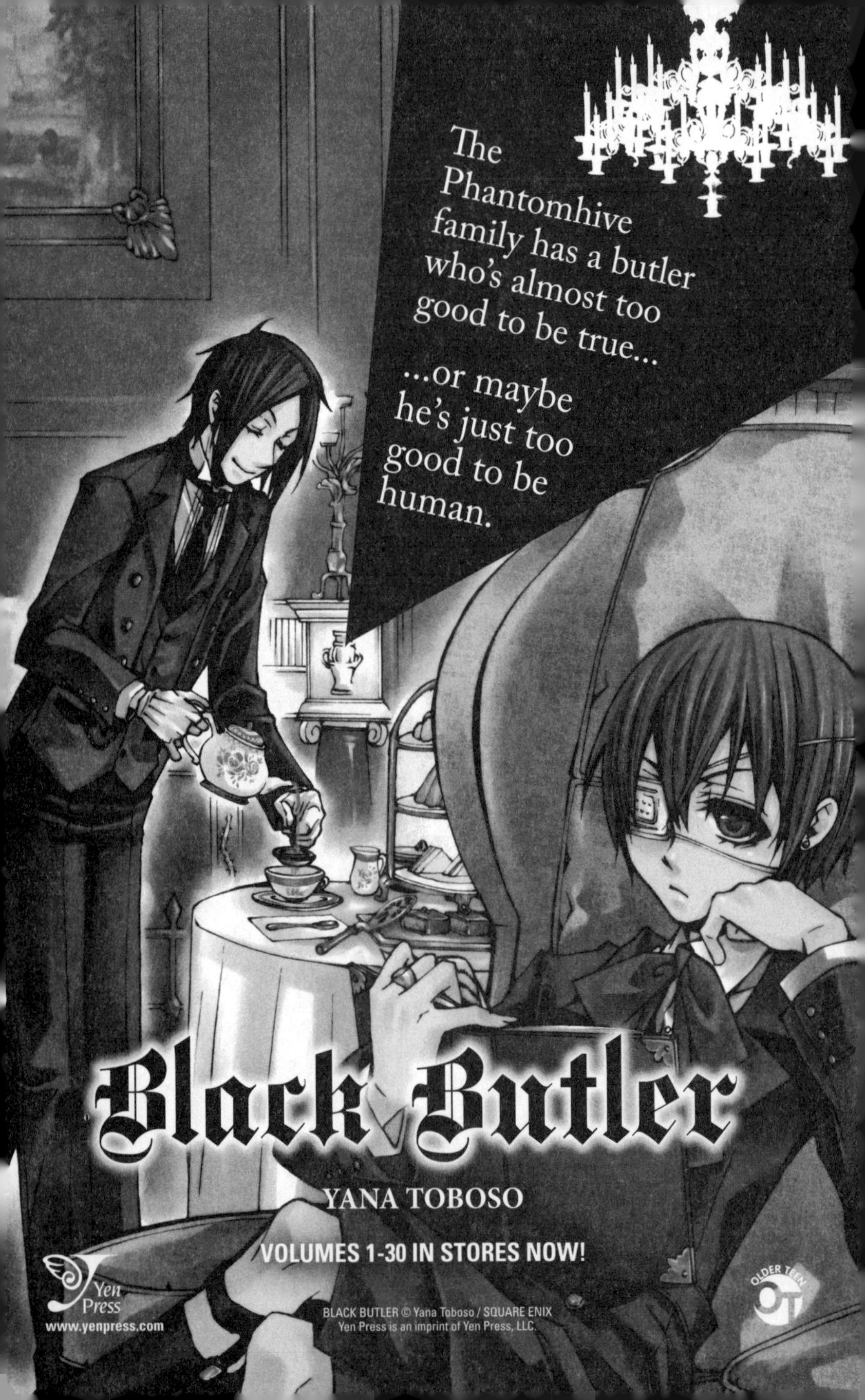

The Phantomhive family has a butler who's almost too good to be true...
...or maybe he's just too good to be human.
Black Butler
YANA TOBOSO
VOLUMES 1-30 IN STORES NOW!
Yen Press
www.yenpress.com
BLACK BUTLER © Yana Toboso / SQUARE ENIX
Yen Press is an imprint of Yen Press, LLC.
OLDER TEEN
OT

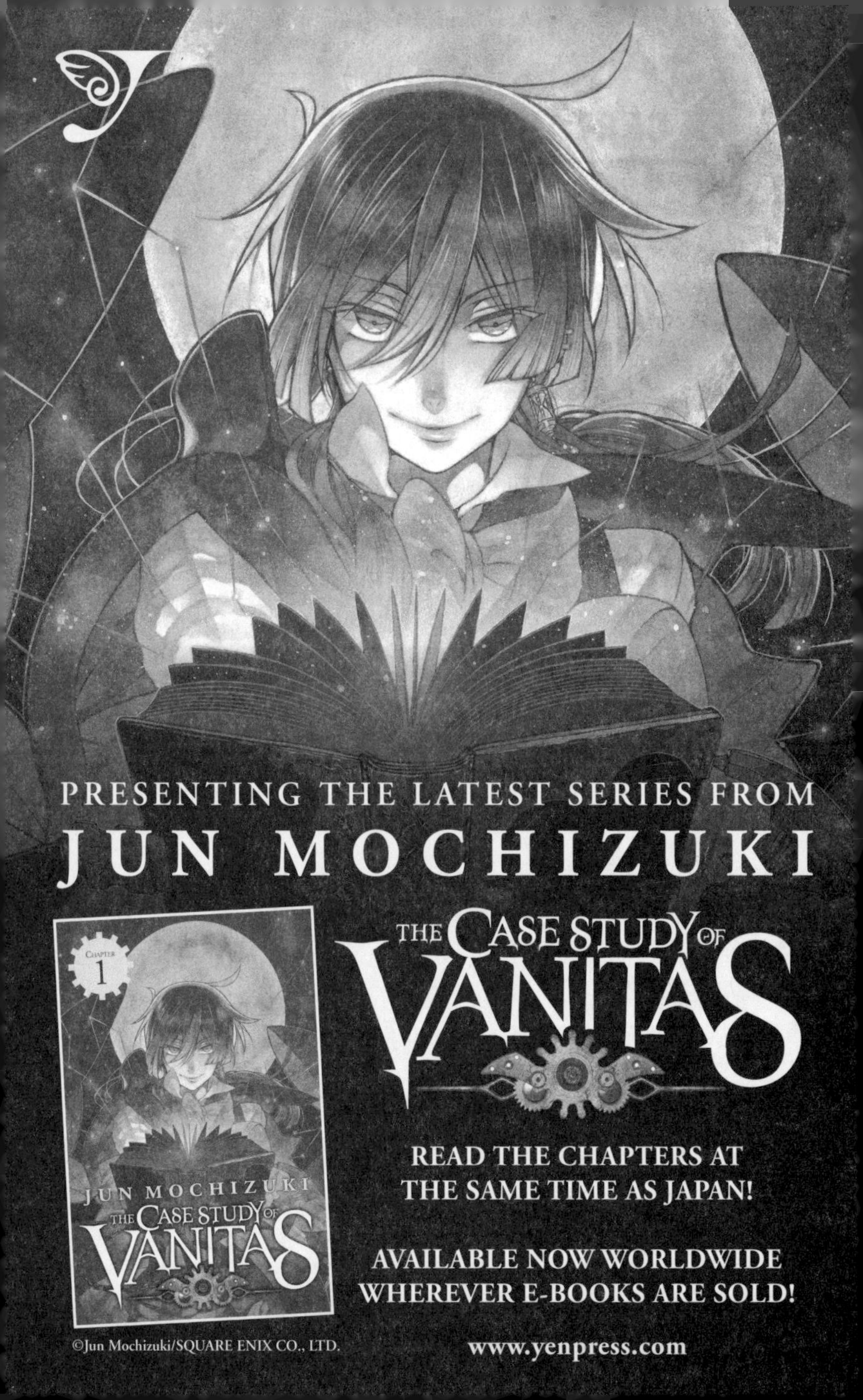
PRESENTING THE LATEST SERIES FROM
JUN MOCHIZUKI
CHAPTER 1
JUN MOCHIZUKI
THE CASE STUDY OF VANITAS
THE CASE STUDY OF VANITAS
READ THE CHAPTERS AT THE SAME TIME AS JAPAN!
AVAILABLE NOW WORLDWIDE WHEREVER E-BOOKS ARE SOLD!
©Jun Mochizuki/SQUARE ENIX CO., LTD.
www.yenpress.com

L INDEX ㉔

Kazuma Kamachi
Kiyotaka Haimura
Chuya Kogino

Translation: Andrew Prowse

Lettering: Phil Christie

TOARU MAJYUTSU NO INDEX Vol. 24
© 2020 Kazuma Kamachi
© 2020 Chuya Kogino / SQUARE ENIX CO., LTD.
Licensed by KADOKAWA CORPORATION ASCII MEDIA WORKS
First published in Japan in 2020 by SQUARE ENIX CO., LTD.
English translation rights arranged with SQUARE ENIX CO., LTD.
and Yen Press, LLC through Tuttle-Mori Agency, Inc.

English translation © 2021 by SQUARE ENIX CO., LTD.

Yen Press
150 West 30th Street, 19th Floor
New York, NY 10001

Visit us at yenpress.com
facebook.com/yenpress
twitter.com/yenpress
yenpress.tumblr.com
instagram.com/yenpress

First Yen Press Edition: September 2021

Yen Press is an imprint of Yen Press, LLC.
The Yen Press name and logo are trademarks of Yen Press, LLC.

Library of Congress Control Number: 2015373809

ISBN: 978-1-9753-2443-8 (paperback)

10 9 8 7 6 5 4 3 2 1

WOR

Printed in the United States of America